The drawing room of "Woodford" (1756), Fairmount Park, Philadelphia. Although "Woodford" was a rather small one-story house when it was built, subsequent additions made it one of the most charming examples of colonial architecture in America. Before restoration, the chimney-breast was boarded over while the drawing room served as a police court for offenders of the Philadelphia vehicle code, but it has survived in its original state. A fine pair of early knife-blade andirons are on the hearth. The tongs, shovel, and brass jamb hooks were found in the house during restoration. *Courtesy Fairmount Park, Philadelphia. Endowed by the Estate of Naomi Wood. Photograph by Alfred J. Wyatt*

The American Fireplace

The research for this publication was partially supported
by a grant from the Penrose Fund
of the American Philosophical Society

The American Fireplace

CHIMNEYS, MANTELPIECES, FIREPLACES & ACCESSORIES

Henry J. Kauffman

Introduction by
Joe Kindig III

GALAHAD BOOKS   NEW YORK CITY

dual.
T.98

Contents

Acknowledgments

M any authors have found that their work, particularly one as wide in scope as this one, is in reality the result of the combined efforts of many persons. Although an author starts his survey with certain facets in mind, using certain resources, these matters change as work progresses. Unknown sources of information appear, and some which originally seemed to be useful contribute little to the project. Much of such activity is dependent on the interest of friends and organizations who are willing to broaden your horizon with gems of information undreamed of before the survey was started.

I am grateful to all who have made suggestions and who helped me in an endless variety of ways. They have contributed much that is pertinent and interesting. Any shortcomings of the survey should be laid at my doorstep.

Among those who helped are:

Mr. & Mrs. William Ball
Willis Barscheid
Teina Baumstone
Louise Belden
Helen Belknap
Quentin Bowers
Paul Buchanan
John Burke
Jacqueline Chapman
John Curtis
Raymond Dey
Mr. & Mrs. Frank Fisher
Mr. & Mrs. John Fisher
Mr. & Mrs. Reginald French

Clyde Groff
John Grubb
Ray Hacker
Mrs. Norbet C. Hansen
Robert Hartman
Lowell Hess
Mr. & Mrs. Walter Himmelreich
Carroll Hopf
Harold Hopper
Frank Horton
Mr. & Mrs. John Hoy
Charles Hummel
Donald Hutslar
George Jackson

C. R. Jones
Mr. & Mrs. James A. Keillor
Alison Kelly
Joe Kindig III
Mr. & Mrs. Gerald Lestz
John Maass
Cyril Marshall
John Milner Marshall
Leland Richard Meyer
William H. Pierson, Jr.
Kent Reeves
John P. Remensnyder
Nancy Richards
Rodris C. Roth
John Rouse

Parke Rouse, Jr.
Frank Schmidt
Gretchen Sharp
Joan Sheldon
Bradley Smith
Richard F. Smith
John Snyder
Charles Spotts
Mrs. Frederick Stocker
Mr. & Mrs. M. W. Thomas
Alec Tiranti (Co.)
Ray Townsend
Gertrude Weber
Eliza Wolcott

The following organizations and companies supplied or permitted the use of photographs, drawings, or photostats:

The American Philosophical Society
Antiquarian & Landmarks Society, Inc. of Connecticut
Bucks County (Pennsylvania) Historical Society
Cincinnati Art Museum
Colchester and Essex Museum, Colchester, England
Colonial Williamsburg
Deep South Specialties Company
Dover Publications, Inc.
Edwin Jackson, Inc.
Hammond-Harwood House
Harvard University (Baker Library)
Henry Francis du Pont Winterthur Museum
Historic America Buildings Survey
Historic Charleston Foundation
Historical Society of Delaware
Historical Society of Pennsylvania
Hopewell Furnace

Lancaster County (Pennsylvania) Historical Society
Mariners Museum, Newport News, Virginia
Majestic Company
Marblehead (Massachusetts) Historical Society
Metropolitan Museum of Art
Minneapolis Institute of Art
Museum of Fine Arts, Boston, Massachusetts
National Park Service
New York Museum Commission
New York State Museum
Old Salem Inc., Winston-Salem, North Carolina
Philadelphia Museum of Art
Pennsylvania Historical and Museum Commission
Pennsylvania State Library
Plimouth Plantation
Rock Ford Foundation
Shelburne (Vermont) Museum

Sleepy Hollow Restorations
Smithsonian Institution
Stanton Hall
Structures Publishing Co.
University of North Carolina
 Press
Victoria and Albert Museum,
 London, England
Virginia Chamber of Commerce
Wheatland Foundation
York County (Pennsylvania)
 Historical Society

Permission has been received from The University of North Carolina Press to quote from *The Dwellings of Colonial America* by Thomas Tileson Waterman; from George L. Phillips to quote from *American Chimney Sweeps;* from Little, Brown, and Company to quote from *The Colonial Architecture of Salem* by Frank Cousins and Phil M. Riley; from The Metropolitan Museum of Art to quote from *A Handbook of the American Wing* by Halsey and Cornelius; and from Colonial Williamsburg and the Earl Gregg Swem Library of the College of William and Mary in Virginia to quote from St. George Tucker's accounts and receipts of July 15, 1788—Tucker-Coleman Papers.

Introduction

From the beginning of time and since the discovery of fire with its miraculous potentials, man has attempted to perfect methods for harnessing this great power to accommodate his own personal needs. Probably no single discovery has affected his physical comforts more; and, by reason of his self-centered character, no inventive means was overlooked to bring heat and comfort into his environment during cold winter months. It is interesting, therefore, to realize that from the dawn of human history relatively little permanent improvement was achieved in the field of heating till the eighteenth century when Benjamin Franklin perfected his "Franklin" stove and the six- and ten-plate stoves evolved from the earlier five-plate form, all depending on convection for the distribution of heat. Within this long period of history, man came close to a solution in the steam-heated rooms of the villas of ancient Rome but these were lost for almost 1,500 years to be reinterpreted by the archaeologist of modern times.

With the fireplace evolving from the hearths of medieval great halls of Europe, where a small opening in the roof offered the only means of escape for the smoke, to the masonry constructed chimneys of the Renaissance, an entirely new concept in interior architectural design was born. The stone ornamentation of this fireplace and, later, the carved and molded woodwork became the focal point of the room, both esthetically and socially. In the domestic dwelling house of the period, the entrance doorway became the prime exterior architectural feature, telling one and all of the material success of the master of the house; in the interior, the fireplace wall further established this success and invited the guest to share in the physical warmth it offered.

The fireplace, with its European ancestry, seems to influence and dominate architectural design in America more than any other architectural element. In the cold climates, we find it invariably utilizing the entire central part of the building and becoming the heart of the house. In milder areas, the chimneys move to the end gables of the house and are still internal. In the South, they are sometimes in the end gables, but frequently of external construction. The kitchens are often located in wings or even in separate buildings to reduce the heat in the main building.

The fireplace afforded opportunities for artisans of many crafts and trades to pursue their individual talents. The carver with his ornamented chimney-breast; the potter with his tiles; the marble-cutter with his mantlepiece; the brass-founder with his andirons; the whitesmith with a trivet; the coppersmith with a firebox; the needleworker with a chimney cloth; the bellows-maker; the china-maker with a garniture; the looking-glass-maker with a chimney-glass; the artist with an overmantle painting; the lowly house painter with a fireboard; and the cabinetmaker with a settle, an easy-chair, or a fire-screen. There was hardly a trade that did not furnish some useful object related to the fireplace. It was the heart of the household and benefitted every merchant of the period. Family life centered around it; a mother wrought a new set of crewel bed furnishings; a father talked of current news from the coffee house and moralistic issues; a son conjured up visions of a sailor's career in the dancing flame and smoke; a daughter caressed and loved a new baby sister on her lap; and grandmother mentally visualized the far-better days of her generation.

The role of the architectural historian today is that of an expert dissecting and analyzing physical forms in order to present a completed picture depicting the dwellings of man throughout various periods of history. His tools are a sound knowledge of specific architectural styles, period design books, local and regional fads and a practical and logical eye. He is well read in the architectural as well as cultural traditions and heritage of the region in question. And he recognizes the importance of archaeological material from the site and relates it to his final conclusions. From this, those of us aspiring to be students of the given period attempt to expand the sociological story of the people and their times. Only then can we recognize the contributions of a society to the overall pattern of civilization and experience man's continual striving to refine the environment within which he lives. Authors who honestly produce the above level of expertise in their specific fields are too infrequently encountered, and therefore I welcome the scholarly depth and the encompassing range of subject to be found in this volume.

Jan. 9th, 1972   Joe K. Kindig III
Hellam, Penna.

The American Fireplace

Seventeenth Century

*I*t is very evident that these three facets of architecture—chimneys, fireplaces, and mantelpieces—are intimately interrelated. And, since they evolved together, their style and function must be discussed together. Such facilities, long used and fondly remembered from their homelands, were copied by the English, Dutch, Swedes, and Germans for their first permanent dwellings in America. Dissent concerning architecture was not a motive for emigration, but the practical view of emigrants was not blinded, however, and changes from European modes were made in accord with American climatic conditions and the available building materials.

Permanent houses were, of course, preceded by temporary shelters, most of them lacking such refinements as fireplaces. Immediate pressing needs for erecting shelters forced colonists to utilize easily available substances, such as mud, withes, stones, sod, bark, and skins. But primitive structures of crude materials were soon replaced by more substantial ones, reminiscent of dwellings in Europe. Derivative building of such kinds accounts for the delay of almost two hundred years, to the turn of the nineteenth century, before a truly American type of domestic architecture appeared, despite unique regional styles in Virginia and Pennsylvania.

Of course there was European precedent for even the temporary structures. English shepherds, farmhands, and burners at the charcoal kilns found protection from the weather in conical huts covered with bark or thatch, so it may be presumed that such structures were used in early America. If more room was needed, the plan of the shelter was elongated. John Smith reported that a church was built at Jamestown, Virginia, on "cratchets," long poles with a forked end set vertically in

Indian longhouse reconstructed at Jamestown, Virginia. The framework was fastened together with thongs and covered with mats which were rolled up in the summer to allow air to circulate. The smoke hole is located in the center of the roof.

the ground to support a ridgepole. Today, it is thought that Smith meant "crucks," which were poles set into the ground slanted together to cross at the top, and held laterally in place by purlins. Neither the conical nor the elongated structures had chimneys; instead there were flat hearths of stone on the floors of the structures, and smoke holes at the top. The buildings themselves functioned as chimneys. The smoke could easily be blown crosswise within them, and the danger of destruction by fire was always present.

Early Connecticut Houses by Isham and Brown suggests that the first structures in that state were cavities, called "cellars," dug into a hillside. They say that:

> These cellars were made by digging a shallow pit in the ground, preferably in a bank, and then lining the sides of the excavation with stone walls carried above the ground enough to give a height of about seven feet, or by setting against these sides upright logs long enough to give the same height. These stone or wooden walls were then banked high with earth on the outside, and were roofed over with logs laid close together and plastered with clay, or with bark or thatch on poles. The probability is that the roofs were of considerable pitch and were thatched.

A shelter built at Salem, Massachusetts, shown in *A Reference Guide to Salem, 1630,* is more sophisticated, employing saplings, woven grasses, bark, stones, and timber. This one was built by placing two rows of saplings in the ground possibly eight or ten feet apart, each one being two to three inches in diameter. These stood upright and the tops were bent inward until they overlapped. This arched chamber was covered with woven mats of grass, over which bark was placed to make the shelter waterproof. This arrangement resembled an Indian longhouse. Its particular advantage was that it provided adequate headroom in all parts of the shelter.

At one end of the chamber a framed doorway was installed, probably with a batten door hung on hinges of leather or wood. The other end was enclosed by a large fireplace with a hearth, back, and sides (jambs) of stones. The whole assembly was probably laid up with mud mortar, for at that time little, if any, lime was available for mortar. The stone back and sides were about four feet high, at least to the lintel; from there upward, a chimney was built of sticks notched at the ends and laid coblike before they were daubed with clay to make them reasonably fireproof.

Such shelters, of course, exist today only in restorations and are doubt-less the result of considerable research; but the forms of their fireplaces are almost too refined for the balance of the building. The question re-volves around the use of jambs and a lintel—the best current evidence indicates that primitive fireplaces had neither. As a matter of fact, some very well-built stone homes in the Hudson Valley, New York, have jambless fireplaces. The construction there might be attributed to tra-ditional practices in Holland; but similar fireplaces have been reported also from other parts of America. Thus, one is led to believe that the fireplaces of the crude buildings of Salem, Massachusetts, should have neither jambs nor lintels. They probably should have a stone hearth with a stone wall at the rear as high as was necessary to reduce the hazard of fire.

It is reported that a different type of shelter was contrived in New Amsterdam (New York City) by the first settlers. There they dug a hole in the ground, the size naturally determined by the number in the family to be accommodated. Sometimes partitions were set in these holes to divide the area and thus give some privacy. The entire inner wall of the cavity was sided with vertical timbers, which were covered with bark to keep loose ground from falling onto the floor. A pitched roof was built over the cavity and covered with bark or sod. While sod for a roof may be considered an ancient device, a sizable number of similarly covered houses in Scandinavia are in use today. These dwellings also had a flat stone hearth on the floor and the chimney facility was a smoke hole in the roof.

In contrast to these temporary shelters of New England and New York, the Swedes and the Finns are believed to have built log houses im-mediately after they arrived in the Delaware Valley in 1638. Again con-trasting with such houses were the temporary shelters of the Philadel-phia region at the time of English settlement when caves were dug along the banks of the Schuylkill and Delaware rivers. These were possibly elongated by projecting lean-tos to accommodate a growing family. The site of a cave thought to have been occupied by Pastorius is marked at Front Street below South Street, and an ancestor of the Morris family reportedly lived in another cave near Front and Market streets. Smoke escaped from such shelters through smoke holes in the roofs or through cracks and crevices in the walls to give some relief to the occupants.

The first permanent houses in Virginia were framed with heavy timbers with studs in the walls over which withes were entwined. These were plastered with wattle and daub, as were also the chimneys.

House at Jamestown, Virginia, with hearth and chimney away from the wall of the house. In this case the hearth was located in line with the entrance to the house. *(Inset)* The hearth was formed by a few stones and a kettle was supported over it from a tripod of wood.

Within years more substantial shelters were built in the first settlements. Several chimney plans can be observed in Jamestown, Virginia, houses, all of which had counterparts in medieval England. The houses were framed of heavy timbers with studded outer walls interwoven with twigs covered with mud and called "wattle and daub." Logs were hewn square with axes and adzes; a frame was built by laying sills, erecting corner posts, and tying the mass together with plates and girts. Rafters for a roof were held in place by purlins to which thatch was attached in the traditional manner. The homes had no cellars, the first floor had only one room (called a hall), and the half story under the roof was known as a loft. But, most importantly for our subject, these structures did have chimneys.

One would expect these chimneys to have been a very primitive type. Virtually no improvement had been made in construction methods since they first appeared in the houses of English yeomen in the fifteenth century. The dramatic vista of a town with many wooden chimneys is

Fireplace at Jamestown, Virginia, with a stone wall at the back, but without jambs. A hood is dropped from the ceiling over the hearth to facilitate the exit of smoke. Notice the very crudely built hearth of fieldstone. This fireplace is within an end wall.

emphasized by Henry Chandlee Forman in *The Architecture of the Old South*, which contains a chapter, "A Landscape of Wooden Chimneys." Forman points out that in 1400 practically all the houses of London had wooden chimneys, and that in 1419 an ordinance forbade future construction of that type and directed that those already built be reconstructed of stone, brick, or plaster.

In America, wooden chimneys were built in different ways. The most common method was to build a framework of wood interlaced with twigs and covered with mud. Despite the illegality of this type of chimney within towns, it was used in rural areas for many years. As late as April 10, 1752, a proclamation of Lieutenant Governor Dinwiddie was printed in the *Virginia Gazette*, "An act to prevent the Building of Wooden Chimneys in the town of Walkerton; and also, to prevent the inhabitants thereof from raising and keeping Hogs."

Another method was to lay small logs coblike and cover them with mud. Fiske Kimball reports in *Domestic Architecture of the American Colonies and of the Early Republic* that in 1640 William Rix's chimney was to be "framed without daubing to be done with hewn timber." Those in reconstructed Jamestown are of woven twigs and mud, but destruction by fire is not likely since the houses are unoccupied.

Architectural plans of buildings of Jamestown illustrate the early locations for hearths. In one house it is near the center of the room, with a smoke hole or short chimney above it in the roof. This arrangement was sometimes improved by building a chimney down to the ceiling (if the house had a loft) of the first floor. One advantage of the earlier plan was that the circulating smoke under the roof helped to prevent rodents and insects from living there. Reasons for moving the hearth from the center of the room to an outside wall are not entirely clear. It has been pointed out that when a cellar was dug under the floor, there was no longer support for the hearth in the middle of the room; to keep it there a foundation of stones had to be provided. But it is also very evident that a similar support was needed when the hearth was moved to an outside wall, so there seems to have been little gain from that point of view. It might also be pointed out that, while the fire was in the center, all sides could be used, whereas it was only half as useful when placed against a wall. Possibly the ease of building a chimney on a wall

A row of houses at Jamestown, Virginia, the center one on the left having a chimney built outside the house wall. This procedure was frequently followed in building houses in the South.

was an important factor, in addition, of course, to the reflection of heat from the wall.

But whatever the reason, all fireplaces were eventually moved against a wall with a hearth of stones and a back wall of stones called a "reredos." The reredos was built as high and wide as necessary to minimize the hazard of fire. Chimneys were built from the ceiling of the first floor up through the loft and extended two or three feet above the roof. Such construction minimized the chances of sparks settling on the thatch and increased the draft. Sparks on the exterior of a roof presented little danger, however; it was those sparks which escaped through the cracks of the chimney inside the house which started most of the fires. Some of the chimneys at Jamestown were built outside the walls of the house. This practice became a tradition in the South in contrast to the North

Hopkins House, Plymouth, Massachusetts, rear view showing lean-to. Note chimney details. Howland House beyond is in the course of rethatching. *Courtesy Plimouth Plantation*

where most chimneys were built inside house walls. All the chimneys of Jamestown are built of wattle and daub.

Despite the fact that wattle and daub is the major construction technique used in the restoration of houses at Jamestown, it was not employed in reconstructing the houses at Plymouth, Massachusetts, except in chimneys. The supposition that wattles were not originally used at Plymouth for some houses cannot be completely discounted, although the hostility of New England weather possibly led them to adopt a more substantial mode of construction. Furthermore, wattle and daub was reasonably long lasting in the chimneys because most of the chimney was within the walls of the house, and little was exposed to the weather.

The floor plan of most of the reconstructed houses at Plymouth provides for one main room on the ground floor and for a loft, reached by a ladder. This arrangement of rooms seems to have been used by most colonists in their first permanent dwellings. The corners of the Plymouth houses were not joined with a mortise and tenon, as later New England houses were, but are interlaid in a manner which seems expedient and reasonably sound. Exteriors of the houses are covered with vertical siding, sawed fairly uniform in thickness and width and pegged with wooden "treenails" or "trunnels" to the frame. The original roofs were all probably thatched, although in the restoration some are covered with long boards or shingles. The frame of the house is exposed on the inside.

A representative floor plan shows a huge fireplace, completely within the walls of the house, occupying a large area at one end of the room on the ground floor. Seemingly, a more judicious use of space would have placed the chimney outside the wall; but, on the other hand, it has been pointed out that it would not have lasted long when unpro-

Interior view of Hopkins House, Plymouth, Massachusetts, showing fireplace with kettles suspended by trammels from lug poles in the chimney. The ladder at the right side of the fireplace was the only means of reaching the loft. *Courtesy Plimouth Plantation*

tected from the weather. It was also believed that a chimney within the walls functioned better than one located outside.

Stone hearths are common, some extending into the rooms and bordered with puncheon floors. But with an earthen floor the hearth could be shallow for there was little danger of fire. Later fenders were used to keep hot coals on the hearth, but such luxury was not known at early Plymouth.

Stones were also used to build a foundation for the chimney to a height of about three feet, the upper parts of the assembly being made of sticks and mud upon a tapering framework of four corner posts held together by cross-members with tenons. The entire assembly of wood was covered with mud to make it reasonably fireproof. Unfortunately there was always a danger of fire when the mud fell away at spots. The occupants presumably knew the signal for necessary repairs, and the survival of such chimneys can probably be attributed to the fact that a roaring fire was rarely permitted in these primitive buildings. As a matter of fact, only a modest fire was needed for cooking and roasting.

The cavernous fireplaces found at Plymouth are probably typical of those used in England during the same period. The fire-chamber walls

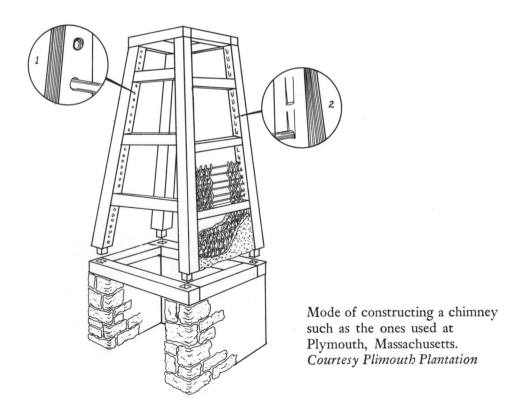

Mode of constructing a chimney such as the ones used at Plymouth, Massachusetts. *Courtesy Plimouth Plantation*

Rear view of framework for the jambs and lintel for a fireplace (in construction) at Plymouth, Massachusetts. Notice the chamfer on the inside bottom edge of the lintel. *Courtesy Plimouth Plantation*

are vertical and the corners are squared. The tapering throat and the flue are located directly over the fire. Naturally, with such an arrangement most of the heat went up the chimney; although the facility was adequate for cooking, it had limitations for heating. Reaching from the hearth to the ceiling were jambs faced with heavy hewn timbers, between which a massive lintel was placed. The wooden lintel was both notched and tennoned into the jambs. The lower inner corner of the lintel was chamfered to reduce the chance of igniting it and to allow an uninterrupted flow of air. There was *no* mantel shelf and *no* ornamentation of any kind.

No cranes were used in these fireplaces to hold pots and kettles. Instead, two green lug poles were installed crosswise in the throat of the chimney, about six feet above the hearth, on which trammels and pothooks were attached to support the required utensils. In later times, the wooden poles gave way to metal members, which never needed replacement. As a matter of fact many iron rods can be found today surviving in the throats of chimneys. The andirons would have been massive ones of cast iron, similar to the ones found among the archaeological remains at Jamestown, Virginia.

It is evident and logical that the "second round" of permanent houses built in the colonies would be an improvement over those built earlier. The abundance of wood in Virginia (contrasted with a dearth in England), combined with the need for frequent repairs to the daub of the exterior walls, led to the covering of the frames with boards or planks. It is likely that the first houses were covered some time later, but subsequently the dwellings were built that way. A hypothetical sketch shows the planks fastened horizontally on the first story and vertically on the gable end above the end girt. The wattle and daub chimney was retained. This projected procedure might be questioned because of the availability of bricks.

From the early use of natural materials, a change was made to brick within decades of 1607, although a lone example, the Adam Thoroughgood House at Norfolk, Virginia, is thought to have been built of brick in 1636. Two bricklayers are known to have arrived with the first contingent of settlers, and bricks certainly were being produced before midcentury. Remnants of four brick kilns found at Jamestown are thought to indicate operation in the seventeenth century. It is probable, therefore, that the practice of importing bricks from Europe has been grossly overstated by historians. In any case, it is now known that local production was considerable in the seventeenth century.

The Adam Thoroughgood House, Norfolk, Virginia, is the oldest brick house in America (about 1636). Its refined form and elaborate architectural details suggest construction at a much later date. *Courtesy Virginia Chamber of Commerce*

A typically large fireplace in the Adam Thoroughgood House in Norfolk, Virginia. The squared corners at the rear and the smoke channel are typical features of the period. This fireplace is obviously within the walls of the house. *Courtesy Virginia Chamber of Commerce*

Another residence may have been a transitional type between the framed house and one made entirely of bricks. This house would have had a timber framework filled with bricks. It was used widely in Europe, but sparingly in America.

Here a study of the Adam Thoroughgood House focuses attention on the chimney and fireplace arrangement of that period. When a second room, a "parlor," was added to the "hall" in New England, a second fireplace was butted against the existing one, with some saving of space and materials. In Virginia, however, the second room was attached to the end of the house opposite the fireplace, creating a need for another complete fireplace and chimney. Doubtless this was a little more elegant way of solving the problem, and a natural transition to a later house with a center hall. The added chimney was usually located outside the house. Both chimneys were built completely of bricks. The Thoroughgood House has two chimneys, one exterior, the other built within the wall of the second gable.

It should be noted here that the Thoroughgood House is not an example of two-step building. The receding shoulders (known as "weatherings" to architects) suggests that a reasonably large fireplace was built on the first floor and a smaller one on the second floor, with a two-flue chimney extending upward from the second floor.

A marked change is evident in the fireplaces of the Thoroughgood House from earlier examples. They are much larger than the earlier examples at Jamestown and are built completely of brick. At least one has a curved lintel of brick in a manner found in many houses built later in Virginia. The face of the lintel and jambs are plastered; possibly the whole interior of the fireplace would have been similarly treated. The opening is framed with a large bolection molding.

An improved technology is evident in the construction of an all-masonry fireplace. The masonry, of course, reflected more heat because bricks and stones properly arranged in a fireplace have no peers in this efficiency. They have been the most widely used materials for fireplaces in America ever since. Continuances from the past appear to be the square, boxlike form of the chamber with considerable depth, and a horizontal axis similar to the fireplaces of reconstructed Plymouth. The accompanying hearth could have been made of stones or brick; however, stones were scarce in Virginia.

The focus on the fireplaces of the first permanent dwellings in Pennsylvania is less precise than the rather clear image of those in New England. This condition arises from the fact that few buildings of the seventeenth century have survived there and there have been no important restorations, except the restored 1704 house near West Chester, Pennsylvania, obviously built in the style of the seventeenth century. Only a little reliable information about the first buildings in settlements can be gleaned from surviving legal documents. All else, of course, are merely hypothetical opinions about architectural activity here. This dearth of information is particularly unfortunate because Pennsylvania was settled by several nationalities who may have possibly evolved unique solutions to the problem of heating a room. The later use of the stove there confirms such an hypothesis.

One support for such a theory is the use of corner fireplaces in Pennsylvania, but in no other contemporary communities. Amandus Johnson comments as follows in *The Swedes on the Delaware, 1638–1664:*

> About May (1638) the ramparts which were constructed of palisades and earth, were completed. . . . Two houses were erected inside the palisades, one of which was probably used for a dwelling house, the other for a magazine or store-house. They were built of unhewn logs, and in the dwelling house were loopholes and probably two or three windows. The roof was gabled and most likely covered with small timbers split in two. In the corner of the dwelling house a fireplace was made of bricks brought over on ships. Rough benches, chairs, and tables were constructed of split timber, and it is likely that the beds of some sort were made.

The fact that this statement is not documented indirectly lends some credence to the writer's belief that few, if any, of these well-constructed buildings were erected immediately upon the colonists' arrival. In the case cited, the implication is that they were built within months of the landing date. Fortunately, a survey entitled *The Log Cabin in America*, by C. A. Westlager, does include documented evidence that between 1643 and 1653 ten structures were built of logs in Delaware. The list includes dwelling houses, forts, a gristmill, blockhouses, a bathhouse, and a church. It is disappointing that such a survey contains no specific information about fireplaces, particularly since other sources document the existence of early houses with unique corner installations.

In 1679-80 two Dutchmen, Jasper Dankers and Peter Sluyter, stopped

Swedish log cabin on Darby Creek near Darby, Pennsylvania. This view shows the location of the chimney over a corner fireplace. Surviving examples are virtually nonexistent today in the Delaware River Valley. *Courtesy Historic American Buildings Survey*

overnight in a log house while enroute from New York City to New Castle, Delaware. They wrote that the house in which they slept was built in the Swedish mode: "These houses are quite tight and warm, but the chimney is placed in the corner." Later the botanist Peter Kalm visited the Delaware Valley and called attention to fireplaces located in the corner of the earliest log houses: "The chimneys were masoned in a corner, either of gray stone (or in places where there were no stones, of mere clay), which they laid very thick in one corner of the House." Thus, although the dwellings in this area were probably very similar in size and shape to those in the other colonies, the placing of the fireplace in that corner position differs. Furthermore, it is interesting to note that European travelers specifically mention such an arrangement, which probably would have elicited no comment had the usual plan been followed.

The reason for putting the fireplace in a corner rather than on a straight wall is unclear. The precedent could, of course, have been long established in Scandinavia, based on factors peculiar to northern Europe. It could have been a procedure of convenience, for instead of building three walls as in a common fireplace, only one diagonal wall had to be built for the corner arrangement.

Interest attaches to this arrangement because it is unusual and because of its adoption in later houses. The use of corner fireplaces in the Letitia House in Philadelphia (c. 1690) could have been the result of Swedish influence. Presumably the Swedes followed the same mode in the eighteenth century and possibly conveyed the scheme to German, English, and Scotch-Irish pioneers as they built their cabins westward into the Northwest Territory. It is also evident that other influences shaped the fireplace facility in later cabins.

Although the residents of New Amsterdam (New York City) started their life in the New World in a hole in the ground, these enterprising Dutch soon built some of the best houses in America at that time. Wartenbaker states in his *The Founding of American Civilization, The Middle Colonies:*

> There seems to be no evidence that the Dutch built log cabins in the Hudson Valley. . . . But with timber houses they were thoroughly familiar, and we may imagine them, broad axe in hand, felling trees, squaring great beams, setting up the framework, covering it with crude boards, erecting wooden chimneys. . . . Most of the quaint little houses stretched along the bank of the East River in the Prototype View of New Amsterdam of about 1650, are obviously of wood.

Thus it is evident that the first houses of the New World were more homogeneous than one would suspect. Most of them consisted of one room with a loft and one fireplace to reduce the chill and provide a cooking facility. As early as 1628, however, brick kilns were in operation in New Amsterdam and Dutchmen were impatiently waiting for the day when they could build more refined houses of bricks. Their skilled masons were less accustomed to building with stone, but beautiful stone was available at quarries and they utilized this medium also. The brickyards soon turned out pantiles for the roofs of these substantial buildings and New Amsterdam was well along the way to look like old Amsterdam.

Unknown and undated artist's sketch of buildings located between York, Pennsylvania, and Baltimore, Maryland. The one in the foreground has a centrally located chimney, while the chimney seems to be on the corner of the building on the right. *Courtesy The Mariners Museum, Neport News, Virginia*

Time has been very wasteful with a knowledge about floor arrangements in New Amsterdam showing the location of early chimneys and fireplaces. The typical architectural procedure in having the gable end of the house facing the street suggests a chimney against the middle of the front wall, but openings, such as doors and windows, would not permit such an arrangement.

Although these old jambless fireplaces, wherever they were located, had some charm, they were highly inefficient as heating devices. They had no jambs to help direct the heat into the room or to prevent the smoke from being blown crosswise, and the vast flues built over them conducted most of the heat up the chimney. They seem to have been peculiarly Dutch, and it is likely that they continued to be built and used long after New Amsterdam was taken over by the English, who were very tolerant of Dutch cultural customs.

A dramatic and very primitive fireplace of this style can be seen in Washington's Headquarters at Newburgh, New York. The hearth of large stones is eight feet long and four feet eight inches wide. Much more spectacular, however, is the stone wall behind the fireplace, for it is eight feet wide and rises eight feet to the hole in the ceiling. There is no hood and the hole is framed with ponderous interlocked timbers which support the massive chimney whose base is approximately eight feet by four feet, big by any residential standards. Although this house was built in 1750, it doubtless has one of the most dramatic, primitive fireplaces of those surviving in America.

The fireplaces and chimneys described thus far certify to regional differences of style and construction along the eastern seaboard. But certainly one of the most striking sectional developments took place in New England, where a rather standardized plan developed in the last half of the seventeenth century. Probably because population spread from Massachusetts to Rhode Island and Connecticut, and to the north, a marked similarity in building practices is found throughout the region. The firmness of the image might also have occurred because more houses have survived from the seventeenth century in New England than in the remainder of the seacoast areas combined.

The type of house reconstructed at Plymouth probably continued to be built long into the seventeenth century and, in outlying districts, into the eighteenth. Increased time for building, a more affluent society,

Fireplace in Washington's Headquarters at Newburgh, New York. Although built in the eighteenth century, many of this type must have been built in the region during the seventeenth century. Its gigantic size is suggested by the average-sized kettles and andirons on the hearth. *Courtesy New York Museum Commission*

and other factors combined to effect changes in the plan and construction of houses after the mid-seventeenth century. The "faire house" (an English term indicating refinement and enlarged size) was built as early as 1641 in Connecticut. No doubt the number of such houses must have proliferated in the following decades.

Most of the houses were built on stone foundations which supported a carefully fashioned frame of oak. Walls were covered with rived clapboards, tapering toward one edge so they could be overlapped to provide tight protection against wind and rain. Although thatching was outlawed by the Pilgrims in 1627, the thatching of roofs continued for many years for houses on the coast. But in the interior, away from the ocean and large rivers, a scarcity of marsh grasses caused builders to use shingles and long boards on the roofs.

The living quarters consisted of one room on the first floor and a half story above, reached by a winding stairway instead of the earlier ladder. In one end was constructed a massive fireplace and chimney, spreading across about two thirds of the width of the room, the rest of the area being taken up by the entry and the stairs, which was called a "porch." Stone was used first for construction of chimneys, according to Isham and Brown in *Early Connecticut Houses:* "In the old Connecticut colony the chimney is usually of stone." They also cite a number of references proving that brick production had begun in the Hartford area as early as 1638. It is possible that availability determined whether stone or brick was used. Records of quarrying begin at about the same time as those of brick production but, of course, one must remember that field stone was used for masonry purposes long before. Much of the masonry was laid up in mud with straw or hair binders, the color of the hair indicating the breed of cattle raised in a particular area. Mortar replaced mud as the binding material soon after mid-century. Its basic ingredient was lime, much of it produced by burning shells from the ocean, according to old records. Isham and Brown comment that:

> The employment of it [lime] gradually spread till, in the better houses of the third period, we find it universal in the older towns. Clay was still used, however, for a long time in outlying settlements, and for inside work, in the more ancient towns also.

First-floor plan of the first-stage house, and the first-floor plan of the second-stage house in New England. From Isham and Brown: *Early Connecticut Houses. Courtesy Dover Publications, Inc.*

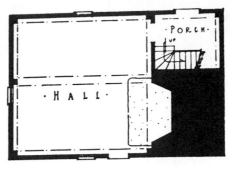

·FIRST FLOOR PLAN·
·FIRST STAGE·

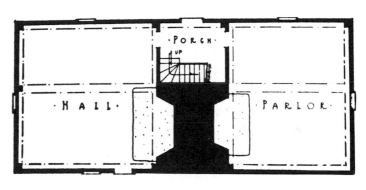

·FIRST FLOOR PLAN·
·SECOND STAGE·

As a matter of fact, even foundations were laid up with mud late in the seventeenth century. Recently when repairs had to be made to some early masonry, the mortar was removed with hose and water. In the eighteenth century, chimney repairs above the roof line were done with lime mortar, the rest of the stack retaining its early application of mud.

While it is known that large stones were laid for hearths, little is known about the size and shape of the opening and the depth of the chamber, because so few of the original one-room houses have survived. However, one might safely assume that the old English rule was invoked: a small opening should be taller than wide, and a large opening should be wider than tall. This rule is evidently sound, for many tall fireplaces are known to have functioned very satisfactorily. The larger the reflective surface in the back, the more heat was projected into the room. There were obvious limitations on the height of a fireplace eight or ten feet long when located in a room having a ceiling height of only seven feet. The long, low openings in the Whitfield House in Guilford, Connecticut, are evidence of this fact. There is no mention of ovens in the fireplaces of one-room houses under discussion, so it must be presumed they came along later, with other refinements.

The next architectural change that involved the construction of chimneys and fireplaces occurred when the second room (called a "parlor") was built against the fireplace-end of the first room. The porch was retained as an entry to both, and the original stairway gave access to both lofts. It was not customary to build fireplaces in loft rooms and even after full rooms were built on the second floor many were without them.

When fireplaces finally did appear on the second floor they were usually smaller than those on the first, for a number of reasons. In the first place, bedrooms naturally needed less heat than the first-floor living quarters. Secondly, the cross-sectional size of the chimney diminished as the whole became taller; and, since there was a direct relationship between the size of the fireplace and its flue, it was unwise to put a small flue on a big fireplace. Finally, the reduced size of the upper stack permitted offsets at the floor level to support the hearth of only a small fireplace. An alternate support was to corbel the masonry outward under it, a plan often used in cellars for first-floor fireplaces, but rarely for those on the second floor.

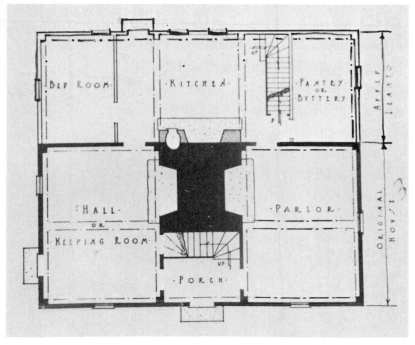

First-floor plan of the third-stage house with a large central chimney and a lean-to. From Isham and Brown: *Early Connecticut Houses. Courtesy Dover Publications, Inc.*

The last and most spectacular development in chimneys and fireplaces occurred when the final addition was made to the earlier two-part house completing what has come to be known as the saltbox house. To increase the number of rooms a lean-to was built across the back wall. A break in the roof line suggests that the lean-to was indeed added, whereas a continuous roof line is strong evidence that the house was probably built complete at one time.

In either case, the lean-to was approximately one third of the total width of the house. It was divided into three parts: a bedroom on the warm or sunny end, a large kitchen in the middle, and a pantry or buttery on the other end. Because all kitchens needed a fireplace, an additional chimney was required. But no change was made in the size and location of the earlier two-part stack. Instead, a third flue was built crosswise against its back side. Of course, after houses were built with an integral lean-to, a solid chimney stack was erected rather than one of three different segments. When chimneys had two flues they were usually regular in shape; but when a third was added the rectangle was changed to an "L" or a "T" shape.

Kitchen fireplaces were always of very generous dimensions, although the width was partly controlled by the size of the stack against which it was built. Some fireplaces, however, were actually wider than the original stack, ranging from six to nine feet long and from four to five feet high, with an approximate depth of three feet. Most of those built in the seventeenth century were made of stone, with massive wooden lintels with a cross-sectional size as much as seventeen inches by ten or fifteen inches. For smaller openings stone lintels were often used, but neither type had mantels or ornamentation of any type.

The major refinement appendage of the late seventeenth-century fireplace was an oven, with some of the large fireplaces having two. Most of them in the seventeenth century were placed in the back wall of the fireplace, usually to one side but occasionally centered, with their floors about thirty inches above the hearth. The interior of most was oval in shape, about thirty inches deep and eighteen wide. The floor was always flat and the top domed, but there was no flue leading to the flue of the chimney stack. Location of the oven was dictated by the fact that live coals had to be lifted into them from the hearth to start the heating action, which in turn coated the roof heavily with soot. When the soot was burned off, the hot coals were raked out onto the hearth. Food was then placed within, the opening closed, and the baking proceeded.

Preoccupation thus far with construction and function of the fireplace must now give way to its refinements and ornamentation. It is a truism of man's adjustment to his environment that problems of physical survival have to be solved before he can give much attention to esthetic matters. Thus, making the interior of the house attractive seems to have come only by the latter part of the seventeenth century.

Interestingly, this decorative process seems to have started with the fireplace, possibly preceded only with chamfered beams and plastered walls. One of the outstanding examples of the new trend is the Buttolph-Williams House, in Wethersfield, Connecticut. The base of its chimney stack is of stone. The upper part and the fireplaces are of brick, considered a more refined medium than stone (by many connoisseurs). The kitchen fireplace, however, is quite "plain," the design becoming the decorative elements of that part of the house.

The fireplace in the "Great Hall" had details reminiscent of fine examples in England, particularly in its greater height than width, a quality shared by others in New England and a few in the South. This uncommon ratio (compared with those of later times) creates an attractive opening and a very effective heating device. The wall brickwork has rounded corners in the rear of the fire chamber, a feature found also at the Hart House of Ipswich, Massachusetts, now located in the American Wing of the Metropolitan Museum of Art in New York City.

The Hart House was built about 1640. Just above the hearth in the back wall the bricks are set in a herringbone pattern, also an old English design. Another interesting detail in the back wall is a recess about two feet wide and six inches deep, called a "smoke channel." This recess presumably directed the smoke toward the center of the chimney flue.

Equally compatible with fine brickwork of the fireplace of the Buttolph-Williams House is the bolection molding placed around the opening. The contour of this molding is very bold, and its massive size is well suited to its function as a decorative device. Only one example among others from the seventeenth century in New England, its use continued well into the eighteenth century. Notable are the flush edges of the brick jambs and the molding, a procedure rarely copied in modern examples of colonial architecture.

A fine example of a seventeenth-century fireplace in the Thomas Hart House of Ipswich, Massachusetts, built about 1640; now located in the Metropolitan Museum of Art in New York City. The radius form between the back wall and the jambs is a very attractive and functional feature. The hearth is frugally furnished as most of them probably were at that time. *Courtesy of Metropolitan Museum of Art*

The really advanced feature of the fireplace in the "Great Hall" of the Buttolph-Williams House, however, is a mantel shelf mounted midway between the bolection molding at the top of the fireplace and the ceiling. Although not found as an original part of this fireplace, a mantel shelf was found on a similar fireplace on the second floor. An excerpt from the brochure entitled *The Buttolph-Williams House* states that:

> There are few counterparts—that is, in the scale—existing in Connecticut of the great moulding used on these two fireplaces [the great hall and the room above it]. A little above where this moulding had been, there was also the clear outline of a shelf (mantel) supported by a moulding.

A similar molding and mantel shelf were placed in the Letitia House in Philadelphia soon after the turn of the eighteenth century. Appearance of such a refinement at this time is very rare, for mantel shelves were not widely used over fireplaces until decades later.

Another distinction of the "Great Hall" of the Buttolph-Williams House is plastering instead of the walls being covered by vertical sheathing, the common procedure at this time. In some cases the fireplace wall was sheathed, even though other walls were plastered, a procedure followed in the kitchen of the house under consideration. More formal types of paneling were not used widely until the first decades of the eighteenth century.

A word about fireplace terminology should be given here since there is confusion in definitions in encyclopedias and dictionaries. Some authorities make "mantel" synonymous with "mantel shelf," some with "mantelpiece," and some make the three terms interchangeable. The author has concluded that in the first half of the eighteenth century there were chimney-breasts or chimney-pieces which rarely had a "mantel shelf." In the second half of that century mantel shelves on the chimney-pieces and low "mantelpieces" began to appear. The mantelpieces were constructed framings, consisting of moldings, colonnettes, *and mantel shelves*, around and above the fireplace opening. By the beginning of the nineteenth century the chimney-breast or chimney-piece had virtually disappeared, and was replaced by the mantelpiece which rarely extended above the mantel shelf.

Therefore, in this work the word "mantel" will not be used by itself; "mantelpiece" will be used when referring to the whole ornamental structure of wood, marble, etc., above and around a fireplace; and "mantel shelf" will be used when referring to the shelf on the chimney-breast or when referring to that specific part of the mantelpiece.

Eighteenth Century

Everyone knows that styles in architecture develop gradually. Rarely is there a date which can be regarded as the precise time when a complete change from one style to another occurred. For purposes of organization, however, some divisions in the subject must be made. It is generally agreed by architectural historians that the first major change in America came at the turn of the eighteenth century. At that time European medieval characteristics were being abandoned, and Georgian features were slowly coming to the fore. And, to further define the evolution in style, the eighteenth century is often divided into halves, making 1750 the dividing line between the simply functional and the later, more fastidious, Georgian. Needless to say, some elements of Georgian architecture appeared late in the seventeenth century while certain facets of the medieval style were continued well into the eighteenth century.

Regional differences in architectural style in America became minimized throughout the eighteenth century. This trend can be accounted for partially by the fact that the entire Atlantic seaboard had become a vast English colony, dominated by all facets of English culture. Migration from other countries slackened, but a steady stream continued to flow from the motherland. The major exception to this English dominance occurred in Pennsylvania, where the hinterland rapidly filled up with people of Germanic origin from the Rhineland. This migration had a profound effect on the developing architectural styles in Pennsylvania. It might also be pointed out that communication between the various colonies increased, a process which tended to minimize differences. The trend toward English styles was abetted by the importation of books on the subject of English architecture. And, finally, a number of

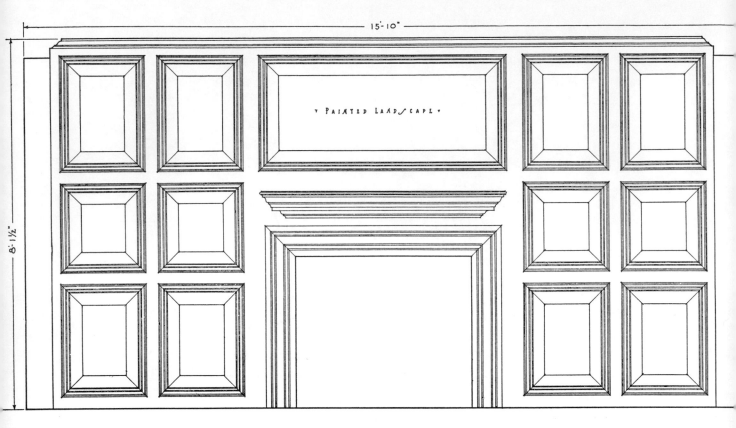

A typical arrangement of stiles, rails, and panels one might logically find in a fireplace end of a room about 1700. This plan is from the Forbes or Barnes House, East Haven, Connecticut. From Kelly: *The Early Domestic Architecture of Connecticut. Courtesy Dover Publications, Inc.*

English builders who came to America successfully imprinted English concepts on the architecture of the New World.

The survey of architecture in the seventeenth century terminated with a description of styles found in New England and, because of the continuity which occurred there, it seems to be the logical starting point for a study of styles of the eighteenth century. It has been mentioned that the culture of the region was English because most of the colonists were of English stock. The house plan usually called for a construction of wood built around a large central chimney in which a number of fireplaces were built. Although this arrangement was satisfactory from many points of view, styles eventually change, even those of chimneys and fireplaces. Attention had been directed toward the functions of the fireplaces and the chimney with only a little evidence pointing toward increased interest in ornamenting these important adjuncts of the house.

In the last half of the century fireplace walls were covered with wainscot (vertical sheathing as in the Hart House) which was unpainted with molded edges, although installations of this type later were often painted. This treatment of the fireplace wall was well suited to the trend of the time, for it was reasonably easy to install and it provided some decorative quality to an otherwise uninteresting room. Of course, in some houses all the walls of important rooms, and even the ceilings, were covered with an inner layer of wood.

The floor plan of the seventeenth-century house was carried along into the eighteenth century, and the use of sheathing was continued, particularly in outlying districts. In the first quarter of the eighteenth century a new treatment for fireplace walls appeared, consisting of inter-secting horizontal and vertical strips of wood called "stiles and rails" with openings between them into which beveled panels were fitted. The whole arrangement was usually made of white pine, free of knots, and well seasoned, as there is little distortion after the assembly was made. The rails and stiles were mortised together and fastened with two wooden pegs in each joint. The panels were of various shapes and sizes, and most of them had a beveled edge about one or one-and-a-half inches wide. Stiles and rails were generally about one inch thick, the panels of thinner boards. The front surfaces were always planed, but the back side, facing the outside chimney wall, was left rough and unplaned. This arrangement of strips and boards is generally called "paneling," in con-

Examples of bolection moldings found in various houses in Connecticut. From Kelly: *Early Domestic Architecture of Connecticut. Courtesy Dover Publications, Inc.*

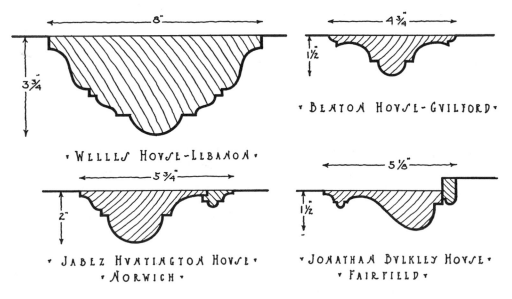

Fireplace wall in a room from Newington, Connecticut, now located in the Metropolitan Museum of Art, New York City. The skewer holder on the left column and the pipe tongs on the right side are outstanding in quality. The andirons are in the style of the period and are of a very attractive design. *Courtesy Metropolitan Museum of Art*

trast with the earlier vertical boarding which is properly known as "sheathing."

The arrangement of the earliest panels often shows the craftsman's love for asymmetrical balance, or possibly his disregard for careful planning. He appears to have started working at one end of the wall, solving his problems as he met them. There seems to have been little concern for locating the fireplace in the middle of the fireplace wall, and the door to the porch was not always balanced by a closet door on the other side of the fireplace.

The fire chamber of the fireplace was usually built of brick, with stone remaining the favorite for large kitchen fireplaces. Stone and wood were continued for lintels, wood being preferred for very large openings. Virtually none were arched to eliminate lintels, as was done occasionally later in the century. Openings have an axis as in earlier times, when some were dominantly vertical. The grander openings were framed with a large bolection molding, above which on rare occasions a shallow mantel shelf was added. Above the shelf were placed two horizontal panels, the larger one often being covered with an oil painting. An alternate overmantel treatment was to construct three small vertical panels with shaped tops.

An interesting example of a fine fireplace wall of the second quarter of the eighteenth century from Newington, Connecticut, is now located in the Metropolitan Museum in New York City. The following description has been taken from *A Handbook of the American Wing* by Halsey and Cornelius:

> In architectural character the room marks a distinctive change from the earlier type which we have just visited. It illustrates the visible effect of the new influence which came to the Colonies early in the eighteenth century. Here is stile and rail paneling set with beveled panels. Here are fluted pilasters (one on each side of the fireplace), a shell cupboard and mouldings different from those of the Gothic tradition. In other words, we have a quaint provincial expression of Renaissance forms whose basis was classic in contradistinction to Gothic.
>
> The immediate inspiration of our paneling was no doubt English, and the English of the Queen Anne period. The arched panels, which are the most distinctive feature of the woodwork, are strongly reminiscent of a treatment usual in work of the reigns of Queen Anne and George I. The crossed stiles in the lower part of the wainscot and doors forms a design peculiar to Connecticut River towns, while the carved round flower at the top of the pilaster is a detail found frequently in both the exterior and the interior of Connecticut houses of the eighteenth century.
>
> The bolection moulding around the fireplace is another English inheritance from the time of William and Mary and Queen Anne, while the carved shell in the wall cupboard is of good quality and recalls similar details of those periods.
>
> The raised hearth would suggest that this room was an upstairs room, although the considerable elaboration of treatment would

seem unusual in any but a principal room in the house. The fireplace lining and hearth are of Connecticut brownstone, a not too permanent material for such a purpose but one generally used.

The preceding description of the fireplace wall points up several important details. In the first place, it is very evident that the flat paneled wall with its pilasters, while it was more elegant than earlier examples, was much less sophisticated than those of the later Georgian period. To many connoisseurs this style of paneling represents the epitome of taste, particularly as far as the American tradition is concerned. It was a perfect setting for the Queen Anne furniture of the period. It might also be noted that in the arrangement of stiles and rails the level of design and craftsmanship was improving. The raised hearth is almost unique for New England, as well as for the rest of the country, except for portions of Pennsylvania settled by Germanic peoples.

Thus, in the early part of the eighteenth century embryonic evidence of change appeared, which came into full bloom in a later dramatic relocation of rooms and fireplaces. This transformation brought increased interest in ornamenting the fireplace wall, particularly in the important rooms of the house. Kitchen fireplaces were little changed although the kitchen itself was moved to the rear of the house.

There was also a marked variation in the style and number of fireplace fittings in the early eighteenth century. The andirons, now made by the blacksmith, were ornamented with scrolls and finials more delicate and profuse than formerly. Brass finials and plates were added to make them compatible with their surroundings. Early jamb hooks of iron were frequently replaced by those of cast brass. Fire tools of iron with brass finials became very popular. In 1753 James Smith advertised in the *Pennsylvania Gazette* in Philadelphia (May 3) that he sold, "all sorts of brass work, viz. Brass dogs, shovels, and tongs, heads for dogs, shoe buckles . . . ." Fenders were utilized to prevent live coals from rolling onto the floor near the hearth; however, few are found in inventories before the end of the eighteenth century. A bed warmer of brass with its iron handle hung on the molding, where it was easily available for use at bedtime. The utensils of the kitchen fireplace were multiplied, although not to the excess found on many hearths today.

The main axis of a new house plan remained parallel with the road, as it was in the salt-box style; however, the lean-to was dropped and the

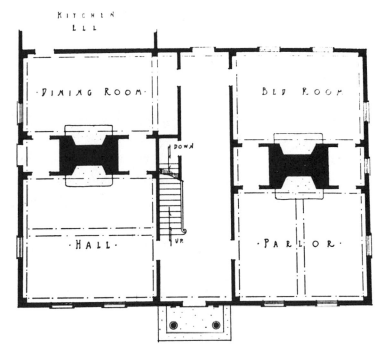

· TYPICAL FIRST FLOOR PLAN ·

♪ CENTRAL HALL TYPE ♪

First-floor plan of the fourth-stage house construction in New England. The kitchen ell was attached at the rear left side, but is not shown on this plan. From Isham and Brown: *Early Connecticut Houses. Courtesy Dover Publications, Inc.*

First-floor plan of a house with the chimneys located in the gable ends of the house. This plan is of the Sheldon Woodbridge House in Hartford, Connecticut, about 1715. From Isham and Brown: *Early Connecticut Houses. Courtesy Dover Publications, Inc.*

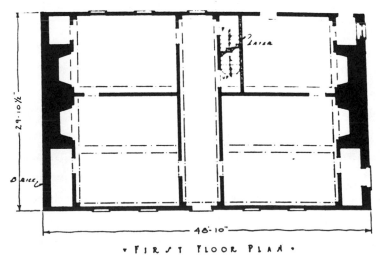

· FIRST FLOOR PLAN ·

♪ SHELDON WOODBRIDGE HOUSE - HARTFORD ♪

kitchen relocated as an ell attached to the rear of the house. The major change was the placing of a commodious hall crosswise in the center of the house. On one side of the hall an attractive staircase was built. Two rooms were located on each side of the hall on both the first and second floors. The intent of the new plan was to make an orderly arrangement of rooms, to ensure privacy for members of the family as they occupied the various rooms, and, perhaps not incidentally, to provide an advantageous space to display attractive household furnishings. The entire revamping of the house reflects the increased prosperity of the colonists, as well as the continued acceptance of English refinements relating to their daily lives. The Georgian house was a trim, well-balanced, attractive, and, above all, a comfortable dwelling.

The creation of the center hall in the Georgian style of architecture naturally demanded that the chimney stack be relocated, but necessarily retained, since fireplaces continued to be the major source of heat in New England. At least one diary of the region mentions the use of stoves, but little is known about their construction and the extent of their use.

In the new plan two chimney stacks were built, one each in the center of the partition wall between the rooms on the first and second floors. This plan provided four fireplaces, one for each room on each side of the hall. In this way the symmetrical arrangement of features was maintained in a true Georgian fashion. The two chimney stacks were built on strong foundations in the cellar, and extended upward through the house until they projected through the roof, midway between the center and the gable ends. The kitchen ell was attached to the rear of the house, unlike the practice in the South, where the kitchen was a separate building; and it had a fireplace with a separate chimney stack. This facility, of course, being a cooking fireplace, was larger than those located in the main house, which were principally for heating.

Although relocated, there was little change in the form and size of the fireplaces. The trend toward greater width and less height in the opening became well established. Those in the main house were neither inordinately large nor very small, the factor determining their size usually being the size of the room in which they were located. Most lintels were straight, and continued to be made of stone or wood. A more leisured approach to building permitted the lining of the fireplace chamber and the hearth to be made of local stone more carefully fitted together than had been done heretofore.

A variation of Georgian houses previously described featured gable ends of brick or stone. Such houses had the usual central hall flanked with two rooms on each side on both floors, but the fireplaces were built into the end walls of masonry instead of into the partitions between the rooms. This arrangement was economical to build, and provided an attractive exterior appearance in the contrast of the two building materials, but it lacked the formal balance of the original plan, and caused the fireplaces to be located off-center near the corner of each room. The space on the fireplace wall not used for the fireplace was utilized for closet room, giving the builder an excellent opportunity to embellish the balance of the wall with a paneled door surrounded with typical paneling of the period.

The modest elegance of the early Georgian mode virtually required that the walls of the important rooms be plastered, all except the fireplace wall, which was paneled. For some time a low band of sheathing was used around the lower portion of three walls, terminating on the level of the window sills and topped with a molded edge known as a chair rail. In more elegant houses the chair rail was retained, and below was an arrangement of stiles and rails fitted with appropriate panels. Finally, the "dado," as this low wall paneling was called, shrank to the low baseboard found in houses of the twentieth century.

The next area to come under scrutiny in this survey is the eastern region of the present state of New York. Although some English cultural patterns seeped into this area from nearby New England and New Amsterdam, now occupied by the English, the region was essentially Dutch in character throughout the first half of the eighteenth century. The Dutch held stubbornly to their customs, and this trait is reflected in their architecture. It might be pointed out that this Dutch architecture has had little nationwide impact, being virtually unknown beyond the region where it is located. Its influence has been minimal in comparison to Georgian and Cape Cod styles.

Despite the fact that its history is relatively obscure, one of the major impressions of the region is erroneous, namely, that the Hudson River

Valley was filled with great manors which were operated in the fashion of European feudal estates. It is true that possibly a dozen examples existed (one having a thousand square miles of land), but there were no castles and only a few remnants of the manor houses survive. These show little evidence of living on a grand scale in America. The bulk of the houses were inhabited by farmers, merchants, and traders, who built substantial and long-lasting dwellings. Holland was the most prosperous country in Europe in the seventeenth century, and European standards of living were at least partially duplicated here.

Notice has been taken of the early cellars and the later framed houses built by the pioneers of the region. Unfortunately, none of these has survived to be examined today. By the early eighteenth century more affluence and time permitted the building of better dwellings. A bountiful supply of stones, plus a skill in masonry construction, enabled the builders to employ stone for construction in the Hudson River Val-

The massive Jean Hasbrouck House located on Huguenot Street in New Paltz, New York. This is one of the great houses of the Hudson Valley. It is now known as "Memorial Hall." *Courtesy Historic American Buildings Survey*

The hearth support in the cellar of the Jean Hasbrouck House, New Paltz, New York. *Courtesy Historic American Buildings Survey*

The great size of this chimney in the Jean Hasbrouck House, New Paltz, New York, is evident when compared with the smaller objects surrounding it. *Courtesy Historic American Buildings Survey*

ley. The first houses were one-and-a-half stories high, duplicates of those of wood which had preceded them.

Probably the first change was made when the roof was raised, giving the house two full floors with an attic above, such as the Pieter Bronck House at West Coxsackie, New York. This house has a single sharp slanting roof with a chimney built within the wall of a gable end. Expansion also occurred lengthwise, as in the Hendrick Bries House in Rensselaer County, New York. It was originally four rooms long and one room deep with a loft overhead and a hall crosswise in the middle. There were obviously fireplaces in the two outer rooms on the first floor. There were also houses two rooms wide and one room deep with a chimney stack built between them, such as the Vernooy-Bevier House in Wawarsing, near Ellenville. The fireplaces in these rooms were presumably of a conventional recessed type, for it is reported that the openings were wide.

Jambless fireplace in the Ferry House kitchen at Van Cortlandt Manor, near Tarrytown, New York. The hearth is furnished with appropriate objects including an iron fire back to protect the tiled back wall from deteriorating rapidly. *Courtesy Sleepy Hollow Restorations*

Houses continued to increase in size in the Valley, one of the larger ones being the Jean Hasbrouck House in New Paltz. This was built in 1712 and possesses many of its original architectural features. There are four rooms with a central hall on the first floor, two rooms on each side of the hall. In the partitions between the rooms are the fireplaces with large chimneys in the Dutch fashion of the region. On the first floor there is surviving evidence that a jambless fireplace was removed, while in another room a recessed fireplace remains intact. These types will be discussed in more detail later.

A point worthy of mentioning is that many houses in the Valley were built against a hill, thus exposing a portion of the cellar wall above the ground. Often in such cases one of these cellar rooms was used as a kitchen and had a large recessed fireplace.

The houses built in New York City in the early eighteenth century were probably more typically Dutch in character than those of the Hudson River Valley. Although virtually none has survived, due to the furious demolition practices pursued in the past in the city, some old sketches show the types which were originally built there. It is evident that many were built of brick, that they were frequently more than two stories high, and that the gable end usually faced the street. The Dutch used land here as frugally as they did in their homeland, the narrow end of the house requiring less street frontage than broadside. Steps built above the roof line in the end walls have been facetiously referred to as steps for chimney sweeps.

No chimneys have survived for examination. However, from sketches it is evident that all of them were built within the walls of the house. This procedure is consistent with traditional practices in building chimneys in the North. Generally speaking, fireplaces were large. One author comments that those in the Hudson River Valley accommodated logs drawn in by a horse or an ox, and that such a log was known to have burned for a week.

The fireplaces known to exist in the region fall into three categories, one of which is the jambless type surviving in Washington's Headquarters in Newburgh. Many of this kind must have been built in the Valley, where pioneer conditions survived longer than in New York City. The use of fieldstone in the back wall emphasizes the primitive quality of these facilities. A less primitive sort was located in the cellar-kitchen of many houses. These were of the recessed variety, with large openings to accommodate the household chores, such as cooking, candlemaking, and soapmaking. They had a massive wooden lintel. The fire chamber was a squared rectangle, the hearth was level with the floor, and there was no ornamentation in the whole assembly.

The Dutch fireplace of most importance and charm, however, was the hooded jambless type like the one in the reconstructed Ferry House at Van Cortlandt Manor, near Tarrytown. For this fireplace a large flue was built with an opening similar to that found in Washington's Headquarters at Newburgh. In addition, a hood was dropped about eighteen inches from the ceiling to funnel the smoke into the chimney. Around the lower edge of the hood was placed a large molding with a wide top edge. This shelf-like facility was an integral part of the molding and was probably not originally intended for the use later made of it. No doubt some enterprising Dutch housewife came upon the idea of displaying pewter or pottery on the ledge, and a typical Dutch mantel shelf came into being. The back wall of the fireplace was covered with tiles, a practice widely followed in Holland in earlier times. As a matter of fact, pictures painted by Dutch masters illustrate the use of the ledge as a mantel shelf.

On the very bottom edge of the molding surrounding the hood was hung a valance of checked linen for the kitchen, or possibly of velvet for the parlor. Valances sometimes matched curtains and other draperies in the room. Dutch houses were kept shipshape by weekly laundering of the light fabrics, with several sets being rotated to keep the decor interesting.

Although these jambless fireplaces were used a long time, it is quite evident that they were inefficient devices. The fire was built directly under large flues, and most of the heat went up the chimney. In this respect they were little different from fireplaces used in other regions of the country. There were no jambs to direct the heat into the room or to prevent the fire from being blown sidewise onto adjoining walls and nearby furnishings. Pots were suspended from overhead and there is no evidence that cranes were used to assist the housewife when she wanted to remove cooking utensils from the fire. Their death knell sounded when the best features of Dutch and English fireplaces were merged into a more efficient unit.

Fireplace from the Hewlett House removed from Woodbury, L.I., New York. Built about 1745, this fireplace has a crane with a teakettle suspended from it. The andirons are brass in the Queen Anne style, and on the left end of the hearth is a brazier of copper with iron legs. *Courtesy Metropolitan Museum of Art, gift of Mrs. Robert W. de Forest, 1910*

It is very evident that over the years changes would be made in the style and construction of fireplaces, particularly when they are located in the area of merging English and Dutch cultures. There is an admixture of the two in the Van Cortlandt House which was built in New York City in 1748. At least one fireplace contains many elements of the earlier Dutch examples found in the Hudson River Valley. It is impossible to ascertain at this time whether function or national preference was the dominant reason for change, but close observation clearly reveals that a more efficient form was achieved in this example.

The hood, originally dropping only eighteen inches from the ceiling, was extended downward to about half the height of the room and was supported by a lintel in the front and jambs on the sides. This innovation brought a more effective control of the smoke and a greater heat reflection into the room and was aided by the contracting throat above, which kept less heat from going up the chimney. All of these were gigantic steps in improving the efficiency of the fireplace. A narrow mantel shelf was attached to the lintel to display finery.

The real Dutch charm of the facility lay in the profuse use of tiles. The front and inner sides of the jambs were covered with tiles, as was also the hearth. The bright color of these tiles created an excellent display and were quite satisfactory in reflecting the heat into the room. On the rear wall of the fireplace bricks in the center were left exposed, for tiles there would have become quickly discolored from smoke. The walls on either side of the fireplace were plastered and whitened to provide an atmosphere of cleanliness, and to make an attractive contrast with the materials of the fireplace. Although little English influence can be detected in the features of this fireplace, the shape and size of the opening are very unlike earlier Dutch examples, and closely resemble certain English types. The lintel and the mantel shelf might have been used at the same time in New England, or in any other region covered in this survey.

The final example of mid-century style and workmanship is seen in a room from the Hewlett House of Long Island now located in the Metropolitan Museum of Art in New York City. The entire fireplace wall of the room is paneled, although not symmetrically. Around the fireplace opening is a large bolection molding with an overmantel arrangement of one large panel and two smaller ones, each of them having bolection moldings. There are two short pilasters in the overmantel, which curiously do not have a base, but terminate in the conventional manner in the cornice above. On the right and left of the opening are other pilasters which reach from the floor to the ceiling. This architectural unit might as well have been located in nearby Connecticut as on Long Island.

The Dutch tiles on the face and sides of the jambs were typical of those sold in New York City in the 1740s. While some had secular themes, others were known as "scripture" tiles because they depicted religious scenes which prompted the teaching of Bible stories when children gathered around the fireplace. Although the hearth is a block of limestone taken from the region of the house, it is possible that it originally was laid with square tiles in the Dutch fashion.

The fire chamber has a horizontal axis, the corners are squared, and it can be truly said that the fireplace embodies the traditional features of Dutch design while set in a paneled end wall of English concept. The same combination can be seen in a few Georgian examples of a later period; however, the use of tiles became rarer and finally disppeared.

The intent of the introductory remarks (in the chapter "Seventeenth Century") about corner fireplaces in the Scandinavian log house of the Delaware Valley is to point out that there were some differences in the details of primitive type architecture, and that procedures in Philadelphia were also different from those in the hinterland, although a few log houses were built on the site before the English arrived. The settlers in the back country of Pennsylvania came into the region through the port of Philadelphia, but it should be noted that the city itself quickly became a prosperous English prototype, with a grid layout of streets lined with brick houses in the London mode. Since such edifices were ill suited for immediate erection in the countryside, the pioneers of New Jersey, Pennsylvania, and Delaware built log cabins as their first permanent shelters. The shells of these one-room cabins show some Scandinavian influence. However, the location of the chimney indicates a variation, and possibly an improvement.

In this area and period of time the log cabin form was created in America. It was to become a symbol of pioneer life in western Pennsylvania and farther west. It consisted of one room with a loft, a few small openings, a thatched or boarded roof, and a fireplace located in the *center* of the gable end. The first chimneys were possibly built of wattle and daub. *The Early Architecture of Western Pennsylvania*, by Charles Morse Stotz, shows a log cabin with a chimney of cobwork. This procedure involved the building of a chimney with small logs, notched and laid on top of each other in a manner similar to the building of a log cabin. The entire construction was covered with mud to make it fireproof(???). The construction was confirmed by F. A. Michaux who traveled in Pennsylvania in 1802. He states:

Views of the Bertolet House located near Reading, Pennsylvania. *(Top left)* Exterior of the house, the location of the chimney indicating the division of rooms within the house. The smaller room is to the right of the chimney. *(Bottom left)* The giant fireplace with its large hand-hewn lintel. *(Right)* The reconstructed fireplace. The function of the piece of wood on which the lintel rests is not known. *(Below)* The two doorways to the small room and the great tapering throat of the chimney which was enclosed in the loft of the building. *Courtesy Pennsylvania Historical and Museum Commission*

These houses are made of the trunks of trees, from twenty to thirty feet long, and four or five inches in diameter, placed one above another, and supported by letting their ends into each other. . . . The chimney which is always at one of the ends, is also made of trunks of trees of suitable length.

Inevitable improvements were made in the early log houses of the region. One simple method was to build a similar structure of stone; however, the earlier overall dimensions and location of the fireplace and chimney remained with little change. In Pennsylvania a major alteration occurred when the one-room cabin was enlarged and the interior divided into two rooms of unequal size, with a loft overhead. Such a cabin can be seen at the Bertolet cabin on the site of the Daniel Boone Homestead in Berks County near Reading. An important innovation was made on the interior, for the fireplace was moved from the end wall to the wall partitioning the structure. Most amazing is that the fireplace was located in the smaller of the two rooms.

The floor plan of the two-room house was developed into a three-room plan consisting of a *Kuche* (kitchen), a *Stube* (parlor), and a *Kammer* (bedroom). The unusually large kitchen in this plan was later divided into two rooms indicated by the broken lines. The small rectangle of broken lines in the *Stube* indicates the location of the five-plate stove.

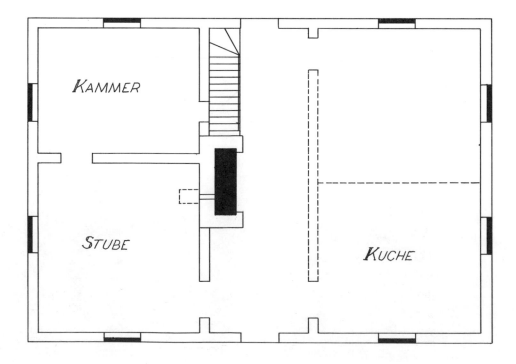

GERMAN HOUSE

Color Plate

Early nineteenth-century fireplace furnished with brass objects typical of the period. The warming pan of sheet brass was made by Hunneman of Boston, and has his name imprinted on the lid. Richard Wittingham, of New York, made the andirons, which have a steeple-top design like the fire tools. The fire tools are not identified by a maker's mark, but are very probably the product of an American craftsman. The mantle is attributed to Robert Wellford, a plaster composition ornament maker of Philadelphia.

Courtesy Henry Francis du Pont Winterthur Museum

A cast-iron five-plate jamb stove, fired from the kitchen room, was used to heat the Miksch Tobacco Shop. This stove, dated 1760, was cast in Pennsylvania by a furnace and has the Low German biblical quotation: "Las Dich Nicht Gelyssten Deines Neststen Gut," translated "Thou shalt not covet thy neighbor's goods." *Courtesy Old Salem, Inc., Winston-Salem, North Carolina*

This small room became the most important room of the house. It served as an entry into the house; and besides containing the fireplace, the steps to the second floor or loft were located here. It really was the all-purpose room. In it the cooking and eating took place and the daily chores of the household were performed because it was kept constantly warm by the fireplace. The fireplace was built of stone over which a large throat and chimney were built to carry away the smoke. But through them much of the heat passed to the outside.

In the countryside, logs continued to be the major building material; however, the log cabin was slowly becoming the log house. The width and length were both increased and the rectangular form became almost a square. Retained was the long, narrow room across one end of the house with its fireplace built as an integral part of the dividing wall between it and the rest of the house. The remaining part was no longer one big room, but was divided into two parts, thus providing a kitchen (the long narrow room), a parlor, and a bedroom on the first floor. In many cases, the same arrangement of rooms was constructed on the second floor, with possibly a small fireplace in one of the rooms. This plan

This large fireplace is located in the Cloister at Ephrata, Pennsylvania, built in the first half of the eighteenth century. Most of the fireplaces in the Cloister have raised hearths similar to this one. The projecting facility at the left end of the fireplace contains a kettle for a constant supply of hot water. *Courtesy Pennsylvania Historical and Museum Commission*

is considered to be a practice brought from Europe by immigrants from Germany and Switzerland. The chimney was usually off-center, and only in rare cases was there a second chimney in the gable end of the house. In other words, in Pennsylvania an off-center chimney suggested a German occupant, two end chimneys an English resident.

It is extremely important to note here that houses with the three-room arrangement were built of both logs and stone, and examples of both survive today in Lancaster County, Pennsylvania. In some houses, to supplement the heat supplied in the kitchen from the fireplace, a hole was cut into the back fireplace wall into which a stove was inserted, the body of which was in the parlor. This was a five-sided box of iron standing on feet, with an open end in the fireplace wall into which wood was placed and through which the smoke moved back into the fireplace and up the chimney. Three of the five plates of the stove were decorated with designs based on incidents from the Bible with an explanation in the German language. After stovepipe was invented (in the 1760s), they became six-plate stoves and were moved away from the wall to improve the circulation of heat. Eventually, they became ten-plate stoves and were used widely in Pennsylvania by most of the ethnic groups living there.

Although most of the residences of the period have not survived with their fireplaces intact, it is important to note that some important buildings can still be examined in their original form. These are the Moravian buildings in Bethlehem and those of the Seventh Day Baptists in Ephrata. Two fireplaces in the Gemienhaus at Bethlehem are notable because they are located in opposite walls of a hall, and appear to have been only facilities for operating stoves in adjoining rooms. This deduction is based on the observation that two fireplace openings were not needed in a relatively narrow hall, particularly not opposite each other. One might also conclude that the raised hearths of these fireplaces were level with the bottom plates of stoves and that the purpose of the whole arrangement was to provide a convenient way for feeding the stoves. It might also be pointed out that stoves could have been the only source of heat in these rooms, for there is no evidence of hearths or other remnants of fireplaces within the rooms. In the same building is located a corner fireplace, rarely found in the "Dutch Country" of Pennsylvania. The fireplaces in the Cloisters at Ephrata are important because they are

Letitia House is certainly one of the earliest and most charming houses in the Philadelphia region. It was removed from its downtown location to Fairmount Park in 1883, and is open daily to the public. *Courtesy Philadelphia Museum of Art*

Fireplace with bolection molding and mantel shelf in the Letitia House in Philadelphia, built about 1715. This is one of the earliest surviving mantel shelves in America. The coving jambs are uncommonly large, and probably aided in projecting heat into the room. *Courtesy Philadelphia Museum of Art*

higher than wide, they are covered with plaster, and they have raised hearths, all practices having earlier roots in European architecture.

Although styles of architecture changed slowly in the hinterlands of Pennsylvania, New Jersey, and Delaware, this conservatism was not typical of the urban areas. In 1687 the Provincial Council of Philadelphia decreed that all caves and crude dwellings were to be destroyed; by 1690 Philadelphia had about 1,000 brick houses. In many of these early houses there were admixtures of architectural details from England, Sweden, and Germany. The use of brick was principally an English feature, spurred by the London fire of 1666. Houses in Germantown and other areas had pent roofs in the German manner, and corner fireplaces in the Swedish mode also found acceptance by residents.

The adoption of corner fireplaces is strikingly explained by Waterman in his book, *The Dwellings of Colonial America:*

> The corner fireplace, almost unknown in Great Britain, France, and the Rhine Valley except in academic designs, was the most common one of Swedish traditional building, and even remained a favorite feature of country and town houses of the gentry while palaces and public buildings were becoming Gallicised. . . .
>
> The earliest example of this plan seems to be the Letitia House, once standing in downtown Philadelphia and now removed to Fairmount Park. . . . At the left are corner fireplaces, back to back, so

they form a triangular chimney (stack). The building is two stories high with much the same upstairs as down. There is little interior trim except a vast bolection or rolling moulding around the fireplace, a characteristic of the region up to about 1750.

Some books on the subject of American architecture do not mention the Letitia House; however, any student of the subject must recognize that its form and interior appendages are important facets in the development of the subject. It is of interest that it is built of brick and has a pent roof, but, most importantly, it has four corner fireplaces. Little needs to be said about the chimney, for it is obviously built of brick and confined within the wall of the house. The chimney cap, however, is highly ornamented in the English tradition. Although the ornamentation is modest in comparison to earlier English examples, it is evidence of English architectural influence in America. The fine bolection molding of one of the fireplaces has been previously mentioned. A point of great interest is the diagonal corner location of the fireplaces in the four main rooms of the house.

Although some corner fireplaces are built flat against the wall, these are not. In a discussion of the Swedish log house it was pointed out that the building of a diagonal one was an economical procedure, for only one wall needed to be added to the existing walls to form the flue and the fireplace. In the earliest structures this consideration could have been of great importance, but time and affluence were now on the side of the builder. The intent now must have been to provide an attractive setting within the house. The importance of esthetics is proved by the presence of the bolection molding, which was certainly not present in the log cabin. The corner fireplace counterbalanced the stairs in the opposite corner. If the fireplace had been placed against one of the walls this nicety of balance would not have been achieved. Also applicable is the notion that fireplaces should be located opposite the entry into a room, so that they could be immediately seen and appreciated. These corner fireplaces were not directly opposite the point of entry into the rooms, but they were certainly more conspicuous than as if they had been located on one of the side walls. Finally, by looking at the floor plan of the house one can quickly see that the corner was an advantageous location for the fireplace, as far as heating the room was concerned. The small

Unrestored first-floor fireplace in the Trent House, Trenton, New Jersey, showing the curved corner section between the jambs and the back wall. Also shows the herringbone arrangement of the bricks. *(Below)* Kitchen fireplace in the basement of the Trent House, Trenton, New Jersey. This one appears to have been plastered at one time, but the bricks are exposed at the back where the heat was the most intense and the plaster deteriorated. *Courtesy Historic American Buildings Survey*

amount of heat projected into the room was well spread, although quite dissipated by the time the farthest corners were reached.

The next house of interest, among many others in the region, is the Trent House in Trenton, New Jersey. The exterior of the house belies its early construction (1719). It is also built of brick, with a symmetrical arrangement of openings in the facade suggesting a Georgian mansion rather than one of the Queen Anne period. Its central hall is flanked by two rooms, each having a corner fireplace—an arrangement not unlike having two Letitia houses with a center hall between them. This arrangement is quite satisfactory. The fireplace in the dining room is small and simply executed. It has the early herringbone arrangement in the bricks of the back wall, and has two panels in the overmantel. The fireplace in the living room is much larger; it has crossetted corners in the molding but not in the panels of the overmantel. It has a paneled dado and an air of simple elegance is present. These features, combined with a beautiful stair in the Swedish style, indicate a trend toward the profuse elegance of later houses in the Philadelphia region.

In passing, some mention should be made of "Graeme Park," twenty miles north of Philadelphia, which was built in 1722. This handsome country house is three rooms long and one room deep, the floor plan of the Swedish *parstuga*. Of course, one would expect this house to have corner fireplaces, but it has none. The fireplaces are neatly placed near the center of each room and are flanked by doors.

Floor plan of the Trent House, Trenton, New Jersey, showing the location of the corner fireplaces. From Waterman, Thomas Tileson: *The Dwellings of Colonial America. Courtesy University of North Carolina Press*

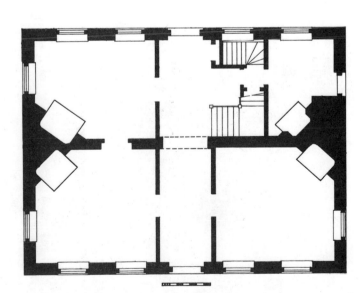

The paneling of the fireplace walls is an outstanding example of design and craftsmanship. The chimney-breast of the "Great Room" projects into the room. The paneling has an entablature reminiscent of fine houses built later in the eighteenth century. Its massive cornice is enhanced with "Wall of Troy" dentils, and the single overmantel panel has a broken pediment with crossetted corners. The corners of the door frames are similarly treated. The fronts of the jambs are covered with slabs of marble, another example of the emerging elegance of the region. The marble is enclosed with a small bolection molding, above which is mounted a narrow mantel shelf.

The opening of the fireplace chamber is almost a perfect square, suggesting proportions found in some earlier examples. The back inner corners are square, and the walls are covered with plaster. The hearth is laid with square blocks of stone or marble and, on the back wall, is a fire back of iron to protect the wall from rapid deterioration.

Front elevation of "Graeme Park" in Montgomery County, Pennsylvania. Although it is more attractive in its presently restored condition, it was obviously an important house in its day. The fancy brickwork in the chimneys is an unusual feature. *Courtesy Pennsylvania Historical and Museum Commission*

The projecting chimney-breast in the "Great Room" in "Graeme Park," which is in a remarkable state of preservation. *Courtesy Pennsylvania Historical and Museum Commission*

In a lesser room the chimney-breast projects only six or eight inches, the cornice lacks the "Wall of Troy" dentil, but the overmantel panel has crossetted corners. The door frames do not. The fireplace opening is essentially the same size and proportion as that in the "Great Room," but lacks the marble facing on the front of the jambs. The woodwork of both rooms is well preserved and are superb examples of paneling around a fireplace.

Two houses built in the immediate Philadelphia area a decade or two later than "Graeme Park" are "Stenton" and "Hope Lodge." "Stenton," in Germantown, was built of brick in the manner of contemporary English architecture. The first floor is symmetrically arranged with two rooms on each side of the hall. Its transverse hall is broken near the center with a wall and a narrow doorway. The width of the doorway

permitted a closet to be built on one side and a corner fireplace on the other. The two chimneys indicate that the flue of the oddly placed fireplace was cut into an adjoining chimney.

Beyond the city limits, in White Marsh, stands the solid brick house called "Hope Lodge," built in the 1730s or 40s. The brochure describing the house points out that:

> The designer of the house, who is unknown, spoke the architectural language of the enterprising and successful eighteenth century merchant, businessman, and man of affairs. It is a forceful and confident style, derived from the classical revival and the humanism of the Renaissance.
>
> Classical forms pervade the house. The symmetry associated with the Georgian [or late Queen Anne] design can be seen in the imposing brick exterior. It has magnificent interior features, vari-

(Top left) The vertical fenestration of "Hope Lodge," near Philadelphia, Pennsylvania, is very evident in this front view of this colonial Queen Anne masterpiece. Its great coved cornice and dormer windows are among its other attractive features. *(Bottom left)* A bedroom fireplace framed with tiles at "Hope Lodge." The inner hearth is covered with tiles, but the outer portion is a huge slab of native marble. The arrangement of the paneling is simple but dignified. *Courtesy Pennsylvania Historical and Museum Commission*

Fireplace in a front room on the first floor of "Hope Lodge." The whole interior of the fireplace appears to have been originally plastered, much of which remains except on the smoke channel in the middle of the back wall. This portion was not protected by the fire back resting on the hearth. *Courtesy Pennsylvania Historical and Museum Commission*

ously molded wainscots, large fireplaces, with blue and white
Dutch tiles [and marble] classical pilasters and pediments with
frame, and cap doorways, and a spacious central hallway bisected
by a prominent arch.

"Hope Lodge" and its outbuildings offer the student an unusual
opportunity to study fireplaces. The ones located in the two front rooms
of the first floor are very similar. The openings are large, about three
feet high by six feet long. The front surfaces of the jambs are covered
with marble obtained from a local quarry, with contours cut into both
the edges and the surfaces. In addition, the hearths have a large slab of
marble, about one foot by six feet, laid on the very front edge, where it
would not be deteriorated by the fire. The remaining area of the hearths
consists of regular bricks, except one, which has square tiles. In the front
corner of the jambs, on each side of the fireplaces, a cove was built either
as a decorative device or for a function not yet identified. This is the
earliest example of this feature found for this survey, but one that became common practice, at least in Pennsylvania. One hypothesis concerning the purpose of the cove is that it was designed as a resting place
for fire tools; a very attractive use, but not a documented one. The fire
chambers have square corners at the rear, and in the back wall is a smoke
channel similar to those found in New England, but less commonly
found in Pennsylvania fireplaces. The walls of the rooms are plastered
with a dado on the lower portion. The ends of the fireplace walls are
covered with simple rectangular panels, in which doors with arched tops
are located. The fireplace with marble surrounds is more elegant than
those of "Graeme Park," but the paneling suggests a less sophisticated
country dwelling.

In other major rooms of the house the fireplaces are very similar to
those described, except that the faces of the jambs and a border under
the lintels are covered with Delft tiles. One of the patterns is that of a
windmill, and when the house was restored in the 1920s missing tiles were
supplied in the identical color and pattern by the same company in
Holland which made the originals. None of the fireplaces has a mantel
shelf, and all are enclosed or framed by the same simple arrangement of
panels. In the basement, however, is a large cooking fireplace which was
used before the adjoining kitchen building was erected later in the century. This fireplace has a large recessed opening with no ornamentation.

A similar small one is also located in a room thought to have been used as an office. There is also a small one in the attic.

The fireplace in the kitchen outbuilding is unusually small for the demands made of such a facility. This one has a bake oven located to one side with a vent into the main chimney, and a slot in the floor where spent ashes were poked down a flue emptying through a hole in the jamb into the hearth of the fireplace. This is a most unusual arrangement, and probably functioned in a very satisfactory manner.

The styles and materials used to build houses in the South in the seventeenth and early eighteenth centuries varied from modest one-room types to reasonably elegant multi-roomed examples. Virtually none was built of stone. The building of substantial houses of brick in this early era is usually attributed to the fact that immigrants of a reasonably high economic level settled in the South, plus the fact that prosperity came quickly through the extensive growing of tobacco which was sold or traded abroad. It is particularly interesting that bricks were used so extensively in the presence of endless woodlands, and in spite of the mild climate of the region. It might be pointed out that despite the use of masonry in the South, most of the surviving houses of seventeenth-century America are located in New England, where they were built of wood.

The constant need for a one-room house explains the continued construction of this type well into the eighteenth century. That they were also enlarged is well illustrated in *Eighteenth-Century Houses of Williamsburg* by Marcus Whiffen. For example, it is assumed that the Benjamin Waller House originally consisted of only one room with a massive chimney, receding weatherings, and an elaborate chimney cap. Subsequently, a hall was added to the end opposite the chimney, and another room was added beyond the hall. Thus, the common procedure in enlarging a southern house was followed precisely. But, to further enlarge the house, another room was added on the north side of the first room, thereby creating the famous "L" shape of many southern houses, a plan also found in the James Getty House at the corner of the Palace Green and the Duke of Gloucester Street. The intent of a house only one room in width was to promote cross-ventilation in the oppressingly hot southern climate.

Builders of the eighteenth century are famous for their ingenuity, and we naturally expect various plans to have been used to enlarge the original one-room house. Making it two rooms wide was an early and logical procedure, as was also making it two rooms deep, with a side hall. In this plan a second room was located directly in back of the front room, with a side hall crossing the ends of both rooms and providing access to each without entering the other. This plan provided privacy in reaching the various rooms of the house, for there was a stairway to the second floor in this hall. In addition, this plan enhanced the proportions and general appearance of the structure.

The chimney is located within the walls of the house, the one stack providing flues for a corner fireplace in each room on the first floor. Because of the attention paid to corner fireplaces, favored by the Swedes in Pennsylvania, a few additional remarks might be made here. A quotation found in *Colonial Williamsburg, Its Buildings and Gardens* by Kocher and Dearstyne warrants inclusion here. They say:

> The corner fireplace was an innovation of the time of William and Mary. John Evelyn speaks of it disdainfully in 1692, saying that this "plan of placing fireplaces in the corner of rooms has come into fashion. . . . I predict that it will spoil many noble houses and rooms if followed. It does only well in very small and triflying room."

The perceptive reader will immediately detect an inconsistency between this statement and one cited earlier by Waterman, who says that corner fireplaces were only an academic concept in Europe (except in Scandinavia) in the seventeenth century. This difference of opinion could well be the subject of an extensive research project; however, this question does not fall within the scope of this survey. Needless to say, many houses in Williamsburg, and probably other parts of the South, have such fireplaces, and some examples might qualify as "noble" houses.

A plan used to enlarge the house two rooms wide with a central passage was to add narrow rooms across the back of the house which Forman

Corner fireplace located in the lower middle room of the Governor's Palace at Williamsburg, Virginia. The location and elegance of the facility refutes the comment that its location would spoil many "noble houses and rooms if followed." *Courtesy Colonial Williamsburg* calls "cells." The front part of the house remained unchanged with its fireplaces and chimneys at the peaks of the gable ends. The addition at the back may or may not have had fireplaces and chimneys; however, they could have been easily omitted because such rooms were used for storage or sleeping. The addition across the back of the house caused the roof line to be elongated, making the form of the house closely resemble that of a New England salt box. The longer back roof of this type is called a "catslide." These additional rooms made the house deeper, and led to the common four-room arrangement of Georgian houses. An example of a such a plan is the John Blair House in Williamsburg.

Another floor plan used in the South to provide houses with an arrangement for good ventilation is known as the "U plan." Such houses were built two rooms wide and two rooms deep, with a center hall between the two front rooms. The back rooms were not connected, and thus the house was built in the shape of a "U," with ample ventilation on three sides of the back rooms. These houses were later changed into a square by enclosing the area between the two back rooms, the floor plan coming to resemble that of a typical Georgian house.

Still another way for slightly enlarging the early eighteenth-century house in Virginia and Maryland was the addition of ingle projections on each side of the chimney, or between two chimneys. The term "ingle nook" refers to a bench or other seating device within the confines of a large fireplace, usually against the jamb. This facility was reserved for old people and/or children who needed the comfort of a warm seat near the fire.

The single projections were really closets built outside the fireplace using the jambs as a common wall for both units. Although most examples were built only on the first floor, a few are known to have been built on both the first and second floors. They are usually deeper than the fireplace chamber, and extend beyond the rear wall of the fireplace. The historians do not comment about the function of these additions; however, they must have been important adjuncts or they would

Projecting ingle nook between two chimneys on the Alexander Craig House in Williamsburg, Virginia. *Courtesy Colonial Williamsburg*

WILLIAMSBURG, JAN. 11, 1770.

JOSHUA KENDALL,

HOUSE-CARPENTER and JOINER,

BEGS leave to inform the Public that he is removed to a house nearly opposite to Dr. *James Carter's*, in the Back-street. All Gentlemen who shall honour him with their commands, in the above branches, may depend on their being faithfully and expeditiously executed, upon the most reasonable terms.

He also makes and carves CHIMNEY PIECES of wood, as ornaments to any Gentleman's apartments; and likewise makes the best and newest invented *Venetian* SUN BLINDS for windows, that move to any position so as to give different lights, they screen from the scorching rays of the sun, draw up as a curtain, prevent being overlooked, give a cool refreshing air in hot weather, and are the greatest preservatives of furniture of any thing of the kind ever invented.

N. B. HOUSE-PAINTING and GLAZING performed in the neatest and genteelest manner.

There are no records or surviving artifacts attesting to the fact that there were fine chimney-breasts in Williamsburg, Virginia, houses. Of course, this man does not claim to make fine ones but at least he made chimney-pieces (chimney-breasts). *Virginia Gazette, January 18, 1770*

not have been built. They obviously would have been excellent places to sleep on a very cold night.

The final development in house planning in the early eighteenth century culminated in the four-room plan, which reached the peak of its development in the second half of the century. It has been pointed out that houses otherwise planned evolved into this arrangement, and its acceptance was overwhelming; after the middle of the century most houses of substance were built in this manner. The plan consisted of a square or almost-square rectangular house with a hall through the center of the house from front to rear. On each side two rooms were located with a partition (often of masonry materials) between them in which fireplaces were built, either centered or slightly off-center. Fireplaces were placed flat against walls or diagonally across corners of the rooms. Thus, in a variety of ways the Georgian style of architecture came into full bloom in America.

It must be noted, however, that even in the first half of the century the four-room plan was used in the South. "Westover," in Charles City

The modest elegance of the Wythe House in Williamsburg, Virginia, is seen in the marble fireplace mantlepiece located in the dining room. *Courtesy Colonial Williamsburg*

County, Virginia, was built with four rooms on the first floor in 1726, and "Carter's Grove," near Williamsburg, Virginia, was built at mid-century, 1751. Both are examples of the finest Georgian architecture in America. It is interesting to observe that the chimneys in "Westover" are built in the end walls and those of "Carter's Grove" are built in the partitions between the room.

Another example of the four-room plan that deserves attention is the Peyton Randolph House in Williamsburg, Virginia, which was built in 1715 or 1716. Although later enlarged, the first portion of the house was essentially square and in 1783 it was described as having "four rooms on a floor." It is reported in *Eighteenth-Century Houses of Williamsburg* by Whiffen that "Inside, the Peyton Randolph House is distinguished by the possession of the best series of paneled rooms in Williamsburg." On the first floor, four rooms and the hall are paneled; on the upper floor, three rooms are paneled. The unique aspect of this house is that the first square portion is served by one chimney stack which has six fireplaces in it, three on each floor. One of the fireplaces on the first floor has jambs faced with marble, a marble mantel shelf, and a marble panel as an overmantel. A marble hearth extends into the room, the inner space being probably laid with bricks. This example is a modest move toward the ornamentation which followed.

Another house to be observed at Williamsburg is the Wythe House, built about 1750, and considered the most handsome house in the town. Architect Richard Taliaferro followed the four-room plan on the first floor with the chimney stacks being in the partitions between the rooms. The house is built of brick with a balanced arrangement of openings in the facade. The roof is hipped, through which the two large chimney stacks extend with ornamented caps.

None of the mantelpieces are original to the house. In the dining room is an attractive marble example with a keystone effect in the center of the lintel-piece. The balance is carved into panels, one on each side of the center and one on each vertical part facing the jambs.

It has been pointed out that enlarging the house in the South was one of the ways of improving it, particularly as families increased in size and prosperity rewarded their efforts in the fields and the counting houses. It was a very natural procedure, also, to enrich the interior of the house with more attractive fittings, such as paneling, cornices, chair rails, etc., with particular attention focused on the decoration of the fireplace.

A pattern of ornamentation seems to have evolved by placing a minimal arrangement of paneling and a mantel shelf of varying width on the fireplace wall, the other walls being plastered. One of the modest arrangements is found in the Keeper's Chamber in the Public Gaol in Williamsburg. There an attractive arched lintel with vertical jambs is framed with a bolection molding in the style of the early eighteenth century. Over the width of the opening are three fielded panels on top of which is attached a narrow mantel shelf. On the shelf is a garniture of pewter plates and candlesticks of the period. The whole assembly is a bit more than half the height of the room, the balance of the walls being plastered and whitened. This example is a very modest attempt to ornament a fireplace opening; the crescendo heightens in other examples in the village.

Another fireplace with an arched lintel and border of fielded panels can be seen in one of the fireplaces of the Market Square Tavern; however, this one has panels on the sides as well as across the top. The room in the Public Gaol has only a chair rail; this one has a paneled dado to add to its modest elegance. A room with panels around the fireplace and across its width, but only half its height, is located in the Nelson Galt House. This one has a double row of panels in its dado, and its decor illustrates a transitional trend toward the higher Georgian fashion which followed.

While the subject of southern chimneys and fireplaces has been dealt with at length, one aspect has not been touched upon—namely, the unusual characteristics of the chimney built outside the walls of the house. This type of construction is by no means universal. On some houses both chimneys are outside the house walls; on others, both are on the interior; and one can find instances where one is within the wall and the other without. But the rarest of all is to find half the chimney within the wall, and the other half outside it. The chimneys on the Gaol at Williamsburg are among the few examples of this type. In other words, the concept that southern chimneys are always located outside the walls of the house is simply not a fact.

However, since a great many outside chimneys (some separate

from the building) are encountered, it is pertinent to examine the reasons for their location. The common theory is that chimneys radiate heat and by locating them outside the walls of the house the interior is kept cool. There seems to be little dispute about this conclusion. In the second place, separating the construction of the house from that of the chimney was an efficient procedure. There was little interdependence of workmen involved, particularly in houses of wood. The carpenter built the house and the mason built the chimney. Additionally, there was no long joint between the chimney and the house to be made weathertight if they were separate. Adjoining surfaces could have presented a difficult problem without the use of modern caulking substances. It is also apparent that by keeping the woodwork away from the chimney flue the chances for fire were minimized, especially since records of many unfortunate fires show the likelihood. As a final point, placing the fireplace and chimney on the outside increased the floor space and gave the room better proportions. How many of these considerations were important to the builder and the owner is a matter of conjecture today. These are but evident reasons and presumably there may have been other legitimate considerations which influenced such a decision.

A second important feature of these chimneys is their shape. A number of alternatives was available. One was to build a straight and uniform stack from the ground to the top of the chimney. The unfortunate esthetic appearance of this construction is immediately evident. The natural alternative was to taper the stack from the bottom to the top. Although this plan afforded only a slight improvement over the straight stack, some examples of this type do exist.

The general practice of the southern builder was to start with a base as large as the size of the fireplace demanded. One fireplace is known to have a lintel span of fifteen feet, but this is an uncommonly large example. A uniform width and depth of the chimney were continued to the second floor level, where the cross-section of the chimney was reduced in size for esthetic reasons, and because the smaller fireplace on the second floor could be accommodated by a smaller flue. This reduction in size was achieved by tapering the walls of the chimney inward, like a small roof, and laying bricks flat on the taper. This procedure was usually followed in reducing the width and depth of the chimney. These slanting

The separation of the chimney from the house is very evident in this view of the Bracken House kitchen at Williamsburg, Virginia. *Courtesy Colonial Williamsburg*

areas are called "weatherings." A similar reduction was often made above the second-floor fireplace, if there was one, and the chimney emerged above the roof line as a slender shaft in comparison to its broad base. The masonry work in these chimneys is an excellent example of the skill of the craftsman and certainly one of the most distinctive features of southern architecture in the eighteenth century.

One would logically think that after a fireplace was built, it subsequently required little attention. The business ledger of Humphry Harwood, a bricklayer in Williamsburg, Virginia, in the late eighteenth century indicates that changes and repairs were a common practice of the time. The need probably arose because brick with lasting qualities comparable to modern firebrick was not available, and it is possible that the constant heat of the fire impaired the quality of the mortar. In any event, the following entries are evidence that his services were required after chimneys and fireplaces were built.

Edmund Randolp Esq. (for Court House) Dr.

1777

January 27 ... To Cuting away Chimney & Working in 2 New
Grates 17/6 & plastering Harth   —/17/6

Two of the three chimneys of the Public Gaol at Williamsburg, Virginia, are partially within the walls of the building, the balance outside. The writer has found very few examples of this procedure in making this survey. *Courtesy Colonial Williamsburg*

Mr. Alexander Purdie (Printer) Dr.

1777		
April 24	. . . To takeing Down kitching Chimney & Cleaning bricks 26/	1/6/—
April 30	. . . To building Kitching Chimney /75/—	3/15/—

Mr. William Hornsby Dr.

1779		
April 3	. . . To laying Kitching Harth	—/22/6
10	. . . To altering fier place in Chamber	—/48/—
May 8	. . . To puting up Crane in Kitching Chimney	/24/—
		1/4/—

The Reverend Robert Andrews Dr.

1780		
May 22	. . . To 12 days of work of my People Moveing House at /2/—Old Price.	
30	. . . To building Chimney /60/— & underpinning House /20/—	4/0/—

Capt. Robert Martin (that married Widow Jackson) Dr.

December 23 . . . To plastering a fireplace /3/9	—/3/9

Mr. James Moir Dr.

1783		
March 5	. . . To building up the Brest of Chimney	—/15/—

General Thomas Nelson Dr.

1783		
June 30	. . . To building a Chimney for Nursery	3/10/—
October 28	. . . To building Laundry Chimney & 2 days labor	
		3/16/—

The Reverend James Madison Dr.

1783		
October 9th	. . . To laying Kitchn harth /3/9 & Layg Kitching (sic) floor /8/9	—/12/6
	To Repairing Kitchn Chimney & Takeing down Stove and Oven /15/—	—/15/—
18	. . . To setting up a Grate /7/6 & lay on a marble slab /2/—	—/9/6
	To repairing Chimney in Parlor /1/6	—/1/6

Mr. Walker Maury (Master of Grammer School) at Capitol Dr.

January 26	. . . To 14 bushs of lime at 1/— & building Chimney in the Capitol 30/— & 6 days labr at /2/6	2/99/—
February 7	. . . To 60 bricks /2/— & laying an harth to Chimney in Capitol /3/—	—/5/—
	To ½ days labor /1/3	—/1/3
October 30	. . . To 160 bricks at /3/— & setting up a grate	—/12/3
	To labours work /2/—	—/2/—

Mr. George Jackson Dr.

1783
December 23 . . . To repairing Back to Chimney & Harth   /5/—

Mr. Henry Nicholson Dr.

August 31	. . . To takeing down Chimney 125/—	1/5/—
Sept. 3	. . . To 7 days labr at /2/6 & rebuilding chimney /70/—	4/7/6

Although many aspects of domestic architecture have been discussed, it is certainly evident that attention has been focused on details which helped to enlarge and enrich the house. The fireplace and chimney played important parts in this evolving process. The emphasis on enlargement and enrichment seems to have been a logical procedure, for man has always sought a better place in which to live. Despite the limitations of the medieval house, it is evident it had much charm. The early twisting streets of Boston were filled with houses of pleasing proportions and had cul-de-sacs which are emulated today.

Despite the fact that the major focus of this survey is directed toward the interior of the house, the exterior becomes significantly more important in the Georgian style which swept the country about mid-century. One of the procedures which became common practice was the use of brick. There were wooden houses in New England and stone houses in Pennsylvania, but the overwhelming number of Georgian houses were built of brick. Bricks have many advantages in building houses, and they are colorful, ranging from pink to deep reds, even to deep blues and almost black, the latter colors being created in the hottest areas of the kilns. Bricks could easily be assembled in such forms as segmental arches and in decorative corner quoins, and they could be laid in either English or Flemish bonds.

The exterior of the house was also made more interesting by a variety of roof styles. The simple and highly efficient gable arrangement was supplemented by gambrel and hipped types. These were ornamented by the addition of dormers in the attics, which increased the usable space within the house, often with the addition of fireplaces. The ridge of the roof was sometimes cut off to accommodate a deck with a surrounding baluster, a "captain's walk."

Certainly one of the most impressive exterior features of the Georgian house was the large chimneys which towered above the roof line. Their great height was necessary because the top of the chimney had to clear any encumbrance to a good draft which the roof might impose. Lacking such clearance, the fireplaces were likely to smoke and be virtually unusable for heating. Tall chimneys are particularly evident when located in the end walls of a house with a hipped roof. Most chimneys were square or rectangular, with adequate provision for the number of flues they needed to hold.

Other exterior elements were added, such as a molded course of bricks as a water table, pedimented windows and doorways, and attractive arrangements of stones or brick leading to doorways with arched fanlights and classical columns. Palladian windows lighted the stair landings, window lights became fewer and large (as larger panes of glass became available), and detailed cornices were re-echoed in the elaborate lintels over the windows. Houses with these embellishments were a far cry from the first huts built at Plymouth and Jamestown.

There was usually some harmony between the tone of embellishments on the outside and on the inside; however, there were also exceptions such as "Kenmore," at Fredricksburg, Virginia, with a plain exterior which completely belies one of the richest interiors in America. On the other hand, motifs in the friezes of fireplaces in the Hammond-Harwood House at Annapolis, Maryland, are repeated in the carved details surrounding the front door. Such exactitude could probably be attributed to the watchful eye of William Buckland, the architect of the house. Regardless of the presence of harmony, or the lack of it, it is perfectly clear that by mid-century the age of elegance in American architecture had arrived.

Although not related to the fireplaces of the house, some comment might be made about the hall and the stairway because of their strategic location and the elegance with which they were executed. The stairway was located on one side of the hall, often toward the rear to provide an entrance area at the front. Sometimes the hall was wider at the rear to accommodate the stairs and continue the spacious appearance of the front area. As a matter of fact, sometimes the stairway was placed off the hall to the right or left, a procedure which maintained the full width of the hall for its entire length, but naturally made one room much smaller than the others.

The stairway usually rose in a long, easy ascent and was bordered with turned or spiraled balusters, on top of which was located a handrail with a finely molded design. Often the staircase became wider at the bottom, and the handrail swung outward, where it was supported by a large and imposing newell post. Beneath the balusters an ingenious arrangement of panels was fitted, and under each step a simple or carved scroll was applied to lend grandeur to the whole arrangement. After viewing this elaborate display of design and craftsmanship, the visitor entered the parlor, where an equal or more fastidious display was to be seen.

The parlor, of course, was only one of the four rooms on the first floor, each having a fireplace, the one in the parlor usually being the most elegant. There were fireplaces with lesser ornamentation in other rooms on the first floor and in those on the second floor and, not infrequently, there was a large cooking fireplace in the basement, particularly in the North where there was not usually a separate kitchen building. There were also fireplaces in attics where children or servants often slept. The latter have virtually no ornamentation, and are simply recessed chambers with a flue to carry away the smoke. In a few rare cases, such as "Stenton" in Germantown (near Philadelphia, Pennsylvania) and the Governor's Palace at Williamsburg, Virginia, corner fireplaces are located in the hall.

To fully understand the ornamentation of the Georgian fireplace one might logically begin by defining the several parts briefly at this point. The area from the hearth to the top of the architrave (molding around the opening) is called the chimney-piece. The portion from the top of the chimney-piece to the ceiling is called the overmantel. Sometimes the whole assembly is referred to as a chimney-piece; other writers call it the chimney-breast. The flat band around the fire chamber opening is called the surround, with squared or crossetted corners, and was made of marble, wood, slate, stone, or brick covered with plaster. The author has not found one original example where brickwork was exposed. The flat surround was usually bordered with a molding of wood edged with designs such as gadrooning, egg-and-dart, or rope. The chimney-piece was superficially supported by trusses or consoles which serve a decorative function only. Immediately above the architrave was a band called the frieze, sometimes plain, but frequently ornamented by applied designs such as flowers, leaves, or drapery. On each end of the frieze a thick console ostensibly supported the mantel shelf. The mantel shelf was also supported by a bed molding with dentils or other decorative details along its bottom edge. Above the mantel shelf was an overmantel panel, enclosed with an architrave with square or crossetted corners. And, finally, above the panel was a broken pediment with square or scrolled ends. There was no standard arrangement of details; some had more, some had less.

Many observations can be made concerning the various details found in American fireplaces of the second half of the eighteenth century. Doubtless one of the most significant is expressed in *Domestic Architecture of the American Colonies and of the Early Republic,* by Fiske Kimball. He points out that the major influence here was Abraham Swan's *British Architect, or Builder's Treasury of Stair Cases.* It was first printed in England in 1745, with American editions published in Philadelphia and Boston in 1775. Kimball points out that many designs for chimney-pieces with consoles (of which there are a great many) were copied, with little modification, from this book. The aid this book gives in dating examples is inestimable since examples bearing a close resemblance to its designs are not likely to predate the book. It also had a direct influence on marble facings made here and abroad, and it is known that some entire mantelpieces were imported and installed in American houses. For sheer elegance no substance was superior to marble for facings. Several exceptions must be noted however; those at "Stenton" (in Germantown, Pennsylvania) and "Westover" predate the publication of the book. It has been previously pointed out that the marble at "Hope Lodge" (near Philadelphia, Pennsylvania) was locally quarried and its installation also predates 1745. This marble is frequently described as a "King of Prussia" type.

Another influence Swan's book might logically have had was in the popularization of mantel shelves. Although such appendages are known

The tapered weatherings on the chimney of the St. George Tucker kitchen, Williamsburg, Virginia, are of two eras. The flat of the eighteenth century, the lower corbeled of the nineteenth century. *Courtesy Colonial Williamsburg*

to have existed in the late seventeenth century, architectural historians are in quite common agreement that they were a rarity until after mid-century. As a matter of fact, Hugh Morrison erroneously points out in his *Early American Architecture* that before 1750 there were "several panels in the chimney-breast, no mantel shelf." Emphasis should be placed here on the fact that at this time there were mantel shelves, and not the later classical type mantelpieces which most persons think of today.

The details of fine Georgian fireplaces are legion. Each one seems to have been a unique array of ornamentation. Architects and builders strive for architectural excellence, and many achieved it by compositions of elements not used in a similar way by another. The following display of chimney-pieces suggests the range from minimal simplicity to the most ornate display. Because there was a lack of chronological sequence in their building, no attempt will be made to arrange them chronologically here. Most regions of the Atlantic seaboard are represented, as well as town and country areas, the concept that grandeur was a city monopoly being dismissed. Kimball says that the most elaborate of all chimney-pieces carved in the colonies was that of the Council Chamber of the Governor Wentworth House at Little Harbor, near Portsmouth, New Hampshire.

The tall Ionic columns of the doorway of the Hammond-Harwood House at Annapolis, Maryland, support an entablature with architrave, pediment, and frieze on which the tobacco-leaf motif is repeated. Carved roses ornament the spandrels and egg-and-dart moldings outline the door and fan-light. *Courtesy Hammond-Harwood House*

(*Below left*) The frieze of the chimney-piece in the "withdrawing room" of the Hammond-Harwood House at Annapolis, Maryland, is ornamented with carved tobacco leaves, an appropriate motif to be used in the rich tobacco-growing state of Maryland. (*Below right*) On the frieze of the chimney-piece of the ballroom love knots and roses are carved in the Adam style. *Courtesy Hammond-Harwood House*

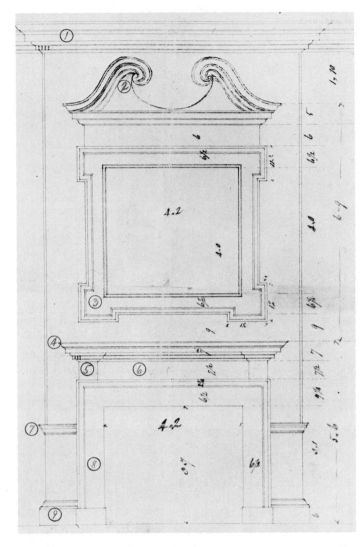

① CORNICE
② BROKEN PEDIMENT
③ CROSSETTE CORNER
④ MANTLE SHELF
⑤ TRUSS
⑥ FRIEZE
⑦ CHAIR RAIL
⑧ SURROUND
⑨ BASE BOARD

Drawing dated 1770, delineating the various parts of a chimney breast. The principal charm of these important appendages of room architecture lay in the fact that there is a different arrangement of details in all of them. *Courtesy Henry Francis du Pont Winterthur Museum*

Fireplace in the banquet room of the Lee Mansion in Marblehead, Massachusetts, built in 1768. Jeremiah Lee was one of America's richest merchants, and his house is a symbol of his wealth. The marble surround of the fireplace opening and the panel of the overmantel are flanked with richly carved consoles. The whole assembly was copied almost exactly from Swan's *British Architect*. Notice that the finials on the fire tools match those of the andirons. *Courtesy Marblehead Historical Society and William Pierson, Jr.*

Log cabin near Ephrata, Pennsylvania, now covered with asbestos shingles, with a massive stone fireplace and chimney, and a window in a side wall. They are called "welcome windows" by some experts; however, their real function remains to be established.

A small fireplace in the Cloister at Ephrata, Pennsylvania, showing the raised hearth and the dominantly vertical opening of the fire chamber with its walls covered with plaster. There were probably many such fireplaces in Pennsylvania in the eighteenth century. *Courtesy Pennsylvania Historical and Museum Commission*

Corner chimney-breast from Lancaster County, Pennsylvania, now located in the Metropolitan Museum of Art, New York City. The provincial style of this example is evident from the primitive painting on the overmantel, and the curious arrangement of the field panels. The chimney-breast and most of the furnishings are of the eighteenth century. The painted tinware and the Shimmel eagle, on the hanging cupboard, are of the nineteenth century. *Courtesy Metropolitan Museum of Art*

The Fisher House in the Oley Valley near Reading, Pennsylvania, is an excellent example of Georgian architecture located in a rural region. The chimney-breast is slightly provincial in character, and is flanked by a cupboard, with arch-topped doors, on each side. The house has a typical floor plan with a fireplace in each room on the first and second floors. They are located in the middle of the partitions with flues rising vertically to the attic floor. There a massive diagonal flue is built to the outer walls of the gable ends, which is a most unusual arrangement. *Courtesy Mr. and Mrs. John Fisher*

FISHER HOUSE

This home, built 1801 by Henry Fisher, is a fine example of late Georgian architecture. Brought from the British Isles, this style is reflected in old homes of eastern and southern Pennsylvania.

The fireplaces in the home of General Edward Hand in Lancaster, Pennsylvania, are interesting because of their variety. One view is of the unrestored fireplace in the basement kitchen with its large crane and stone for sharpening knives in the corner of the left jamb.

The original condition of a fireplace in a second-floor chamber is unusual because it retains its single original coat of paint. The mantel shelf is similar to others located in the house; however, some are connected with the framing around the chamber opening.

The most elegant fireplace assemblage in this house is in the major chamber of the second floor. Its simple Georgian details are compatible with other architectural features of the house, which was built late in the eighteenth century. *Courtesy Rock Ford Foundation*

The provincial charm of Pennsylvania is evident in this room, particularly in the chimney-breast with its carved motifs and scrolled overmantel with its painted jugs holding sprays of foliage. Edward Hick's painting, "The Peaceable Kingdom," and other decorative items are compatible with the major architectural features of the room. The chimney-breast is from a house built in Lancaster County, Pennsylvania, about 1780, and is now located in the Henry Francis du Pont Winterthur Museum near Wilmington, Delaware. *Courtesy Henry Francis du Pont Winterthur Museum*

A simple and charming chimney-breast on the second floor of Belmont Mansion, one of the famous houses in Fairmount Park, Philadelphia, Pennsylvania, built in the middle of the eighteenth century. The simple consoles, the carved shell, and the egg-and-dart molding make this arrangement particularly pleasing. *Courtesy Philadelphia Museum of Art*

105

Chimney-breast in the first-floor front room of "Woodford," located in Fairmount Park, Philadelphia, Pennsylvania. Its beautifully carved overmantel, its coved ceiling, its marble surround, and its excellent proportions establish it as one of the finest in America. *Courtesy Philadelphia Museum of Art*

The chimney-breast of the Powell House of Philadelphia, Pennsylvania, built about 1765, now located in the Philadelphia Museum of Art. The spectacular arrangement of details and the profuse carving amid comparable surroundings establishes it as one of the finest examples of the colonial period. *Courtesy Philadelphia Museum of Art*

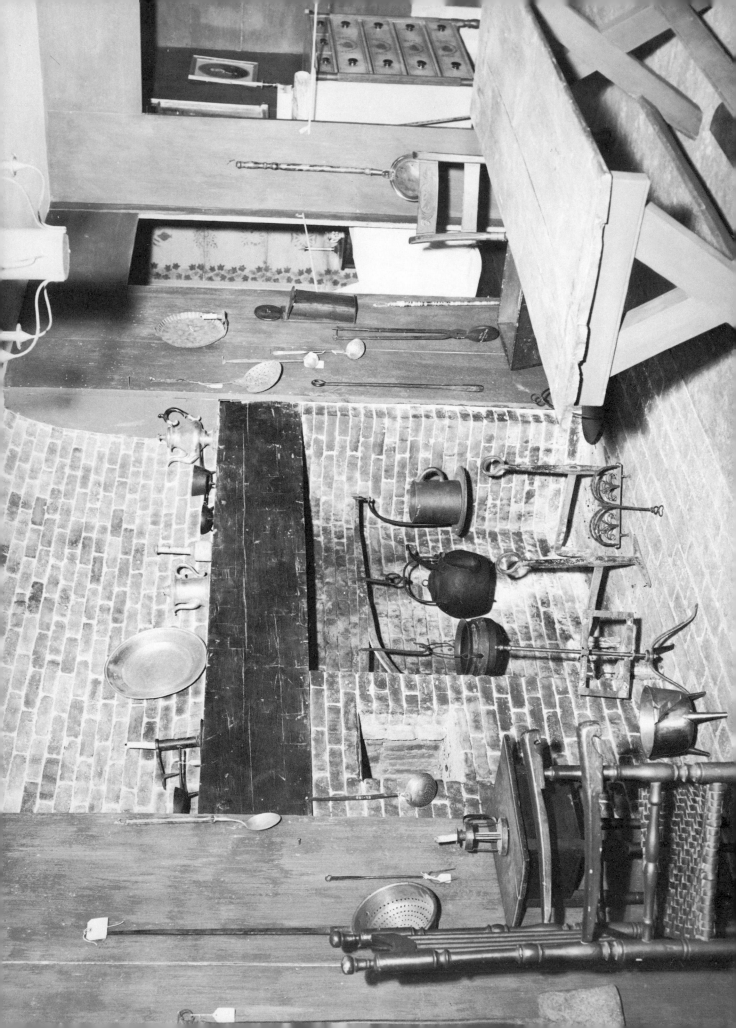

Kitchen fireplace in the Henry Francis du Pont Winterthur Museum, based on the kitchen of a house built at Oxford, Massachusetts, about 1740. The fireplace wall is covered with rails, stiles, and panels while the other walls are plastered. A large piece of granite was used for the lintel. Accessories such as a peel, iron andirons with spit hooks, a bell-metal posnet, and a clock jack with its weight and flywheel were essential for everyday life at that time. The contemporary furnishings are attractively arranged. *Courtesy Henry Francis du Pont Winterthur Museum*

The lintel in the Stencil House in the Shelburne Museum, Shelburne, Vermont, is of particular interest because its slight extension beyond the masonry wall provides a shallow mantel shelf. This idea could have suggested adding shelves to lintels which did not extend beyond the surface of the wall. *Courtesy Shelburne Museum*

The plank inserted in the masonry wall above the fireplace in the "West Room"
of the Wythe House in Williamsburg, Virginia, is called a bressummer. Although
its present function may not have been its original one, it is an attractive feature
today. *Courtesy Colonial Williamsburg*

The refined carving of vines and tendrils on the chimney-breast of the John
Stuart House of Charleston, South Carolina, are evidence of a maturing skill and
sensitivity of American craftsmen. Tall ceilings and white woodwork suggest
adaptation to Southern climactic conditions. The marble chimney-piece is appropriate and is expertly wrought. *Courtesy Minneapolis Institute of Art*

One of the most spectacular fireplaces in America can be seen in the basement of the Single Brothers House at Old Salem in Winston-Salem, North Carolina. Presently it consists of a battery of kettles on the left for heating water, a central fire chamber for cooking, and an oven on the right for baking. *Courtesy Old Salem, Inc., Winston-Salem, North Carolina*

Paneled room end from "Soldier's Joy," a mansion on the upper James River near Wingina in Nelson County, Virginia. The rest of the room consists of wainscoting and cornice with corner pilasters. The style of the chimney-breast is obviously transitional from Georgian to Federal. The fire chamber is lined with soapstone with the facing of the jambs marbelized. *Courtesy Cincinnati (Ohio) Art Museum*

The fireplace wall in the second-floor drawing room of the Branford-Hovey House (1753) in Charleston, South Carolina, is one of the finest of its period in America. There is not unanimous agreement among experts about the virtues of painted paneling versus unpainted; however, the charm and high quality of this unpainted woodwork is evident. Of particular importance is the fact that this unit is made principally of native cypress, to which mahogany and tulipwood have been added. The use of Corinthian columns on each side of the door, as well as the short columns over the mantel, are typical Charleston procedures. *Courtesy Historic Charleston Foundation*

Corner fireplace in an elaborately paneled room of "Marmion," built in the first half of the eighteenth century in King George County, Virginia, now located in the Metropolitan Museum of Art, New York City. Despite the fact that corner fireplaces were thought to be most appropriate for modest architectural interiors, this is an evident exception to that generalization. *Courtesy The Metropolitan Museum of Art*

Coal grate on a metal hearth in the fireplace of a small parlor in the Governor's Palace at Williamsburg, Virginia. The use of this facility was in step with the latest fashion in London. Some of the colored marble used in the chimney-piece was excavated on the site. The small figures are Chelsea. *Courtesy Colonial Williamsburg*

Fireplace in one of the front rooms on the first floor of the Dey Mansion located in Preakness Valley Park, Wayne Township, Passaic County, New Jersey. Probably built during the decade of 1740 to 1750, and used by Washington for his headquarters during July, October, and November, 1780. In many ways this fireplace is a typical one of its period; however, the lintel and the jambs are of local red sandstone, a procedure followed in other houses of the region. The limitations of stone for long lintels is evident by the break in the center of this one. The fireplace is furnished with a contemporary fire back and an elegant pair of andirons. *Courtesy Raymond Dey*

116

The fireplace wall from the Benjamin Hasbrouck House built in Ulster County, New York, in 1752, now located in the Metropolitan Museum of Art, New York City. There is a unique boldness of the paneling in this room which suggests an intermingling of cultures in the Hudson Valley. The bolection molding is a remarkable example of encasing the delicate Dutch tiles. *Courtesy Metropolitan Museum of Art, Rogers Fund, 1933*

Fireplace and overmantel in the Knox Headquarters House (built 1754) located near Newburgh, New York. The fireplace is framed with a small molding suggesting a wider shelf which emerged later in the century. The jambs and back wall are coved in this very fine large fire chamber. This is one room, at least, that was adequately heated by its fireplace. *Courtesy New York State Museum*

An attractive pair of knife-blade andirons are used in the arched fireplace of the John Blair House at Williamsburg, Virginia. Their construction and the style of the finials suggest production about the middle of the eighteenth century. The plastered front of the brick jambs and the curved back of the fireplace are original. *Courtesy Colonial Williamsburg*

Paneled end of a room from Portsmouth, Rhode Island, now in the Metropolitan Museum of Art, New York City. The size and shape of the fire chamber suggests construction about the middle of the eighteenth century. The cupboard over the fireplace is a rare and very attractive feature. *Courtesy Metropolitan Museum of Art*

120

Nineteenth Century

The fact has already been mentioned that it is impossible to determine exactly when styles of architecture change. The transition from Medieval to Georgian was understandably slow and uneven, and subsequent developments were no less so. Needless to say, the division of eras by centuries is also an indefinite method, but it is interesting to note that the beginning of the Federal style of architecture can be pinpointed with some degree of accuracy, an uncommon example of cause and effect. Archaeological expeditions were being conducted in Italy about the middle of the eighteenth century, culminating in the excavations of Pompeii and Herculaneum. This activity attracted world-wide attention. Two Englishmen in particular, Robert and William Adam, were greatly influenced by the finds uncovered there. It appears that English architects and builders were sick and tired of the frivolous appendages of the Georgian style; consequently, the delicacy and grace of design in the new discoveries found quick acceptance there.

A slowly emerging democratic society in America saw elements of idealism in the cultures of the past, and the Georgian mode was gradually losing ground here. This action was due to the fact that after the Revolution the lines of communication with England, severed by the war, were quickly repaired, so that once again English ships brought books, artifacts, and ideas from the motherland. Jefferson's return from France with French concepts of architecture also stimulated an active interest in the oncoming change. America was on the threshold of a new era, which would touch the lives of many people who lived along the Atlantic seaboard. Although English architects and builders were reasonably quick to accept the new Adam neoclassic style, true Adam mantel-

The Loring-Emmerton House in Salem, Massachusetts. This house has many of the qualities found in houses built in Salem early in the nineteenth century. *Courtesy Historic American Buildings Survey*

pieces having appeared in England in the 1760s, decades were required to bring it to its apogee of popularity here.

Nowhere in America did the new trend become more widely accepted than in the town of Salem, Massachusetts. The reason for this incident lies principally in the fact that Salem was a marine oriented community. It had no rich hinterland to provide grain for commerce like Philadelphia and Baltimore, and handicrafts could be easily bought in nearby Boston. So ships built in the Salem shipyards turned to the sea. The hinterland did have rich stores of timber to be cut, the sea had vast schools of fish to be caught, and Indian trappers provided a bountiful supply of furs, all of which were sold on world-wide markets. Trading became the life-breath of Salem, and with it came a sophistication comparable to that of larger urban areas along the coast.

Some trade was carried on with the West Indies as early as the seventeenth century, in 1784 trade with Russia was begun, in 1785 the first ship from Salem arrived in China, and in 1791 a ship arrived at Sumatra. These vessels returned home with such exotic commodities as spices, rum, indigo, and tobacco, but the *pièce de résistance* was Chinese export porcelain, examples of which must have graced every mantel shelf of importance in Salem by the end of the eighteenth century. As a matter of fact, these ornaments became the standard garniture for a Federal mantel shelf, and can be found in most museums today.

The wealth accumulated from these trading ventures was fantastic beyond belief. Trade with the Orient provided not only objects of luxury but also the means to build elegant houses in which they could be displayed. It is reported in *Early American Rooms* by Kettell that:

> Elias Hasket Derby's venture in the "Mount Vernon," which was only 100 feet long and 400 tons burden, carrying a cargo of sugar to the East and returned with silks and wines, netted a profit of about $100,000 on an investment of about $43,000, or about 250 percent.

It seems rather certain with the turn of events after the Revolution in all matters related to life in America, combined with numerous contacts with countries abroad, Salem would naturally become a cosmopolitan community, the locale for the avant-garde in architecture and all matters associated with this activity.

It might be pointed out here that despite the fact that a new architectural form appeared at Salem late in the eighteenth century, until that time architectural progression had been normal there. The crude huts built there about 1630 have been previously described. These were replaced by one-room houses covered with planks. Later, there were salt-box types and many-gabled houses, the latter form being immortalized in Hawthorne's *House of Seven Gables*. These gables were needed to roof the various ells and ends added to enlarge the original houses. Later still, some houses with gambrel roofs were built of bricks with four towering chimneys in the end walls. In the middle of the eighteenth century Salem architecture showed little departure from the styles found in other regions of New England, but by 1780 a new form appeared there, called by Cousins and Riley in their book, *The Colonial Architecture of Salem*, the three-story wood house. In the nineteenth century this unique form was built of bricks.

The exterior of this house might be described as "plain." The floor plan and the facade were usually square, the only imbalance being the fore-shortened row of windows on the third floor to accommodate a low-pitched roof. There was frequently a deck on the roof with a baluster at its edge, where ladies impatiently walked and watched for returning ships bearing their husbands and profitable cargoes. The walls were covered with clapboards, or rusticated boarding to simulate stone. Some distinction was gained in the appearance of these houses by their fine craftsmanship, by the use of quoined corners, and by the addition of porches at the front entry, most of which seemed very small in proportion to the formidable size of the house to which they were attached.

The location of the chimney is of importance in these houses. Although examples exist with a Georgian arrangement of the chimneys in the separating partitions, most now were located in the outer walls of the house. They were built within the wall, and rose majestically above the roof to clear all encumbrances which might cause the fireplaces to smoke. One expert in the field suggests that placing chimneys in the end walls was a better plan for diffusing heat, possibly because the outer walls were naturally colder than partitions. At least, the new arrangement was an alternative plan to the one used earlier, and it might have been chosen for that reason alone.

Some of the interiors had a four-room symmetrical arrangement with evident vestiges of the Georgian era, but the new arrangement of chimneys became the most common. The moving of the chimney to the outer wall combined with the Adam-styled mantelpiece to replace the earlier chimney-breast had a startling impact on the interior decor of

A room from the Ezekiel Hersey Derby House built in Salem, Massachusetts, in 1799 and now located in the Philadelphia Art Museum. The mantelpiece is not an extravagant example of McIntire's work but is a typical product of the period. There are figures in the central panel of the frieze, the two outer panels having swags of leaves and/or flowers. An urn is placed at the top of each column on the ends of the frieze. *Courtesy Philadelphia Museum of Art*

the typical Salem town house of the late eighteenth and early nineteenth centuries. (This will be discussed later.)

In addition to the motivation provided by the seafaring activity of Salem, architectural matters were greatly influenced by a native son named Samuel McIntire. Although McIntire is world famous now, he spent his entire life within a very short radius of the town of his birth. With only the apprentice training he received from his father, he became a craftsman-architect, comparable to his great contemporary, Charles Bulfinch.

The products of McIntire's skillful hands warrant a short digression into his genealogy and training. He was baptised on January 16, 1757, in the First Church of Salem, the son of Joseph McIntire, a respected house builder of Salem for most of his life. He learned his father's trade along with his brothers, Joseph and Angier, and at twenty-one he married Elizabeth Field. They had one son—Samuel Field McIntire, who succeeded his father in trade, but certainly not in achievement.

The first report of his work is recorded in 1776, in partnership with his brothers, but by 1780 his genius must have been evident, for he then became a lone craftsman working for Elias Derby, for whom he built a number of fine houses. In 1782 he designed the Pierce-Johonnot-Nichols House; that and his subsequent work indicate his great love for and his magnificent achievement in architectural endeavors. He also attained considerable skill as a sculptor and is known to have done work both in relief and in the round. The maritime life and technology of Salem led him to carving figureheads for ships; two busts by him are in the collection of the American Antiquarian Society in Worcester, Massachusetts. He also carved eagles in the round for finials on roofs and gate posts. He died February 6, 1811. On his gravestone the following inscription was cut:

In memory of
MR. SAMUEL McINTIRE
who died Feb. 6, 1811

He was distinguished for genius in Architecture, Sculpture, and Musick; Modest and sweet Manners rendering him pleasing; Industry and Integrity respectable; he professed the religion of Jesus in his entrance on manly life; and proved its excellence by virtuous Principles and unblemished conduct.

This short digression into the story of Salem and its master wood-carver, McIntire, might seem unwarranted; however, the clue to the procedure remains to be revealed. The change in the location of the chimney was not, in itself, completely new and revolutionary; it merely made popular a practice which had been followed on a number of occasions in earlier times. Georgian-styled houses were built with chimney-breasts in the end walls, particularly those with diagonal corner fireplaces, like numerous examples located in Williamsburg.

The consistent and dramatic change which occurred in Salem, and elsewhere on a more reduced scale, was the dropping of the eighteenth-century chimney-piece (the various arrangements of moldings on the chimney-breast), and the development of the nineteenth-century mantelpiece. This change did not occur with one strong sweep of the hand or mind. Although only a few scattered examples of Georgian architecture remain in Salem, it is apparent that the style was popular there in its day. The important rooms of "The Lindens" were totally paneled with cornices, a dado, and a chimney-breast in the earlier tradition. As late as 1800 a fireplace in the Putnam-Hanson House was centered and flanked by two doors, one being a closet, the other a passage into the adjoining room. However, the new mode is evident in the use of landscaped wallpaper depicting life in the Orient at that time. The Georgian-styled overmantel is completely lacking in this example, and the new mode is exhibited by the application of flowers and fruit on the frieze of the mantelpiece, painted in natural colors.

An excellent example of the transition from chimney-piece to mantelpiece can be seen in the Pierce-Johonnot-Nichols House. In this house, finished in 1782, both styles are displayed, the western side being executed in the Georgian manner, while the eastern side is regarded as pure McIntire/Adams.

Certain evidences of the Georgian style persist in the latter area. The jutting chimney-breast seems to have been carefully centered in the room, but the flanking doors for closets or passageways are missing. The recessed area on each side of the fireplace was a fine place to hang portraits, but was ill suited for the typical Georgian use of it. The surround is made of marble slabs which are bordered with Corinthian colonnettes, intercepted in the middle by a horizontal molding suggesting a mantel shelf. The wide frieze is ornamented with three panels, the outer

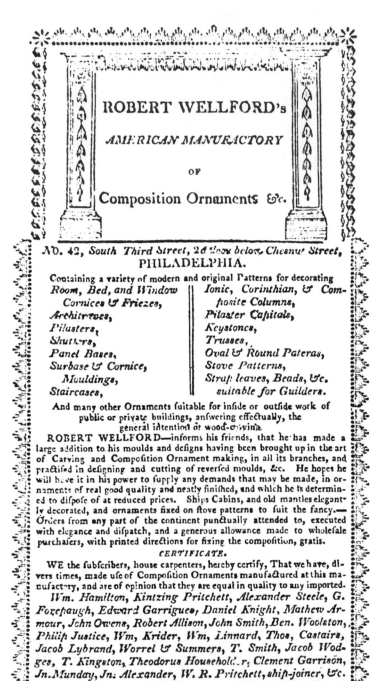

A copy of Robert Wellford's broadside advertising his "American Manufactory of Composition Ornaments, &c." Wellford was obviously a very capable man, for a sizable number of signed and unsigned examples of his work are known today. *Courtesy Historical Society of Delaware*

ones having swags of flowers and leaves while the inner elliptical one has a ship motif. There is a simple overmantel panel, which is neatly fitted with a mirror.

It will be impossible to deal with all the facets of McIntire's work in this short survey. His first work showed evidence of earlier practices, which he gradually abandoned in the development of a McIntire style. In 1807 he made the mantelpiece for the Registry of Deeds which stands alone without lateral or overhead appendages. This work has a dentiled course under the mantel shelf with reeded colonnettes on each side, headed with Adam urns in applied composition panels at the top of the colonnettes. But its popular and most exciting detail is the eagle carved for the central panel on the frieze. His frequent use of the eagle motif suggests his or his clients' enthusiasm for the new nation, and he became very skilled in producing this national symbol. He carved it on a large scale for the Registry of Deeds' mantelpiece.

An eagle was also carved for the frieze at the Woman's Friend Society, where it was embellished with other symbols of patriotism, such as cannon, swords, and flags. A similar piece made for the Kimball House is considered by some connoisseurs to be one of his most extravagant products. This mantelpiece is also of particular interest because the colonnettes on the front of the jambs were repeated on the ends to minimize the broad side appearance of the chimney-breast, where it jutted out into the room. Among other interesting details are the two rows of wooden spheres carved into the edge of the mantel shelf. All the ornamentation on this example is carved from wood.

By 1805 McIntire was reaching the zenith of his career, when he executed some of the finest workmanship on the mantelpieces of Salem. The mantelpieces show a completely separate entity, mounted against a plastered wall, above which was no paneling or continuation of any kind. The example in the David P. Waters House is considered to include some of the finest of McIntire's work inspired by Adam. The following description is excerpted from *The Colonial Architecture of Salem* by Cousins and Riley:

> The former is seen to be an elaboration of much that has been already considered, in response to the desire for richer effect, and gives opportunity for an instructive study in recombining conventional material. Generally speaking, this mantel takes the form of

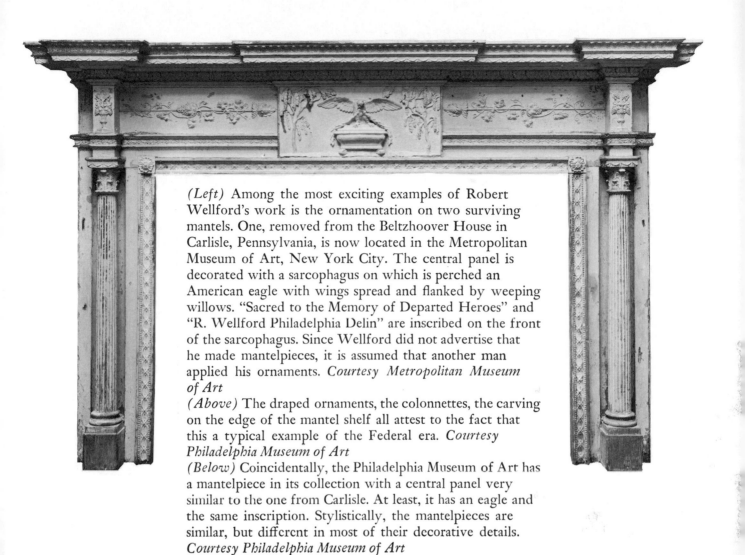

(Left) Among the most exciting examples of Robert Wellford's work is the ornamentation on two surviving mantels. One, removed from the Beltzhoover House in Carlisle, Pennsylvania, is now located in the Metropolitan Museum of Art, New York City. The central panel is decorated with a sarcophagus on which is perched an American eagle with wings spread and flanked by weeping willows. "Sacred to the Memory of Departed Heroes" and "R. Wellford Philadelphia Delin" are inscribed on the front of the sarcophagus. Since Wellford did not advertise that he made mantelpieces, it is assumed that another man applied his ornaments. *Courtesy Metropolitan Museum of Art*

(Above) The draped ornaments, the colonnettes, the carving on the edge of the mantel shelf all attest to the fact that this a typical example of the Federal era. *Courtesy Philadelphia Museum of Art*

(Below) Coincidentally, the Philadelphia Museum of Art has a mantelpiece in its collection with a central panel very similar to the one from Carlisle. At least, it has an eagle and the same inscription. Stylistically, the mantelpieces are similar, but different in most of their decorative details. *Courtesy Philadelphia Museum of Art*

that in the west chamber of the Peabody-Silsbee house. It has the same reeded pilasters and corresponding projection of the entire entablature, the same sunken oval panel with beaded edge and applied fruit and flower basket; also the same cymatiun, corona, and bed molding, in this instance employed with supplementary surrounding square-edged shelf with projections like those beneath the cornice. McIntire's favorite fret-like dentil course is here augmented by his well-known screw bead above it, replacing the plain fillet he often placed there. The sheaves of wheat on the frieze projections, also the architrave motive, recall the mantel of the Home for the Aged Women, although rosettes instead of tiny fruit baskets here alternate with vertical reeded groups.

In conclusion, one might take a perspective look at McIntire's work. Although he was an architect and a builder, it is his work with mantelpieces which is of primary interest here. He, like many other craftsmen of his day, was highly influenced by the books of the period, particularly because he had no formal preparation for his work other than the apprenticeship he served with his father. Despite the limitations of his training, he did develop a style in the making of mantelpieces with which he is identified. Fiske Kimball, in his book *Mr. Samuel McIntire, Carver, the Architect of Salem*, points out that his favorite motif in the central panels of his mantelpieces was a basket of fruit or flowers. The total composition of these subjects was never duplicated, and the contents were always unsymmetrically arranged. There was a grandeur in the details of the side colonnettes and the mantel shelves which stamp him as a master of his craft.

His most spectacular carving, in the eyes of many connoisseurs, was the previously mentioned eagle. He portrayed the bird holding in one claw an olive branch, in the other a sheaf of arrows. In the Clifford-Crowninshield House he varied the theme by carving an array of musical instruments in the central panel. It is possible that these varied themes reflected the wishes of his clients, in which case it is evident he could satisfy them in whatever design they desired.

It is a fortunate circumstance that his products were preserved with such care that they survive to be appreciated today. His work was carried on by his son, who might be described as a faint echo of his father.

It would be unfair to conclude this survey of McIntire's work without mentioning that in addition to his carving, he also used composition ornaments, as did other craftsmen of his era. There is evidence from their use in far-flung places in America that he imported some of them, probably from England and France. There is also documented proof that he carved some molds to make his own.

There is also evidence that other men were engaged in work similar to McIntire's in the principal cities along the eastern seacoast. One of the best known is Robert Wellford, who is listed as the owner of the "original American composition ornamental manufactory," in the *Philadelphia Business Directory of 1811*. Posterity is indebted to Mr. Wellford for a number of signed and unsigned mantelpieces and for a number of advertising broadsides which were issued early in the nineteenth century, one being dated April 6, 1801. One showing a mantelpiece is illustrated and the contents of one directed "To The Public" is reiterated here because of the relevance of the contents to the subject of carving and composition work.

> From the remotest ages of antiquity Carving hath been esteemed an essential decoration to the works of magnificence; with civilization and knowledge, and this liberal art. As they gradually reached perfection they arose to meridian splendor, which the beautiful vestiges of temples and Statues do evince, and will long perpetuate the just celebrity of Greek and Roman artists.
>
> In the modern buildings of this country are specimens of admirable skill which prove the rising merit of American artists.
>
> A cheap substitute for wood carving has long been desirable for some situations, particularly enriched mouldings, etc., and various were the attempts to answer the purpose, the last and most successful is usually termed Composition Ornaments. It is a cement of solid and tenacious materials, which when properly incorporated and pressed into moulds, receives a fine relievo; in drying it becomes hard as stone, strong, and durable, so as to answer most effectually the general purpose of Wood Carving, and not so liable to chip.— This discovery was rudely conducted for some time, owing to Carvers declining every connection with it, till, from its low price, it encroached so much upon their employment, that several embarked in this work, and by their superior talents greatly improved it.
>
> The Subscriber being brought up in the art of Carving and Composition Ornament Making in all its branches, and practiced in designing and cutting of reversed Moulds, &., he has been induced to tender his services to the public in this line. His hopes for success is founded on the execution of the origin of his patterns:

The great encouragement with which he has already been favored with, will call forth the utmost of his exertions to improve the art to greater perfection.

And he trusts there will be found little difference in expense, and his only contention will be for superiority of workmanship.

The invention of Composition Ornaments offers a good embellishment at a moderate price, it resembles in some degree the art of printing and engraving; its utility must therefore be obvious to many, and it is hoped will long receive due patronage from such liberal minds of refined taste as can best discern any efforts of improvements, to merit which shall be the assiduous endeavor of,

Their obedient servant,
Robert Wellford.
April 6, 1801

N.B. The aforesaid factory is now carried on in an extensive line, at No. 42 Chestnut Street, Philadelphia, where his friends may be amply supplied with ornaments to suit almost any fancy, which he presumes will encourage them to call at the said factory.

Orders from any part of the Continent punctually attended to, and a generous allowance made to wholesale purchasers, with printed directions for fixing composition, gratis.

The foregoing statement indicates that Wellford either had, or hoped to have, an extensive business in selling composition ornaments. His printed directions probably instructed embryonic decorators in the art of applying composition ornaments, presumably with some success, for a number of mantelpieces have survived with which he has been identified in some way. The broadside is concluded by listing the names of 25 men who attest to the quality of his products, the last being a ship joiner. [There probably were decorated captain's quarters at that time.]

Perhaps it has been hasty to introduce the discussion of mantelpieces with those which are the most elegant and best known. The procedure is perhaps a commentary on the fact that a new art quickly reached its height, and then slowly deteriorated. There were, however, contemporary evidences of similar workmanship elsewhere. Considerable stature was also attained in Providence, Rhode Island, where square houses were built with small porticos and decks with balusters on the roofs.

View of the south side of "Lemon Hill" in Fairmount Park, Philadelphia, Pennsylvania. The curved central bay clearly suggests the oval rooms within. Some houses of the period have the oval room at the end of the house. *Courtesy Philadelphia Museum of Art*

Although the square three-story house is rarely found outside of New England, there are examples of Federal architecture in other parts of the country. Philadelphia was the capital of the nation from 1789 to 1800, and nothing less than the latest fashions were acceptable in the Quaker City. The city of Washington was laid out by L'Enfant to provide a setting for many houses built in the Federal mode.

The houses built outside of New England were generally three stories high, but were not square. Some exterior walls were plastered; there were tall windows reaching from the floor to ceiling; entrances did have small porticos; and, like examples in New England and elsewhere, many had an elliptical or round room, emulating a contemporary French style.

"Lemon Hill" in Fairmount Park in Philadelphia is another charming house with architectural elements typical of the era. An impressive floor-

to-ceiling window in the Palladian style is located on the second floor over the front door. A large square hall laid with King of Prussia marble is just inside the entrance. The stair is located off the hall in a small library opposite an entrance to the dining room. Opposite the front door is the entrance to an oval drawing room. This shape is evident on the exterior rear wall of the house where a projecting curved bay identifies the inner form.

The focal point of interest here is the oval drawing room, not only because it was a typical architectural form, but because it has unique doors and mantelpieces. The doors, made of mahogany, are curved to fit the contour of the room walls. The wooden mantelpieces are also curved in this most unusual manner. They are ornamented with fluted gouge work, a technique which was destined to become popular in fine houses throughout eastern Pennsylvania, not only in Philadelphia, but in the back-country areas such as Berks, Lancaster, and Dauphin counties. The furniture of the oval room was originally thought to be French, but was later identified as of Philadelphia origin.

To continue the survey of Federal examples along the eastern seacoast, one finds some equally arresting examples as far south as Charleston, South Carolina. There, wealthy residents experienced the same prosperity and Adam influence as did those living in northern seaports. A distinct Charleston style developed there, which is characterized by a narrow house one room wide and three rooms deep, the narrow end facing the street. Nevertheless, they resembled northern houses with their brick construction, three-story height, and tall windows suggesting a typical verticality.

One of the most notable examples is the Nathaniel Russell House, which was built in the first decade of the nineteenth century. The "Age of Adam" is emphasized by Frances R. Edmunds in *Antiques*, February, 1966, who says that "Certainly in the plan of his house he [Mr. Russell] followed the conceit of the brothers Adam in including a square room, an oval room, and a rectangular room." An unusual four-sided bay on the

The mantelpiece in the oval drawing room of "Lemon Hill" in Fairmount Park might be described as a restrained Classical style. The gouge work on the central panel of the frieze is barely visible in this photograph. *Courtesy Philadelphia Museum of Art* garden side of the house contains an oval room on each of the three floors. The house was finished at a cost of $80,000, which suggests an elegance rarely achieved in early times.

One of the outstanding rooms of the house, of a number apparently designed for entertaining, is the oval gray drawing room upstairs. This one is the most sophisticated of all, its carved dentils being originally gold-leafed. The mantelpiece is in the typical Adam style, painted white against a gray wall. The decorations are obviously molded rather than carved, for duplicates appear in other Charleston houses. The two outer panels of the frieze are decorated with geometric designs, while the center panel displays a scene with five human figures.

It was a very natural procedure to utilize the Adam-styled mantelpieces in the elegant detached houses described thus far; however, it is equally important to note that similar mantelpieces were used in city "row" houses which proliferated in number and elegance in the late eighteenth and early nineteenth centuries. The stable government of the new republic brought an era of prosperity and growth to the new nation, particularly in seaports, such as Baltimore, New York, and Boston. Rows of brick houses were built in Boston under the influence of architect Charles Bulfinch, three or four stories high, many with attractive Federal doorways.

The growth and prosperity of the times was particularly evident in Baltimore. The town was founded in 1729 as a storage place for tobacco in the upper Chesapeake region. As late as 1765 it is reported that Baltimore had not more than fifty houses and shipping there was carried on by only one vessel. In 1780 the population stood at 8,000, and the census of 1810 reported it at 35,583 residents. The phenomenal growth started at the time of the Revolution because the port was neither attacked or blockaded. Extensive quantities of grain were brought to the city where it was milled into flour and shipped abroad. This mercantile and related activity brought many entrepreneurs to the city who soon acquired land and erected homes there. Baltimore is described by Rodris C. Roth in her thesis entitled *The Interior Decoration of City Houses in Baltimore 1783–1812,* as follows:

> In Baltimore proper the streets running up from, and parallel to, the harbors were lined with stores, warehouses, shops, and dwell-

Extravagant gouge work on a mantelpiece found in Berks County, Pennsylvania. Such work is usually found in Pennsylvania, or can be attributed to craftsmen who worked in Pennsylvania. The delicacy of the work is evident in the close-up view of the column. *Courtesy Edwin Jackson, Inc., New York City*

Exterior view of the Nathaniel Russell House in Charleston, South Carolina. The oval rooms are within the projecting bay. *Courtesy Historic Charleston Foundation*

ings. Many of them newly built, almost all were of brick, and usually placed wall to wall. Sidewalks were customarily located directly in front of the buildings rather than gardens or grass.

This arrangement of joining facades created a uniformity in both interior and exterior architecture which was followed throughout much of the nineteenth century, many examples from the late portion of the century surviving today. This was an economical plan, for it reduced exterior maintenance to the front and back walls, and effected a saving of heat. The room arrangement on the first floor consisted of a hall running along the sides of two rooms and terminating in a back room. Chimneys and fireplaces were built in the common masonry wall, and rarely in partitions between the rooms. This procedure was a practical one for it kept all the masonry work together, and allowed the fireplace to be built opposite the entrance to the room, a traditional location favored by builders and architects. Also, by placing the fireplace in the

The Federal-styled mantelpiece in the Nathaniel Russell House in Charleston, South Carolina, is an outstanding example of the work done with molded ornaments. Similar ones are known to have been used in other houses of the region. The central panel with the figures and the capitals of the Corinthian columns are other important features of this example. *Courtesy Historic Charleston Foundation*

common wall a doorway could be opened in the center of the partition between the two major rooms on the first floor (double parlor), with an ample opportunity to build closets between the two rooms on the second floor. It should be noted here that the front room on the second floor was often used as a lady's drawing room, and sometimes was more elegantly fitted with mantelpieces and wood trim than the parlor on the first floor. This custom was followed not only in Baltimore, but also in other cities along the Atlantic seaboard. The fireplaces were often flanked by cupboards or niches to add to the versatility and attractiveness of the rooms.

The architect or builder had two major choices in the material of which mantelpieces were to be made—wood or marble. As early as 1786 residents of Baltimore were offered marble chimney-pieces, and two years later a sale was held in the city offering products of Italian marble such as chimney-pieces, jambs, slabs, and flags. The flat jambs and slabs could be decorated in the desired manner by local craftsmen who were working there, and in other cities, at that time. At the turn of the century mantelpieces of Italian marble were being imported, one type being described as "after the English fashion."

Although wooden mantelpieces were probably less elegant than those of marble, it should not be concluded that all of them were an ordinary type. At least a few examples have survived which are typical of the finest ones of the Federal era. They are decorated with composition ornaments on both the side columns and the frieze. On the central panel of the frieze of one is an urn, and on the outer side panels are swags with bow knots. Miss Roth comments about a Baltimore ornament maker who made ornaments which could be applied in desired arrangements on chair rails, cornices, and ceilings, over doors and windows, and on mantelpieces.

It was mentioned that while McIntire carved many of his decorative motifs, he also used molded designs which he made or imported. Thus, one must conclude that the locally made ornaments probably offered

The Classical style is very evident in a doorway into an oval room in the Nathaniel Russell House in Charleston, South Carolina. The cornice, frieze, and door stiles are elaborately ornamented. In contrast, the mantelpiece within the room is very moderately ornamented. *Courtesy Historic Charleston Foundation*

"Sweetbrier" was built in 1797 two miles west of the city of Philadelphia, Pennsylvania, but is now included, due to its location, in Fairmount Park. The mantelpiece in the "Drawing Room East" (Johnson Memorial Room) is in the Wellford style of the late eighteenth century or early nineteenth century. Its applied plaster molds of flowers, swags, and a mythological figure are on a background painted a contrasting color. Other examples of the procedure can be found in houses of the period. *Courtesy Philadelphia Museum of Art. Photograph by A. J. Wyatt, Staff Photographer*

Federal-styled mantelpiece from a Baltimore drawing room, now located in the Henry Francis du Pont Winterthur Museum near Wilmington, Delaware. The mantelpiece is decorated with plaster ornaments, the central panel of the frieze depicting the Battle of Lake Erie. The furniture is of the Classical era. *Courtesy Henry Francis du Pont Winterthur Museum*

147

some variety in designs, while imports tended to standardize the work done on the eastern seaboard where they were used. In either case, they helped to create an atmosphere of elegance and refinement on the interior trim of the houses of the period.

It might also be appropriate to point out that not all row houses were examples of elegance and fitted with elaborate mantelpieces. Certainly many modest homes were built having mantelpieces made of boards and ornamented only with simple moldings. In some examples there was probably a substitution of fluting or reeding for the applied ornament. The walls were papered, finished with whitewash, or painted with one of over twenty colors advertised in the local newspaper. Among the designs offered in wallpapers were "panel papers" *with landscapes to decorate chimney-breasts.*

This simply carved mantelpiece of wood might have been used anywhere on the eastern seaboard throughout the first half of the nineteenth century. *Courtesy Edwin Jackson, Inc., New York City*

Chimneys, fireplaces, and mantelpieces were important features of Federal architecture, and they continued to be so recognized for another half century. Attention has been directed to the fact that the extensive paneling and the profuse ornamentation of the Georgian period slowly slipped away to be replaced by the delicate and refined ornamentation of the Adam style. The next step was away from the Adam style, or rather a simplification of Adam details in the less elegant houses of the late eighteenth and early nineteenth centuries.

In New England, homes were built both on the coast and in the countryside following one of two major plans. The house with a central hall flanked by rooms on each side was continued on a modest scale. The house with a massive central chimney with rooms on three sides of it also persisted. These were built by farmers and fishermen in all parts of the region; however, they have come to be most frequently called "Cape Cod" houses.

A room from an example of this type is preserved for posterity in the Smithsonian Institution in Washington, D.C. The architectural fittings were removed from a house built at Martha's Vineyard, Massachusetts. Several coats of paint from the central panel of the frieze of the mantelpiece having been removed, intertwined script letters E and D flanking the letter C were found, and the date 1808. This discovery confirms the hypothesis that the house was built by Edmund and Deliverance Crowell in the year indicated.

The exterior of the house resembles a standard Cape Cod type; however, the architectural details of at least one room indicate otherwise. The following description written by Mrs. Howes Norris is taken from *The Dukes County Intelligencer*, Vol. 9, No. 1 (originally published in a booklet entitled *Sketches of Old Homes in Our Village*).

> In the parlor of the house, the wainscoting and cornice is quite elaborate and it is said the work was done with a jack knife, but the most interesting feature of the room is a painting done on wood over the mantelpiece. It was the work of Miss Jane Norton when the house was finished; Miss Norton taught school in the village but belonged to North Tisbury. The picture represents a village street with a field in the foreground; a row of houses three stories high, with a chimney at each end, face us, and men in knee britches and women in old style appear.

A room from the Crowell House, built in 1808 at Martha's Vineyard, Massachusetts, and moved to the Smithsonian Institution in Washington, D.C. The relationship of the mantelpiece and the overmantel are very evident in this photograph. *Courtesy Smithsonian Institution*

There is an obvious folk-art charm in the overmantel painting from the Crowell House. The architecture and the arrangement of the buildings are particularly interesting. *Courtesy Smithsonian Institution*

A coach has dashed up to the Inn, which we know by the sign hanging from a nearby tree; and carts of hay and a dog are seen. The color is extremely dark and it is not a work of art but is most curious and interesting.

This most unusual townscape is painted in oil on an oval pine panel with fan-shaped panels in each corner to fill out the rectangle. It is interesting to note that the artist did not paint the nearby Cape Cod houses, but apparently preferred the "big city" types which were being built in Boston and other nearby cities. Such work was often done by itinerant painters who roamed the countryside earning their "board and room" as they went. A short row of marks in the lower right-hand corner of the panel suggests the possibility of a signature of the artist: however, it cannot be said that it is the signature of Miss Norton.

The mantelpiece is further described by Miss Rodris Roth in Vol. 9, No. 1, of the *Dukes County Intelligencer* as follows:

> The oval theme [of the overmantel panel] is repeated in a medallion centered on the mantel board. A border of hyphens and reeds is seen directly beneath the shaped mantel shelf. The fireplace opening is trimmed across the top with a diamond fret border and flanked at the sides by a pair of pilasters faced with bands of interlaced circles. A continuous border of bound reeds runs around the room at the upper edge of the paneled dado. The plaster walls above are crowned with a cornice ornamented with flattened medallions and set on a wide diamond fret border that is a magnification of the trimming over the fireplace opening. The woodwork is probably of local or nearby mainland origin. It would appear to be the product of a professional craftsman, skilled in carving interior trim, rather than the result of spare-time whittling aboard ship by a carpenter-sailor.

The mantelpiece is obviously attractive, but it lacks the carved or applied decorative patterns of those of Salem, and in their absence it becomes a provincial example. The use of the overmantel panel with its folk-like painting does indicate that elegance was sought and simply achieved. The woodwork was originally painted a rich, blue-green, except for the corner sections of the overmantel which were painted mahogany brown. There is no evidence that the walls were ever painted or covered with paper. Thus, there was a sharp contrast between the painted woodwork and the white plastered walls.

Such an interior arrangement minus the dado, the cornice, and the overmantel panel was used for another half century throughout New England. The detailed carving of the mantelpiece was doubtless reduced or eliminated and, finally, mantelpieces were made merely of a few boards, with two or three bands of molding.

Although there was obviously a wide range of sizes and decorative treatments of fireplaces in all periods in America, it is evident that only a limited number can be described here. These can serve as typical examples, and will hopefully serve in identifying similar ones found in different eras and regions. An interesting example of fireplaces in the late Federal and early Greek Revival periods can be seen in Lancaster, Pennsylvania, where "Wheatland," the home of President Buchanan is located. By Salem (Massachusetts) standards this was a modest house in size and appointments, yet it reflects a provincial interpretation of the merging periods in a very pleasing manner.

It is built of brick with a center "block" containing a hall flanked by a large room on each side, one a living room, the other a dining room. The stairs are located in a transverse hall across the rear, the location of the stairs being the only departure from a symmetrical balance in the interior architectural arrangement. There is a shallow appendage on each end containing a library and a kitchen on the first floor and bedrooms on the second floor.

This house has one of the most interesting complements of fireplaces found in this survey. The kitchen has a large walk-in fireplace with a sturdy lintel of wood about ten inches square. On the front side of the lintel a later shelf has been added. This was a common procedure for those who wanted to update their fireplaces, and incidentally provide a facility for displaying kitchen finery. The opening is about five feet high and seven feet wide. The back corners are squared and the back wall rises vertically to the throat of the chimney. It is fitted with a large crane, and in all respects it is little changed from the earliest type. There seems to have been little deviation in kitchen fireplaces until the cast-iron stove displaced them about the middle of the nineteenth century.

Although there is considerable variety in the styles of the fireplaces at "Wheatland" each seems to fit nicely in the room in which it is found. For example, the more elegant living and dining rooms have mantelpieces made of Vermont marble in what might be called a "country"

Marble mantelpiece in the living room of "Wheatland" in Lancaster, Pennsylvania, with a marble hearth and a coal grate. The columns on the front of the jambs are evidence of Federal influence. *Courtesy Wheatland Foundation*

Plain slabs of slate are the material used to form the mantelpiece of this fireplace at "Wheatland" in Lancaster, Pennsylvania. The fire chamber has a lining of cast iron from Margaretta Furnace. *Courtesy Wheatland Foundation*

Federal style. There is no delicate carving on them because such work would have been very costly as well as incompatible with the surroundings. The one in the living room has two flat slabs of marble as facings for the jambs, with a wide flat slab laid horizontally over them. There is a mantel shelf at the top, a narrower one near the bottom of the horizon-

The mantelpiece in one of the bedrooms of "Wheatland" in Lancaster, Pennsylvania, is made of wood with a marbelized finish. The coal grate was probably a later addition. *Courtesy Wheatland Foundation*

tal slab, and the whole assembly of horizontal slabs seems to be supported by two turned free-standing columns. The columns have vestiges of Ionic capitals, but lack the delicacy of the highest style of Federal colonnettes. They seem to be clearly a transitional form. There is uncertainity as to when the coal-burning grate was installed. One would hardly expect that a conventional wood-burning facility, such as the mantelpiece suggests, would have been installed when the house was built if the intent was to burn coal in a grate. The presence of other wood-burning facilities also suggests that originally all of the fireplaces were intended for wood.

Possibly the most unusual material was used for mantelpieces in the library and two bedrooms. These consist of thick slabs of slate, four vertical and two horizontal, with a mantel shelf across the top horizontal slab. There are large deposits of slate within fifty miles of "Wheatland"; however, only a few examples of slate mantelpieces have been found. There is no ornamentation on the surface of the slate, and one must assume that this medium did not lend itself to such treatment. The surface is not highly polished and, except for a striking black color, the material has little to commend it for such a purpose. However, the broad expanse of undecorated slabs suggests an embryonic form which became popular a decade or two later.

The fireplace in the library is fitted with a stove, which was doubtless installed after the house was built. There would be no point in installing a conventional mantelpiece if the use of a stove had been anticipated. The addition of the stove and the grates for coal suggests that, although the fireplaces were adequate for heating when wood was burned, the whims of fashion demanded they be converted to coal after it became a fashionable fuel.

Finally, in the west bedroom on the second floor is a mantelpiece which is not markedly dissimilar from those made of slate, but this one is of marbleized wood. The intent of this installation was to suggest a costly medium, but to do so inexpensively. It is not likely that anyone was deceived by the substitution. This one is also fitted with a coal grate with an iron border to fill the large opening formerly used for wood. The hearth of this fireplace is laid with bricks, others have either slate or marble.

The W. J. B. Stokes House, built in Trenton, New Jersey, in 1838–40. This is an excellent example of the Greek prostyle with four massive Ionian columns in the front. Its low-pitched roof and tall chimneys are additional facets of its style. *Courtesy Historic American Buildings Survey*

Although the Federal style of architecture seems to have been firmly entrenched on the American architectural scene, it also was destined to be outmoded by the proponents of the Greek Revival style. As a matter of fact, the Greek Revival established its first foothold in America long before the Federal waned. It is generally accepted that the first Greek Revival building in America was the Bank of Pennsylvania, designed by Latrobe and built in Philadelphia, 1799–1801. This example was but the precursor of much activity which followed on the Atlantic seaboard, in western New York and Pennsylvania, the Western Reserve, the deep South, and along the Mississippi River.

The identifying feature of Greek buildings was a portico in prostyle, which means, "a portico in front of a Greek temple, of which the columns stood in front of the building." The ultimate, however, was the peristyle—a plan in which columns were built completely around the building. The prostyle had a pediment only across the front, while the peristyle had a pediment across the rear as well.

Of a less conspicuous nature in houses were elements such as low-pitched roofs, inspired by the roofs of Greece, where steep-sloped roofs to drain off melting snow were not required. Doorways were placed to one side and usually flanked on each side by Greek columns. The multiple paneling of earlier doors was replaced by long vertical panels. The openings for windows were larger and the trim became broad and flat. Cast-iron grills were popular and balconies on southern mansions had balusters of the same material.

The Joel Hayden House at Haydenville, Massachusetts, built about 1830. Its pleasing proportions and simplicity of design make it an outstanding example of its style. *Courtesy William H. Pierson, Jr.*

The double projection of the chimney-breast in the living-room fireplace of the Joel Hayden House provides plenty of depth for the fire chamber. The display of Greek objects on the mantel shelf is particularly appropriate. *Courtesy William H. Pierson, Jr.*

The interior arrangement of the rooms was dominated by the "T" or "L" shape in which the entire house was laid out. Sometimes the plan consisted of a central block with wings on each side. The formal balance of rooms had been broken by the earlier introduction of oval and round rooms combined with others, either square or rectangular. Chimneys were usually built in the outer walls of houses, a plan which permitted windows to be inserted in the side walls of a room and large doorways to join the important rooms on the first floor. Free-standing columns on each side of the opening between the rooms brought the flavor of the exterior into the interior, and seemed to unify the whole architec-

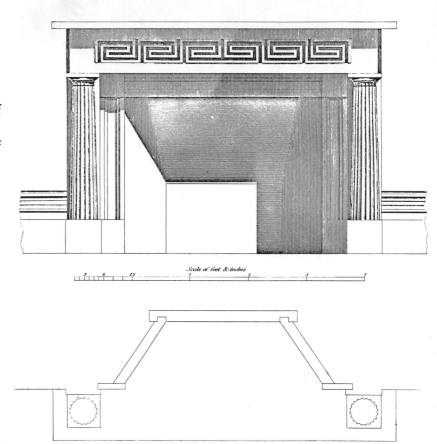

Plan for a chimney-piece from *The Practical House Carpenter* by Asher Benjamin. The use of Doric columns and a fret design on the frieze of the mantelpiece stamp this design as Greek in character. *Courtesy Dover Publications, Inc., New York City*

tural assemblage of the house. Although the exterior was basically the plan of a Greek temple, the interior was designed to create a setting for the owner's personal needs. Instead of the four unnamed rooms on each floor of the Georgian house, the Greek Revival house contained rooms such as the conservatory, library, breakfast room, kitchen, reception room, servants room, flower room, pantry, ballroom, and study. The purposes of these rooms reflect the rise as a class of cultured entrepreneurs, most of whom made their money in the fast-growing industries of the Northeast, land speculation of the Western Reserve, or the cultivation of cotton in the South, which followed on the heels of Whitney's invention of the cotton gin at the turn of the century.

Houses in the Greek Revival style were built in most regions east of the Mississippi River, in sizes ranging from modest dwellings to the vast residences such as those found in Natchez, Mississippi. A fine example of a Greek Revival house is the Joel Hayden House at Haydenville,

Greek Revival mantelpiece of gray marble with a raised rectangular panel cut into the frieze. The slabs of marble on the sides have an anthemion carved in the top section and a fret design in the bottom. *Courtesy Mr. and Mrs. Gerald Lestz*

Massachusetts (about 1830). Hayden was doubtless connected with the Hayden Brass Works and later probably shared in the financial return from the spinning of brass buckets, a process patented by Hiram Hayden in 1851. The templelike central portion of the house has four Doric columns across the front of the portico, and three nicely scaled smaller ones on the porches of the one-story wing on each side. The chimney end of the living room contains two doorways with broad flat moldings with crossetted corners, an obvious hangover from the earlier Georgian period. Between these two doorways the fireplace and mantelpiece are located. They are of the conventional size and shape for the period and are made of black marble. There is a projecting chimney-breast with a panel in the overmantel, but of less significance and importance than those of the Georgian style.

The use of marble or a substitute resembling marble was widespread in the Greek Revival era. This procedure can at least be partially attributed to Asher Benjamin who wrote *The Practical House Carpenter*, which had a number of printings from the early part of the century until 1830. The suggestions for mantelpiece styles in his earliest publications had a definite Federal flavor, but those in the 1830 printing are clearly in the style of the Greek Revival. He comments as follows:

> In the decoration of chimney pieces (mantels) the wildest fancy has been indulged. Their composition should conform to the style and character of the room in which they are placed, whether of marble or of wood. If of wood, they may be painted black and varnished, which will give them a neat appearance, and render them less liable to be soiled with smoke than when painted a light color. . . . The jambs and back are intended to be made of soap stone, but may be made of any other kind of stone which will stand the heat of the fire, or of iron.

He further comments about the proportions of fireplace openings for burning both wood and coal. It is obvious that the use of coal grates was a matter of increasing importance in 1830.

Marble mantelpieces in the drawing room of Wormslee Plantation near Savannah, Georgia. The sculptured supports of the frieze are strong evidence of Greek influence. The house was built about 1820. *Courtesy Historic American Buildings Survey*

An example of American Gothic Victorian architecture with perforated vergeboards. Its six chimney tops suggest that it has a number of fireplaces. From *John Maass: The Gingerbread Age. Courtesy Holt, Rinehart, and Winston*

Chimney tops on the Bishop House located at George and Bartlett Streets, New Brunswick, New Jersey. *Courtesy Historic American Buildings Survey*

Open fire places for burning wood ought to be proportioned in some degree to the room in which they are placed. It is however difficult to lay down any precise rule for their proportion. An open fire place cannot be made much less than three feet in breadth, if the room be not more than twelve feet square, and should never exceed three feet nine inches in any room, whatever be its size. A fire place of three feet opening between the jambs, should have an opening from the hearth upwards of about two feet seven inches.

Where open fire places are made for burning coals, the grate in them should be about one inch in length for every foot in the length of the room; that is to say, if the room is twenty feet square, make the grate twenty inches long, and about ten inches deep. The top bar of the grate should not be less than eighteen inches, nor more than twenty-four from the hearth.

Although no examples of mantelpieces have been found by the author which show a direct influence from the three designs which Benjamin offers in the 1830 printing of *The Practical House Carpenter*, there is evidence that a source for a pure Greek style was available at that time. As he mentions, these could be made of wood or marble. The post and lintel construction of Greek temples is very evident in his suggestions. The vertical and horizontal parts suggest the framework for a building. They were decorated with recessed panels, a molded central section, or a fretwork design similar to those found on Greek ceramic products. His most elaborate design has additional small Doric columns on each side to support a projecting frieze.

One of the most extravagant examples of domestic Greek Revival architecture in America is at "Andalusia," near Philadelphia, Pennsylvania. Nicholas Biddle, the owner of the estate, visited Greece and upon his return engaged Thomas U. Walter to remodel his forty-year old Regency house to conform to his recently acquired taste for the Greek style. The marble mantelpiece in the music room was brought from Italy. Composed of two levels of flat marble, the outer level consists of a mantel shelf supported by two sculptured figures. Over the mantelpiece is located a massive mirror in a gold-leafed frame to lend further elegance to the arrangement. A coal grate with a brass frame completes the setting as it is today. The mantelpiece in the dining room is relatively plain, with its broad molded side columns and similar frieze under the mantel shelf.

Although there is a sprinkling of elegant mantelpieces in Greek Revival houses, a slow but inevitable trend was becoming evident. This matter is brought into focus by Thomas E. Tallmadge in his book *The Story of Architecture in America*. He comments:

> The fireplace had lost much of its importance [in the Greek Revival style]. The over-mantel disappeared, giving way to the mirror. The fireplace itself, however, was usually of marble, and sometimes elaborately carved with figures taken from Flaxman or Wedgwood. Mirrors imported from France became very popular. Their height and width, and the elaboration of the gilt frame were in some degree an estimate of the financial standing of the owner. They occupied important places, as at the end of the drawing-room between two windows or over the fireplace reaching to the ceiling.

Mantelpiece in "Stronghold," New Brunswick, New Jersey. Although built in the second half of the nineteenth century, its style is transitional between Greek Revival and Victorian. The central panel is a fire-board which was removed when a fire was lighted. *Courtesy Historic American Buildings Survey*

A simple Romanesque-style mantelpiece made of gray marble, located in West Chester, Pennsylvania. When built it had a grate for burning coal. *Courtesy Mr. and Mrs. William Ball*

This author was obviously talking about conditions in the city where wood for fuel was becoming expensive, and stoves were gradually replacing open fireplaces. At this time, however, America was essentially a rural country and Lewis F. Allen comments differently in his *Rural Architecture* (1852).

A farm house should never be built without an ample open fire-place in its kitchen and other principally occupied rooms; and in all rooms where stoves are placed, and fires are daily required, the open Franklin should take the place of the close or airtight stove, unless extraordinary ventilation to such rooms be adopted also. The great charm of the farmer's winter evening is the open fireside, with its cheerful blaze and glowing embers; not wastefully ex-pended, but giving out that genial warmth and comfort which, to those who are accustomed to its enjoyment, is a pleasure not made up by any invention whatever; and although the cooking stove or range be required which—in addition to the fireplace, we would always recommend, to lighten female labor—it can be so arranged as not to interfere with the enjoyment or convenience of the open fire.

Thus, it is evident that a battle for and against the fireplace ensued, a contest which the adherents for the fireplace finally lost. Throughout much of the Victorian era of architecture, however, fireplaces continued to appear in the floor plans drawn for houses and they were built in the principal rooms, at least.

It has been shown in the architectural eras previously discussed that there was a relevance between the architectural style of the houses and the fireplaces within the houses. The logic of such a procedure is very evident. It would have been obviously anachronistic to place a primitive fireplace in a Georgian house, and vice versa. Thus, one must logically expect that Victorian fireplaces were stylistically compatible with the architecture of the period.

In view of the foregoing statement, some attention must be given to the domestic architecture of the Victorian era. A number of factors were involved in bringing this new style to the fore. One was the fact that men seem inevitably to become disenchanted with current styles and yearn for a new one. This procedure has deep psychological founda-tions which can only be recognized and not scientifically explained here. Despite the great appeal and use of the Greek Revival style A. J. Downing explains, in *The Architecture of Country Homes*, that it fell into disfavor.

> It has been observed by modern critics, that there is no reason to believe the temple form was ever, even by the Greeks, used for private dwellings, which easily accounts for our comparative failure in constructing well arranged residences in this style.

It might be truthfully said here that Downing had "an ax to grind" in making the above statement, as it was a very logical procedure for him to downgrade the Greek Revival style and to embellish the Victorian with its attractive elements.

In addition to the psychological whim for change in architectural style, it must be recognized that the pulse of America was quickened at mid-century. Transportation and communication were greatly improved by the digging of canals and the building of railroads. Such facilities were instrumental in spreading designs and distributing materials to relatively remote regions. Machines for processing wood were invented, which provided cheap lumber and millwork for a new architectural era. America was on its way toward popularizing the pointed arch, the barge-board, and the veranda in new and romantic ways.

The virtues of stones and bricks for building houses were well established by this time, and many of the so-called villas were built of these better and more costly materials. But the humble cottages and the houses for the vast number of middle-class families were built of wood. Both clapboard and vertical siding were used. There were also variations of the Victorian style. The pointed arch, or American Gothic, seems to have been the most popular, but Italian or Tuscan villas were built, and there was a mansardic style which John Maass described in his book *The Gingerbread Age* as "handsome without and comfortable within."

The size of the house and the decor of the interiors usually reflected the economic stature of the owner. Small houses had only a parlor, kitchen, and bedroom, while a giant villa had halls, bedrooms, servants rooms, and closets, as well as a kitchen, dining room, pantry, library, parlor, and finally bathrooms. The modern house of the second half of the century had most of the amenities known today (except a television antenna). The furnishings are described by Maass.

> A floral carpet is underfoot, and large-figured wallpaper all around; there are overstuffed chairs, ottomans, marble-topped tables and carved sideboards; the remaining space is garnished with potted plants, bronzed statuary, plaster casts, wax flowers under glass domes, shellwork, beadwork, fringed cushions, gilt-framed pictures and petit-point mottoes; souvenirs and bric-a-brac are ranged on fret-work brackets and tiered whatnots. Stripped of this overgrowth, the Victorian parlor with its parquet floor, high ceiling, tall windows, strong moldings and an ample fireplace emerges as a very handsome room.

An unusual mantelpiece in the Romanesque style made of cast iron. Originally it was painted black with gilt outlining the contour of the various panels. *Courtesy Mr. and Mrs. William Ball*

It is interesting to note that Maass includes a fireplace as one of the standard appendages of a Victorian room. It has been pointed out earlier that after mid-century the furnace in the cellar was slowly pushing the fireplace out of the living room; however, at least one example is known which has both, and this one is probably not a rarity. It has been noted that most of the houses designed by Downing and illustrated in *The Architecture of Country Houses* have fireplaces, at least in the important rooms of the first floor.

As a matter of fact, it is very evident that Downing loved fireplaces and chimneys. It is evident that chimneys went through the fancy-to-plain-to-fancy stages, and their status in numbers and ornamentation reached its zenith in America in the Victorian era. Downing states that:

> A common brick chimney gives no pleasure by its form, because that form is *lumpish* and unmeaning. To make a chimney form interesting, however simple it may be, it must be divided into three parts, viz. a base, a shaft, and a cap. A chimney should never spring out of the roof with no apparent preparation for it, but a base more or less wide should always be shown, upon which the part exposed may evidently rest and obtain a solid foundation to withstand high winds. After dividing a chimney top into three parts, the next

point of art is to *proportion* the whole so that it may, in the first place, have the most agreeable form, and in the second place, a form in keeping with the rest of the dwelling.

Later, in Downing's description of a large villa he comments that

> The chimney tops of this design should be formed of moulded brick, if such can be obtained. If not, chimney-tops of the Garnkirk fire-clay, of the patterns shown in Fig. 155, may be had of Jas. Lee & Co., New York or Boston.

There probably was a considerable variety of designs available in chimney-tops, one of those on the Bishop House in New Brunswick, New Jersey, is very similar to those illustrated by Downing. Most of the houses which Downing illustrates have a profusion of chimney-tops ranging in numbers from one to eight.

Doorway in the Victorian-Romanesque style located in Lancaster, Pennsylvania. The relevance between the design of the mantelpiece and doorways is very evident.

Although distinct styles of mantelpieces were developed in the Victorian era, it is entirely logical to expect that the earliest ones closely resembled those they were slowly displacing. As a matter of fact, Downing illustrates a "Grecian style" with many evident vestiges of the earlier period. The facing on the front of the jambs are broad flat slabs of wood or marble, as are also the frieze and the mantel shelf. There appears to be a dentil-like ornamentation supporting the mantel shelf. The whole arrangement distinctly resembles the post-and-lintel construction of a Greek temple.

The embryo of the ultimate Victorian style is evident in another of Downing's examples which he describes as "simple Gothic." The major change in this one from the previously described Grecian style is that the top of the fire chamber opening is a pointed Gothic arch instead of the earlier straight lintel. The pointed arch creates a three-cornered spandrel between the arch and the mantel shelf, which appears to have

A page from *The Baltimore Advertiser and Business Circular for the Year 1850* showing two advertisements of marble workers, both of whom supplied marble mantelpieces.

This mantelpiece is one of several in a house built in Cooperstown, New York, in 1875. It was originally equipped with fireplaces and a furnace. The fireplaces have small grates for burning coal. The one shown here has its "summer" fire-board in place. The designer of this mantelpiece virtually exhausted the shapes of panels which could be used on such a facility. *Courtesy Mr. and Mrs. M. W. Thomas*

been left undecorated at first, but ultimately became the center of attraction in a Victorian mantelpiece.

Finally, a third style of mantelpiece must be mentioned, the Romanesque, which ultimately seems to have become the most popular of all. However, a sizeable number of hybrid Gothic/Romanesque examples are known to have been used. The Romanesque is identified by the round, or half-round arch at the top of the chamber opening. The round arch top of the chamber opening created bigger spandrels than those of the earlier Gothic style, which were filled to overflowing with fruits, flowers, and vines, all carved with amazing skill and delicacy.

The large number of illustrations in contemporary publications, and the surviving examples of Victorian fireplaces indicate their use through the second half of the nineteenth century. Each one was made in a style appropriate for the room in which it was to be used. There was considerable flexibility in materials and styles. Fancy ones were made of marble, plain ones of cast iron, and vice versa. Most of them were made of wood, stone, slate, bricks, cast iron, or marble. Although improved methods of transportation made most materials available throughout the country, some specialization did occur.

One of the most interesting examples of specialization occurred in Baltimore, which is widely known for marble front-door stoops. The common use of marble in Baltimore is attested by the fact that in *The Baltimore Advertiser and Business Circular for the Year 1850*, there is a section entitled "Importers and Manufacturers in Marble." In this section nine dealers are listed who supplied a variety of objects made of marble, including steps, platforms, sills, lintels, frontispieces, tombs, table tops, and mantelpieces. These items could be made from Egyptian, Irish, Italian, or American marble. One company specified a brand known as "Baltimore White Marble." Bevan & Sons indicated they were "prepared to execute all orders in their line"; however, they mentioned that they "constantly have on hand, a variety of exquisitely CARVED MANTELS." Possibly those of the latter type were imported.

The Victorian style was the last important one in which fireplaces and mantelpieces were essential components; however, they continued to be used on a small scale throughout most of the century. Unfortunately, it must be admitted that their exit was not made in a flash of splendor. They came upon the American scene as simple functional devices, they reached a "high art" status in the eighteenth and early nineteenth centuries, and finally disappeared as unattractive and little-used appendages in the late nineteenth century.

Twentieth Century

*A*lthough this book is designed to serve many purposes, the two principal ones are to inform the reader concerning the styles and technology of fireplaces of the past, and to provide basic information relating to contemporary procedures in building chimneys, fireplaces, and mantelpieces. This chapter will be concerned with the second objective. It is quite evident in the twentieth century, that the fireplace has not lost its charm, since it continues to be the focal point of interest in many interior arrangements. Modern heating devices have made it less necessary; nevertheless, not only have the old styles been continued, but new ones have appeared.

There is an undefinable mystery about the construction and function of a fireplace, and most people who own one want to understand it. The information provided will assist people who are planning a home, as well as those who want to build a fireplace with their own hands. In both cases certain fundamental decisions must be made, and they should be made on the best advice available. There is no unanimous agreement on all the facets discussed; however, there is value in recognizing the problems and following them to logical conclusions. For many years fireplaces were built on hearsay methods, which has led to the construction of devices stingy with heat and productive of smoke. Hopefully, such a result will be avoided, but no guarantee is advanced with the prescription.

Assuming that correct architectural data are available for details such as size and proportions, two problems must be solved simultaneously; namely, the location of the fireplace and the style of the fittings—the mantelpiece, hearth, etc. Each fireplace must have a separate flue, and as many flues as practical should be built in one chimney stack. As a word

Construction Sketch of Successful Fireplace

See Table of Dimensions on Opposite Page

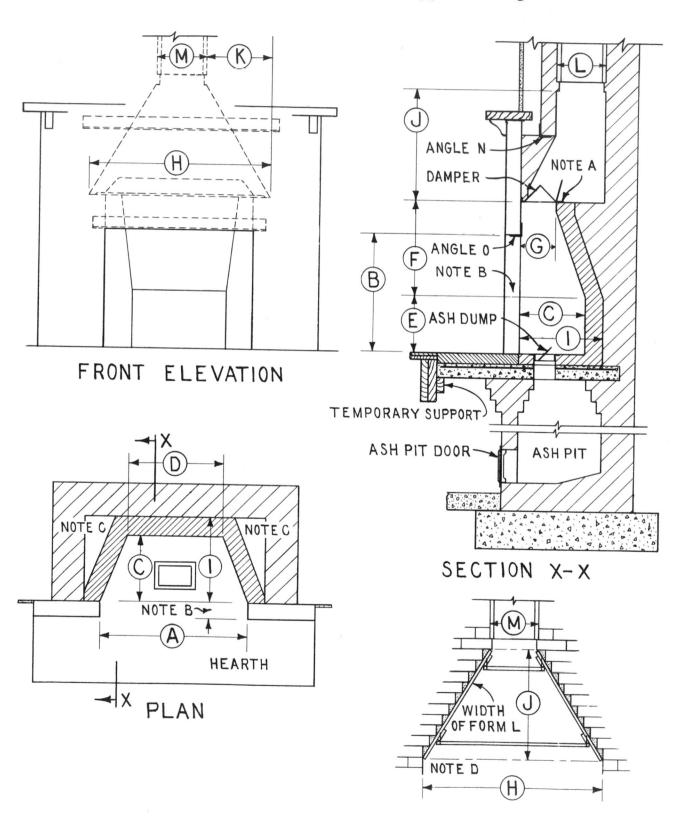

FRONT ELEVATION

PLAN

SECTION X-X

Table of Fireplace Dimensions

Finished Fireplace Opening				Rough Brickwork and Flue Sizes									Ash-pit Door	Equipment	
											Flue Sizes			Steel	Angles *
A	B	C	D	E	F	G	H	I	J	K	L	M Round	Door	N	O
24	24	16	11	14	18	8¾	32	20	19	10	8×12	8	12×8	A–36	A–36
26	24	16	13	14	18	8¾	34	20	21	11	8×12	8	12×8	A–36	A–36
28	24	16	15	14	18	8¾	36	20	21	12	8×12	10	12×8	A–36	A–36
30	29	16	17	14	23	8¾	38	20	24	13	12×12	10	12×8	A–42	A–36
32	29	16	19	14	23	8¾	40	20	24	14	12×12	10	12×8	A–42	A–42
36	29	16	23	14	23	8¾	44	20	27	16	12×12	12	12×8	A–48	A–42
40	29	16	27	14	23	8¾	48	20	29	16	12×16	12	12×8	A–48	A–48
42	32	16	29	14	26	8¾	50	20	32	17	16×16	12	12×8	B–54	A–48
48	32	18	33	14	26	8¾	56	22	37	20	16×16	15	12×8	B–60	B–54
54	37	20	37	16	29	13	68	24	45	26	16×16	15	12×8	B–72	B–60
60	37	22	42	16	29	13	72	27	45	26	16×20	15	12×8	B–72	B–66
60	40	22	42	16	31	13	72	27	45	26	16×20	18	12×8	B–72	B–66
72	40	22	54	16	31	13	84	27	56	32	20×20	18	12×8	C–84	C–84
84	40	24	64	20	28	13	96	27	61	36	20×24	20	12×8	C–96	C–96
96	40	24	76	20	28	13	108	29	75	42	20×24	22	12×8	C–108	C–108

NOTE. * Angle Sizes: A—3×3×³⁄₁₆; B—3½×3×¼; C—5×3½×³⁄₁₆.

Note A: The back flange of the damper must be protected from intense heat by being fully supported by the masonry. At the same time, the damper should not be built solidly at the ends but given freedom to expand with heat, as shown in the front elevation.

Note B: The drawing indicates the thickness of the brick fireplace front as four inches. However, no definite dimension can be given for this because of the various materials used—marble, stone, tile, etc., all having various thicknesses.

Note C: The hollow triangular spaces indicated in the plan, behind the splayed sides of the inner brickwork, should be filled to afford solid backing. If desired to locate a flue in either space, the outside dimensions of the rough brickwork should be increased.

Note D: A good way to build a smoke chamber is to erect a wooden form consisting of two sloping boards at the sides, held apart by spreaders at the top and bottom. Spreaders are nailed upward into cleats as shown. The letters H, M, and J correspond to letters in the elevation and in the Table of Dimensions. The form boards should have the same width as the flue lining.

Note E: A ruler is a convenience in using the table. Select the number in the left-hand column that corresponds to your proposed width of fireplace opening. Lay the ruler on the line below it and read the figures to the right on the same line. They give you the complete recommended dimensions and installation of the fireplace for the chosen width of opening. From *The Book of Successful Fireplaces. Courtesy Structures Publishing Company* of caution, the writer has seen some very unfortunate locations for fire-places merely to keep all the flues in one stack. Whenever expedient, all the flues should be built in one stack, since one is usually cheaper than two, and sometimes equally attractive.

Fireplaces are found in many locations in a house, but the overwhelm-ing number are built today in a living room or family room. They can be placed on a long or on a short wall, with the long wall getting the nod in most cases. The choice of location could be influenced by a desire for utilization of heat, or simply by what the owner likes best. In tra-ditional houses fireplaces were usually built in the center of a long wall or across a corner. There is no claim that this rule cannot be broken; however, it is a reasonably safe one to follow. In all decisions concerning the location of fireplaces a thorough look should be taken at past prac-tices, for they are the distilled experience of generations of builders of fireplaces.

Assuming the central location is selected, the next step is choosing the design of the fireplace. For example, the question of a flat wall versus a projecting chimney-breast must be resolved. In the opinion of the writer a projecting chimney-breast is preferred in many cases. This type of construction catches the eye and focuses attention on the region in which the fireplace is located. It provides recessed areas on each side, which are often filled with book cases or cupboards. Narrow cupboards can be built into the projecting sides of the breast; these traditionally were used for the storage of candles. Possibly the sides can remain un-adorned except for candelabra mounted there to provide additional light, if such an effect is desired. Furthermore, a projecting breast creates a panel area above the mantelpiece which can be utilized for hanging a portrait, a mirror, or an enclosed cupboard. Candelabra can also be mounted there, although their use on the sides and the front simulta-neously should be discouraged. If the chimney-breast is completely cov-ered with wood, an excellent opportunity is provided for a color contrast with the other walls in the room. Needless to say, the use of a chimney-breast creates a very "formal" appearance, and should be furnished with a limited number of tools, only andirons, shovel, tongs, fender, and possibly a warming pan.

One major decision concerning the fireplace remains to be made—the size of the opening. Although personal preferences can hold sway in this matter it goes without saying that very small openings should not be made in large walls and vice versa. In cases of a living-room fireplace caution should be used lest it serve merely as a backdrop for the display of tools and utensils. Traditionally, living-room fireplaces are moderate in size with the intent of heating and decorating the room.

One of the indiscretions found in fireplaces in the author's community is massive displays of stone and brick in jambs and lintels in a room with furnishings which are otherwise reasonably sophisticated. Fireplaces such as these were used in houses of the seventeenth century, or later log cabins, but never in the refined houses of the eighteenth century. One reference book has a chapter entitled "A Short Chapter About Taste." This is a subject of great importance, and should not be skipped over lightly by either the owner or the builder.

For the sake of variation, one might decide that a larger kitchen-type fireplace could be built in the family room. One must not conclude, however, that a large fireplace always produces a great amount of heat except when a consistently large fire is kept burning. Heat is radiated from the walls of the fireplace and, if the walls are unheated because they are too far away from the fire, there will be little radiation into the room. The large fireplace of this type might be built of stone or brick and left unplastered.

The fittings of this fireplace would be different from those of the living room. An interesting appendage might logically be a crane, from which a variety of kettles would be suspended. A reflecting tin oven or bird spit might be on the hearth, along with a waffle or wafer iron. Andirons might be made of iron, two or three feet high, depending on the size of the opening, with spit hooks for roasting a joint of meat. A recess in the jambs might provide a storage place for containers holding ingredients for seasoning.

Ornamentation, other than the objects used for cooking and normally displayed there, should be kept to a minimum. Betty lamps might hang from the mantelpiece, but the profuse gathering of equipment for permanent display is a procedure of doubtful merit. The popularity of fireplace cookery today increases the need for utensils of many kinds, but they might be stored more conveniently in a nearby cupboard.

Although a number of ideas might be discussed in tentatively planning fireplaces, when actual construction begins some final decisions must be

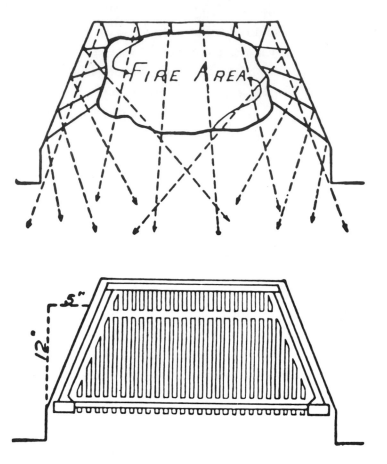

The Hearth Plan: Count Rumford, whose work as a fireplace designer has never been surpassed, conceived the fireplace interior as a sort of reflector. His first measure was to splay the sides and thus narrow the hearth from front to back. Plans call for a splay of five inches per foot.

Back is Sloped: The reflector concept is further carried out by sloping the back of the fireplace forward from a point 14 inches above the hearth to the level of the damper, as indicated in the drawings. This deflects both flame and heat forward. Products of combustion pass off through the damper, but a maximum of heat is reflected into the room.

Damper Placed Forward: The sloped back contributes to other important design factors. It brings the damper forward of and not directly under the flue and to a position just back of the breast wall of the fireplace. It leaves room for an ample smoke shelf behind the damper. Where the damper has a rear position, no shelf is possible. Soot falling down the chimney comes through the damper opening and often into the room. There is no barrier to the down-draft, and smokiness ensues. If the damper is at the rear, much heat is sacrificed.

Sloping back, damper well forward, and a roomy smoke shelf are all important None can be sacrificed without impairing the other. The smoke shelf, with the upturned damper valve-plate, forms a deflector for any down-draft, so that it eddies upward in the ascending column of smoke.

The recommended location of the damper is four to eight inches above the fireplace opening of the fireplace front (which is supported by a stiff steel angle). To sacrifice this safety margin in order to support the masonry by a damper flange is to incur risk of issuance of smoke into the room.

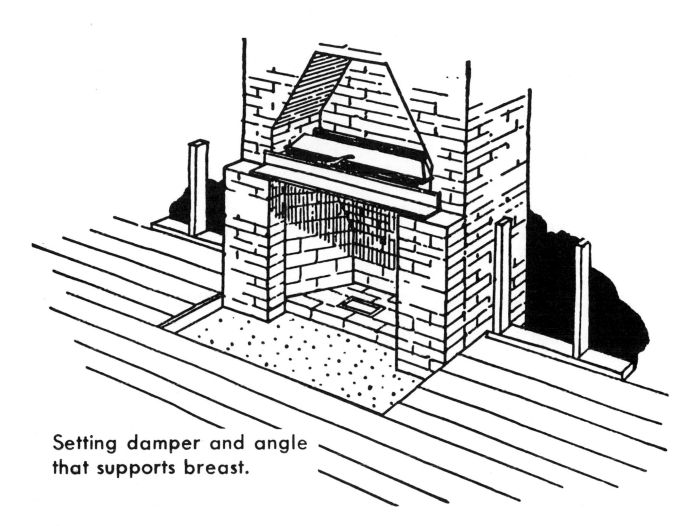

Setting damper and angle that supports breast.

Choice of a Damper: The damper should be a co-ordinated part of a properly designed fireplace interior. It should afford a smooth metal throat for the passage of smoke and fumes. A vertical front flange will permit it to rest snugly against the masonry of the fore wall, and a narrow opening (front to rear) will continue the plane of the slope of the back masonry and leave room for the smoke shelf. Its sides should be splayed to conform to the fireplace design. It should be easy to adjust and easy to close during seasons when the fieplace is not in use. Choice of a means of control is a matter of preference. Poker control is less conspicuous. Rotary control is simpler to operate. From *The Book of Successful Fireplaces. Courtesy Structures Publishing Company* made. One, of course, is the number and location of the fireplaces to be built and their actual size, at least as far as width and depth are concerned. Houses with a basement have a footing below the basement level, others must be built below the frost line. A footing must be provided for each chimney stack, and the size of the footing is determined by the area required for the base of the stack. The footing should be a concrete slab at least eight inches thick, and six inches larger than the stack on all sides. A chimney stack is usually massive and adequate support is necessary to prevent sinking and cracking of the walls. Cracked walls could be a hazard and, in extreme cases, could minimize the draft of the chimney as well. Chimneys can be planned to stand free, as they were in the South, or to be supported by house walls.

The mix for concrete for the footing should be one part of cement, two parts of sand, and four parts of crushed stone. At least a week should be allowed for it to set before construction of the chimney stack begins.

Probably at the bottom of the stack will be an ash pit, with an opening on either an inside or an outside wall. The back wall of the ash pit can be the wall of the house, while the inner wall should match the front wall level of the fireplace. A cleanout door must be placed near the bottom to remove the ashes that fall through the ash dump in the hearth. Bricks obtained from a local supplier of building materials are usually used for the masonry work. In addition, a mortar box will be needed along with a trowel, mortar board, hoe, hammer, level, and a stout string to check alignment. The mortar should be composed of one part Portland cement, one part hydrated lime, and six parts of clean moistened sand. The consistency of the mortar should be satisfactory to support the weight of a brick, but be thin enough to permit tapping for proper alignment.

The walls are built upward from the footing to within about a foot of the bottom of the hearth level, where courses are corbeled inward to provide support for the hearth slab. This slab is supported at the rear by the lower stack, and at the front by a piece of timber fastened to the floor joist. The underpinning of the slab consists of bars of iron on which sheet metal is placed before the concrete is poured. All parts of wood should be kept at least four inches away from areas which will become very hot.

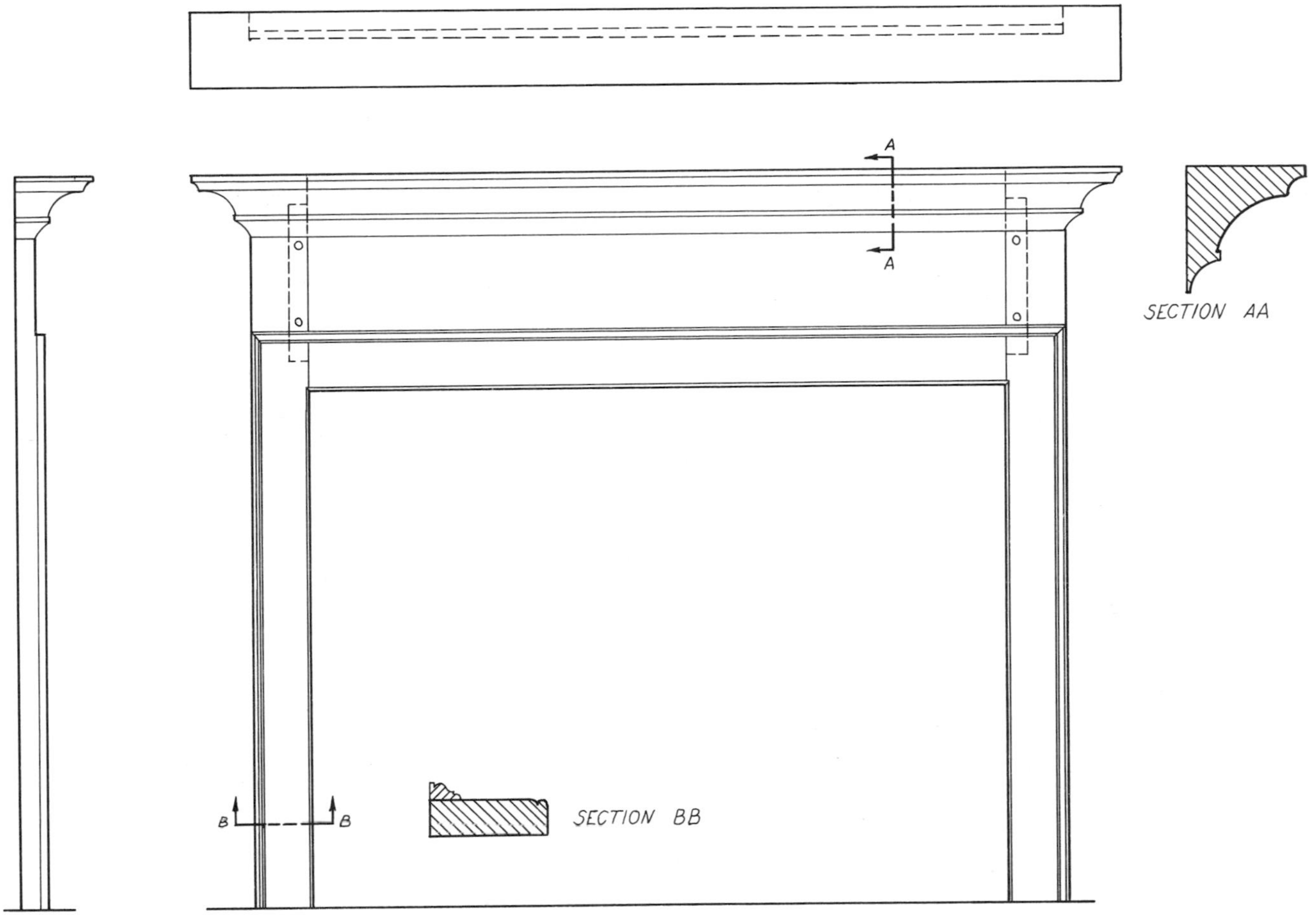

SECTION AA

SECTION BB

Plan for constructing a simple mantelpiece of wood. A "stock" molding can be substituted for the design suggested at A A. *Courtesy Donald Hutslar*

The thickness of the concrete slab is of considerable importance, for provision must be made to accommodate the covering desired. The back hearth might logically be laid with firebrick, for that will probably never need replacement even though great amounts of heat are generated. The firebrick on the hearth and the back of the fireplace might be laid in fireclay; however, common practice is to use the regular mortar used in the balance of the masonry work. The covering of the fore hearth is a very important consideration because it reflects the taste of the owner and is an important part of the decor of the room. The simplest solution is to fill it with red brick. An alternate procedure would be to use flat thin stones (commonly called flag stones) which is an attractive procedure, but suggests a provincial setting. Flat slabs of marble can also be used, but this requires a formal setting. Perhaps the best compromise is

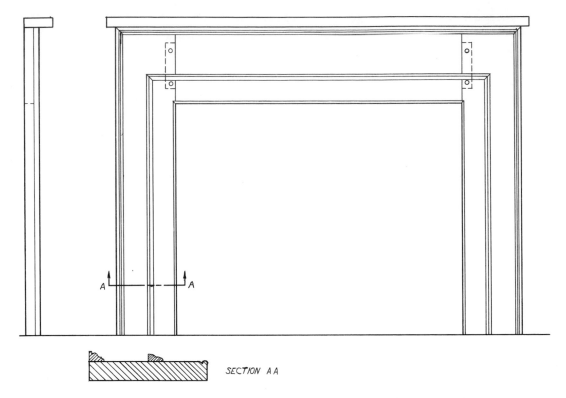

SECTION A A

Simple mantelpiece of wood which can be completely fabricated from stock board and moldings from a local lumber dealer. *Courtesy Donald Hutslar*

to use square glazed red tiles. They quickly acquire a polished patina, and seem appropriate for most settings. Of course, if time is needed to secure the desired materials the hearth does not need to be laid until after the rest of the fireplace has been completed. Sometimes such work is deliberately left for attention on a "rainy day."

Two choices are available in the building of the side and back walls from the hearth to the lintel. A masonry shell can be built which is later filled in with a back wall and jambs, possibly by a professional who is experienced in such work. This is probably the safest procedure for an inexperienced mason. Or the finished form can be built into the walls as they are carried upward. In either case the back wall should be vertical for about fourteen inches, depending on the size of the fireplace, and then cove forward, leaving an adequate open space for the damper about six inches above the level of the lintel. The side walls are built vertically, slanting inward toward the center of the fireplace at the rate of about four inches for each foot of depth. The top level of the back and side walls should be level, forming a smoke shelf to function in conjunction with the damper. At about the same time the lintel must be put in place, with much concern about the size of the fireplace opening. Not only must a pleasant ratio of height to width be provided, but all provisions must be met to prevent the fireplace from smoking.

In case a stock mantelpiece is to be used from a lumber supply company, the height and width are predetermined by the dimensions of the mantelpiece. Or, a simple mantelpiece can be made by a clever craftsman from stock supplies which need to include only flat boards and moldings. As a matter of fact, it is known that in colonial times such work was part of the contracts for building a house. Additionally, the builder must also be concerned with the materials used to cover the front face of the jamb. Although bricks were left uncovered in some early kitchen fireplaces, in living rooms they were usually covered with tiles or plaster. Of course, the most elegant procedure was to cover the masonry jambs with slabs of marble, which usually matched the marble used in the fore hearth. Because this is an uncommon procedure today, considerable difficulty might be experienced in getting the proper size and the desired color. In other words, if marble is to be used, explore sources before provision is made for its installation.

Above the smoke shelf the inner walls taper inward to meet the tile flue centrally located over the fireplace. This wall should be smooth, possibly made of firebrick, with no offset between the masonry and the flue lining. The size of the flue lining is determined by the size of the fireplace opening, and can be ascertained by referring to the chart on flue sizes. It is a common rule that if the direction of *any* flue must be changed, that of the heating plant should be kept straight. However, modern practitioners do not follow this rule absolutely. Flue linings should be built before the bricks are laid and should continue to the very top of the chimney. At least a four-inch space should be maintained between all flues in one chimney stack.

The chimney at the peak of a gable roof should extend at least two feet above the peak; if not at the peak, the distance should be two feet six inches. The top of a chimney should extend three feet above the level

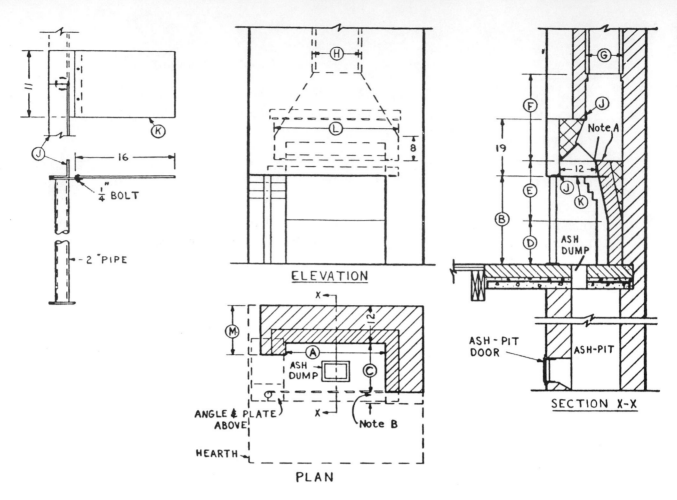

ELEVATION

PLAN

SECTION X-X

Table of Dimensions and Equipment for Projecting-Corner Fireplaces

A	B	C	D	E	F	Flue Size				Ashpit Door	Angle * (2 req'd) J	Plate Lintel K	Corner Post Height
						G	H	L	M				
28	26½	16	14	20	29⅓	12	12	36	16	12×8	A–36	11×16	26½
32	26½	16	14	20	32	12	16	40	16	12×8	A–42	11×16	26½
36	26½	16	14	20	35	12	16	44	16	12×8	A–48	11×16	26½
40	29	16	14	20	35	16	16	48	16	12×8	B–54	11×16	29
48	29	20	14	24	43	16	16	56	20	12×8	B–60	11×16	29
54	29	20	14	23	45	16	16	62	20	12×8	B–72	11×16	29
60	29	20	14	23	51	16	20	68	20	12×8	B–78	11×16	29

Note: * Angle Sizes: A–3×3×³⁄₁₆; B–3½×3×¼.

Note A: The back flange of the damper must be protected from intense heat by being fully supported by the masonry. At the same time, the damper should not be built in solidly at the ends but given freedom to expand with heat.

Note B: The drawing indicates the thickness of the brick fireplace-front as four inches. However, no definite dimension can be given for this because of the various materials possible—marble, stone, etc., all having various thicknesses. From *The Book of Successful Fireplaces. Courtesy Structures Publishing Company*

Table of Dimensions and Equipment for Double-Opening Fireplaces

Width of Opening A	Height of Opening B	Damper (2 req'd) Height E	Smoke Chamber F	Flue Size		Angle * (2 req'd) J	L	Tee	Ashpit Door
				G	H				
28	24	30	19	12	16	A–36	36	35	12×8
32	29	35	21	16	16	A–40	40	39	12×8
36	29	35	21	16	20	A–42	44	43	12×8
40	29	35	27	16	20	A–48	48	47	12×8
48	32	37	32	20	20	B–54	56	55	12×8

Note: * Angle Sizes: A–3×3×³⁄₁₆; B–3½×3×¼.

Note Y: The damper and the steel tee should not be built in solid at the ends but given freedoom to expand with heat. From *The Book of Successful Fireplaces. Courtesy Structures Publishing Company*

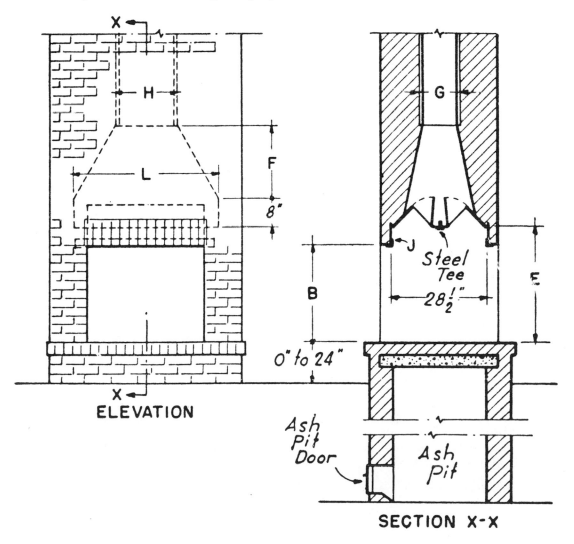

ELEVATION

SECTION X-X

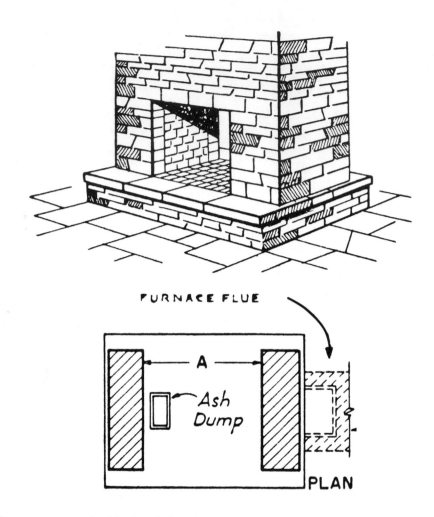

FURNACE FLUE

A
Ash Dump
PLAN

A two-way or double-faced fireplace. In this design two dampers are mounted back to back, their rear flanges resting on a steel tee section which is supported at each end by masonry, but the ends of the tee and dampers must be left free to expand under the heat. From *The Book of Successful Fireplaces. Courtesy Structures Publishing Company*

Two-way contemporary fireplace showing the use of different materials in its construction. Styles of this type are particularly appropriate for rooms with contemporary furnishings. From *The Book of Successful Fireplaces. Courtesy Structures Publishing Company*

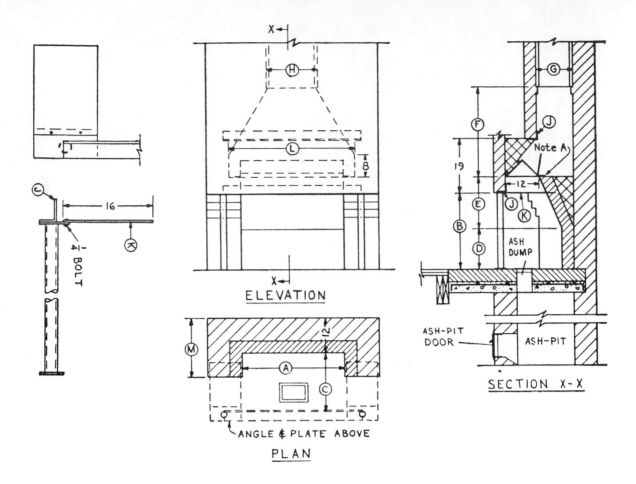

ELEVATION

PLAN

SECTION X-X

ANGLE & PLATE ABOVE

Table of Dimensions and Equipment for Three-Way Fireplaces (Type 1)

A	B	C	D	E	F	Flue Size				Ashpit Door	Angle * (2 req'd) J	Plate Lintel (2 req'd) K	Corner Post Height (2 req'd)
						G	H	L	M				
28	26½	20	14	18	27	12	16	36	20	12×8	A–42	11×16	26½
32	26½	20	14	18	32	16	16	40	20	12×8	A–48	11×16	26½
36	26½	20	14	18	32	16	16	44	20	12×8	A–48	11×16	26½
40	29	20	14	21	35	16	16	48	20	12×8	B–54	11×16	29
48	29	20	14	21	40	16	20	56	20	12×8	B–60	11×16	29
54	29	20	14	23	45	16	20	62	20	12×8	B–72	11×16	29
60	29	20	14	23	51	16	20	68	20	12×8	B–78	11×16	29

Note: * Angle Sizes: A—3×3×³⁄₁₆; B—3½×3×¼.

Note A: The back flange of the damper must be protected from intense heat by being fully supported by the masonry. At the same time, the damper should not be built in solidly at the ends but given freedom to expand with heat. From *The Book of Successful Fireplaces. Courtesy Structures Publishing Company*

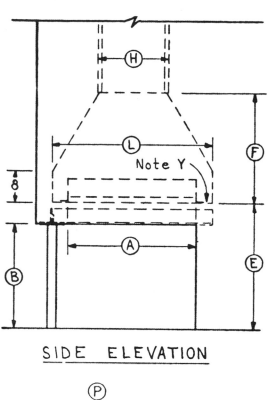

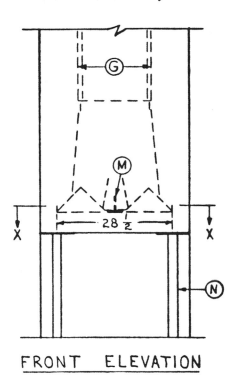

SIDE ELEVATION   FRONT ELEVATION

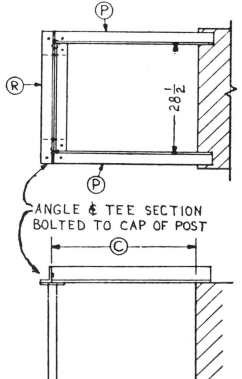

ANGLE & TEE SECTION
BOLTED TO CAP OF POST

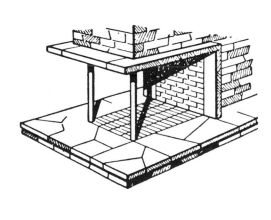

Table of Dimensions and Equipment for Three-Way Fireplaces (Type 2)

| A | B | C | E | F | Flue Size | | Steel Tee | Post Height (2 req'd) | Drilled Angle (2 req'd) | Special Welded Tee |
					G	H	L	M	N	P	R
28	26½	32	32	24	16	20	36	35	26½	36	34
32	26½	36	32	27	20	20	40	39	26½	40	34
36	26½	40	32	32	20	20	44	43	26½	44	34
40	26½	44	32	35	20	20	48	47	26½	48	34
48	26½	52	32	35	20	24	56	55	26½	56	34

Note Y: The dampers (2 required) and the steel tee should not be built in solid at the ends but given freedom to expand with heat. From *The Book of Successful Fireplaces. Courtesy Structures Publishing Company*

Three-way contemporary fireplace with a hearth and overmantel built of bricks. This type usually has corner posts supporting the overmantel. From *The Book of Successful Fireplaces. Courtesy Structures Publishing Company*

of a flat roof. A cement cap should be placed on top of the chimney with an overhang called a drip edge, so that moisture does not readily seep downward along the wall of the chimney.

Possibly the most popular type of fireplace today is built in what might be termed a contemporary style. Many are located and constructed like the traditional examples, but they are usually flush with the wall with a shallow molding surround and a very shallow mantelpiece. These, like all modern furnishings, are built to serve a function rather than to elaborately decorate a room. Their simplicity usually demands that considerable insight be directed toward their size, location, and fittings. Fittings should be held to a minimum, and be contemporary in style. To the writer, it seems inappropriate to place antique andirons, fenders, or fire tools at a contemporary styled fireplace.

A more pronounced departure from traditional style is to construct a corner fireplace which is open on two adjoining sides, the front and an end. This type is usually built with a corner post, although a cantilever plan can be employed if adequate provision for support is made in the rear wall. Most examples have a corner post and an angle-iron lintel to support the usual masonry walls above. The back should be coved toward the front to assist in promoting a draft and to minimize the possibility of smoke drifting out into the room. A damper, of course, is required in all fireplaces, not only to retain as much heat in the room as possible, but also to prevent dust, debris, and cold air from entering the room when the fireplace is not in use.

A third type of fireplace which might be considered contemporary is one with a double opening serving two adjoining rooms. In such cases, the chimney stack can serve as a divider between two rooms, with an opening in each room. For example, such a fireplace could be built in the wall between a hall and a living room. An open fire in the hall not only assists in heating the house, but also creates an atmosphere of hospitality for visitors. The hearth may be raised or low, as in all fireplaces, but with the knowledge that extremely few colonial examples were raised. Adequate flues must be provided for the two openings—in other words, double the flue space for a single opening—and each flue must have a damper. The table of dimensions provides information about sizes and arrangements.

Three-way fireplaces are among the popular contemporary styles. These can be built in a projecting chimney-breast, an arrangement not too dissimilar to the early jambless types used in the seventeenth and eighteenth centuries, but usually on a smaller scale. With the front completely open, a shallow jamb on each side is recommended to minimize the chance that smoke or flames will be blown sidewise into the room. A forward position for the damper is advised, with or without a mantelpiece. The most common practice is to carry a vertical unbroken wall upward from the lintel to the ceiling. Again, a cantilever type of construction is possible, but support by two front posts is recommended. The proper flue size is suggested in the accompanying table of sizes. Another type of three-way fireplace can be built by projecting a pier into a room with three sides open, a plan similar to that of a two-way fireplace, but with only one supporting wall. Corner posts and steel angles carry the weight of the overstructure. Two dampers are centrally located over the middle of the hearth for adequate ventilation of the fire chamber.

A final type of contemporary fireplace is a circular or square model of sheet steel which can be placed in any location in a room. They are usually mounted on tall legs to protect the floor, they have a fire resistant hearth, and at the top taper into a cone, which is fitted with a stove pipe. The stove pipe, of course, is attached to a chimney flue, or may rise vertically through the roof. Some examples have a finish of colored enamel and are very attractive in an appropriate setting. They are a departure from the traditional fire on the hearth, but they are a reasonably good substitute.

Finally, some consideration must be given to a modern fireplace shell, built of two layers of steel with an air chamber between the two walls. At the bottom is a cool-air inlet and either in the top front or side is a hot-air outlet. This device not only heats by radiation from the fire chamber but also by circulation of hot air throughout the area to be warmed, possibly a room nearby or one on the second floor. Various manufacturers produce these prefabricated shells under trade names, such as "Heatsaver," "Heatilator," and the like. It is best to consult a dealer regarding various available sizes and models before planning a fireplace of this kind. The steel shell is enclosed in a masonry wall and in no way interferes with the appearance of a traditional or contemporary fireplace. It does limit the style, however, to the conventional type built into a wall. In many ways it is a good choice for the amateur builder because it guarantees a good smokeless fireplace and has the additional advantage of circulating heat throughout the room.

Iron Fireplaces

*I*t must again be acknowledged, regretfully, that fireplaces as heating devices were very inefficient. It seems logical that many attempts had been made to eliminate some of the disadvantages, among which was the stove or iron fireplace devised by Benjamin Franklin. The use of the term "stove" is a bit misleading, for his device was not the iron box used for heating and cooking common in America from 1850 until 1950, but really a small iron fireplace, made to fit into the larger masonry fireplaces of the seventeenth and eighteenth centuries.

Franklin, in addition to being one of the country's outstanding scientists, was also an articulate writer and a printer, assets he exploited to the full by publishing in 1744 a pamphlet describing the superiority of his new device. To explain its advantages, he made a critical analysis of the deficiencies of the heating system then in use. In the following paragraphs, these undesirable features will be described, often in Franklin's own words.

He pointed out that large fireplaces had a wide throat and flue which carried most of the heat of the fire up the chimney, and that to minimize the possibility of their smoking, a door or window had to be left open to create an adequate draft. This was the accepted practice to make a fireplace function without smoking. One could avoid the uncomfortable effects of the draft by sitting either within the fireplace [ingle nooks], or on high-backed settles before the fire, and expedient of doubtful value, since it kept needed light and heat from other areas of the room.

Franklin was quite emphatic on the subject of drafts which he claimed were caused by air whistling through cracks and crevices in the openings of the room. He believed that it was very unhealthy to sit near an opening where a sharp draft occurred, pointing out that common illnesses such as "colds, rheums, and defluctions which fall into jaws have destroyed many sets of fine teeth." To sustain his observation he quoted a Spanish proverb,

> If the Wind blows on you thru' a hole,
> Make your will and take care of your Soul.

In addition, it was his observation that blazing fires in the huge fireplaces damaged normal eyesight, shriveled the skin, and brought on an appearance of old age prematurely.

Franklin was aware that others were engaged in the same activity. He cites the invention of the Frenchman, Sieur Gauger, whose arrangement of iron plates for the fireplace was an attempt to solve some of the problems encountered. These plates were placed in such a manner that when cold air was drawn into the arrangement from the outside, there were no sharp drafts in the room. The air, after being heated by circulating through cavities, was expelled into the room, with the result that the room was comfortably heated. Although Gauger's device used little wood, and was quite satisfactory for heating, its efficiency was not beyond improvement, and its cost was high. Franklin's goal was, doubtless, to find a better solution.

He was highly critical of other heating devices used at the time. He points out that the Holland stove [a closed box with doors] made no provision for bringing fresh air into the room in which it was located. Little draft was needed to make the fire burn, consequently the house could be made more airtight. The English loved an open fire; therefore he reasoned that because the fire could not be seen, people became careless in tending the stove, so that the fire was often too low to heat the room or too hot and the room was overheated.

Franklin's particular displeasure was directed against the German stove, perhaps because they were so widely used in the German settlements to the west of Philadelphia. His description of it has been repeated many times. "The German Stove," he said, "is like a Box, one side Wanting." The open end of the box was inserted in the back wall of the fireplace, with the closed portion jutting into an adjoining room. He admitted that this device was very satisfactory for heating, but consistently argued that unchanged air mixed with breath and the odor of

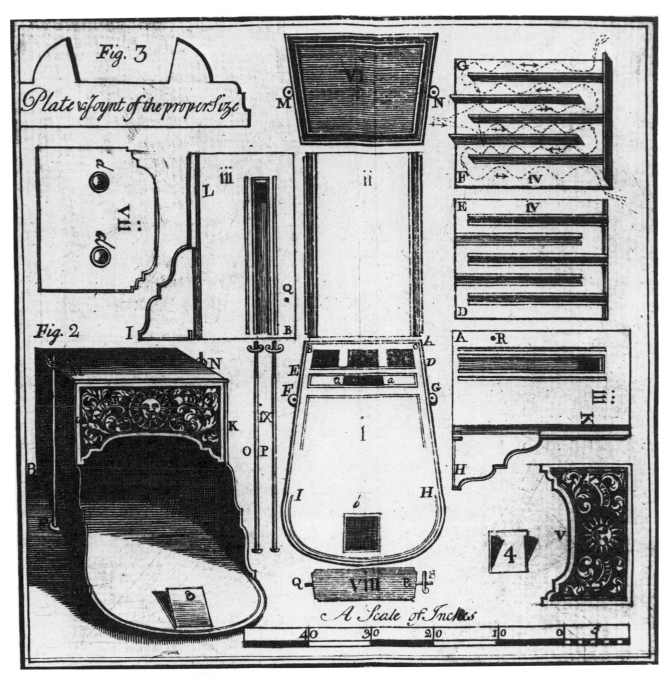

Frontispiece of Benjamin Franklin's brochure about his "Pennsylvanian Fire-Places." *Courtesy The Historical Society of Pennsylvania*

perspiration was disagreeable; besides he complained, one could not see the fire, a severe deprivation to an Englishman.

Finally he pointed out that charcoal fires in pots [braziers] did not permit a change of air in a room, and if they smoked, as they often did, the smoke was also confined within the room. Although they were deemed satisfactory for heating workshops, the fumes from the coals were harmful and were known to produce fatal consequences.

Franklin thought in modern terms about heating. He explained that he devised the Pennsylvania fireplace to eliminate most of the disadvantages of the open fireplace. His device consisted of the following cast-iron parts: 1. a bottom plate; 2. a back plate; 3. two side plates; 4. two middle plates which were joined to form a chamber for heating air; 5. a front plate; 6. a top plate; and 7. a blind (not cast iron).

The names of the various parts of Franklin's fireplace indicate the way it was assembled and the manner in which it functioned. The pieces were cast with grooves or edges to facilitate the assembly of the parts and to keep them permanently in their proper position. The bottom plate had three holes across the back for the exit of the smoke. Immediately in front was one larger hole into which fresh air poured through a channel cut to the outside of the house. This feature presumably saved the lives of many people—at least as Franklin reckoned matters. On the bottom plate two side plates and a rear plate were mounted, with a plate on top. Two bolts running from top to bottom held all parts together. Across the front a decorated plate was attached at the top to minimize the chances of smoking. The remaining opening was fitted with a blind (often called a fireboard) which was to cut off the circulation of air at night and keep a fire smouldering until morning. Near the back an enclosed cavity was placed over the air intake hole through which air was heated and circulated before it was expelled into the room through vents in the side plates. This procedure was very similar to the modern devices which circulate air near the fire and discharge it into the room. The smaller iron fireplace did not reach up to the lintel of the masonry fireplace, and a wall built between the two forced air into the room, which was warmed by the exterior of the iron fireplace. This circulating air augmented that which came out of the side vents.

Franklin was very sensitive about the appearance of his invention. He suggested that after the pointing used to make the joints air tight became dry, it was to be painted black, the paint being made from broken bits of black lead from silversmiths' crucibles mixed with a little rum and water. This solution was also applied to the entire exterior surface of all the plates and, after it was dry, it was rubbed to a black sheen typical of the surface of iron. He believed the area between the fireplace and the lintel should have been plastered and whitewashed, thus forming a pleasing contrast with the black stove and the red hearth. After Franklin had explained the manner of assembling his iron fireplace, he made some comments about its advantages. He pointed out that his device completely warmed an entire room, so that the health of the occupants was not impaired by diseases such as colds, catarrhs, tooth-aches, fevers, pleurisies, and other ailments. The good circulation of air permitted people to sit by a window to sew or read, and unrestricted

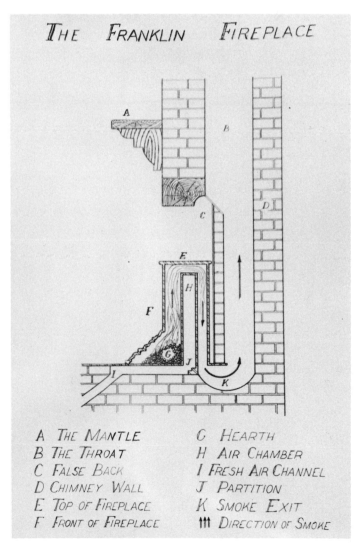

THE FRANKLIN FIREPLACE

Sketch showing the installation of a Franklin fireplace. The air chamber *H* had openings in the sides through which the heated air entered the room.

A THE MANTLE
B THE THROAT
C FALSE BACK
D CHIMNEY WALL
E TOP OF FIREPLACE
F FRONT OF FIREPLACE
G HEARTH
H AIR CHAMBER
I FRESH AIR CHANNEL
J PARTITION
K SMOKE EXIT
⫼⫼⫼ DIRECTION OF SMOKE

Mr. Bearow

Bot of J. D. Paxton & Co

5 Stoves	No 3	11 . 2 . 07
2 ditto	No 2	3 . 3 . 12
1 ditto	No 1	1 . 1 . 20
1 Franklin Stove		3 . 2 . 21

20 . 2 . 04 @ 85/ $187.29¢

W Russell for
J. D. Paxton & Co

Marion Furnace
Aug. 22. 1828

N. B. The feet of the franklin are wanting, we
will send them with the weights, I think
it would be advisable to black 1 or two
of these stoves, it adds very much to
their appearance, say the franklin & the Largest.
4 plates.

W R for
I D Paxton & Co

$1.50 Please pay Mr. McCosh One
Dollar & fifty cents, & charge us
with it

W R for
I D P. & Co

movement was possible in all parts of the room. Crowding around fireplaces to keep comfortably warm was eliminated.

In case of sickness, they functioned very well in the bedroom of the patient. Adequate amounts of fresh air were available, and in no way dangerous or inconvenient. By merely cutting a hole into a chimney, they could be installed in a room without a fireplace, an asset as convenient today as it was in the eighteenth century. He also mentioned that distemper was uncommon among the children of German people from 1730 to 1736, when it raged among other groups. This coincidence was attributed to the fact that Germans used iron stoves, and Franklin regarded his device as equally satisfactory from that point of view.

Because wood was becoming scarce around cities, such as Philadelphia, any saving of fuel was considered commendable. As much as one-half to two-thirds of the wood used in a conventional fireplace was saved in Franklin's new device. He testified that "my common Room, I know, is twice as warm as it used to be, with a quarter of the wood formerly consumed there." Because he foresaw that wood would be used for fuel for many years to come, he calculated that the reduced demand for it would permit the supply to grow as fast as it was used, thus eliminating the need for bringing coal across the Atlantic.

In the eyes of at least one man the Franklin fireplace was particularly effective. Moreau de St. Méry comments in *American Journey (1793–1798)* that rooms were generally heated by Prussian stoves made of sheet iron, but they were slowly being replaced by "stoves perfected by Franklin, because of which they are called Franklin stoves."

He points out that the stove stood in front of the fireplace opening, thus heating the room by radiation and convection. The fact that they were set away from the wall greatly increased their effectiveness as a heating device. He mentions that the wood was placed on andirons, which increased the draft and created a very hot fire. He states:

> In Philadelphia they burn black spruce logs, which shoot out sparks like chestnut; chestnut, which is bad; large acacia logs, which are good for back logs because they burn slowly.

Invoice for some furnace products showing that it was a usual procedure to "black" Franklin fireplaces. *Kauffman collection*

But the best woods are sugar maple, birch, live oak, white oak and, best of all, Northern walnut or hickory. It costs half as much again as the next best wood; but even at that price it is preferable to the others. It gives out great heat, its coals are compact and lasting, and it burns a long time.

Franklin's final comments must be regarded as those of a wise economist and hygienist. He states:

We leave it to the Political Arithmetician to compute, how much money will be sav'd to a country by its spending two thirds less for fuel; how much Labour sav'd in Cutting and Carriage of it; how much more Land may be clear'd for cultivation; how great the Profit by the additional Quantity of Work done, in those Trades particularly that do not exercise the Body much, but that the Workfolks are obliged to run frequently to the Fire to warm themselves; and to Physicians to say, how much healthier thick-built Towns and Cities shall be made, and the Air Breath'd by the Inhabitants be consequently so much purer.

(May his soul rest in peace.)

It appears that Franklin's iron fireplace was an immediate success. Possibly he was providentially blessed for the philanthropic position he took in regard to its financial return. In his *Autobiography* he states:

In order of time, I should have mentioned before, that having, in 1742, invented an open stove for the better warming of rooms, and at the same time saving of fuel, as the fresh air admitted was warmed on entering, I made a present of the model to Mr. Robert Grace, one of my early friends, who, having an iron furnace, found the casting of the plates of these stoves a profitable thing, as they were growing in demand. . . . Governor Thomas was so pleased with the construction of this stove, as described in it [the previously mentioned pamphlet], that he offered to give me a patent for the sole vending of them for a term of years; but I declined it from a principle which has ever weighed with me on such occasions, viz., *that, as we enjoy great advantages from the inventions of others, we should be glad of an opportunity to serve others by any invention of ours; and this we should do freely and generously.*

Franklin was aware that others were not similarly motivated. He referred to an ironmonger in London who worked up a design of his own from Franklin's specifications and got a patent for it there, thereby making a small fortune. Others followed similar procedures, but Franklin did nothing about the situation because he genuinely believed in sharing his invention with others; besides, he hated disputes. (His next thoughts were concerned with the establishing of an academy for educating the youths of the province.)

Not only did he assign the plans for his invention to Mr. Grace, but he also assisted in selling the finished product. As Postmaster at the new Printing Office in Philadelphia, he was able to advertise easily in the local paper, the *Pennsylvania Gazette*. On February 3, 1741, the following advertisement appeared:

> Just brought down from the Furnace A Fresh Parcel of Iron Fire-Places; to be sold at the Post-Office.

News items about the iron fireplace appeared in papers as far away as Boston, where one was offered for sale in 1748.

Oldest example of Franklin fireplace known to have survived. In slightly disheveled condition. Some changes from the original mold are evident. *Courtesy Bucks County (Pennsylvania) Historical Society*

No example of Franklin's original invention is known to have survived. The oldest survivor is located at the Bucks County Historical Society, in Doylestown, Pennsylvania. The frieze of this specimen is decorated with the rays of the sun around a face and bears the Latin motto "Alter Diem," as does the original. Considering the alterations from the original specifications, it is evident that Franklin had not conceived a perfect heating unit. The heating chamber had been eliminated because, when the wind blew directly toward the cold air port in the exterior wall, more cold than hot air entered the room. There simply was not enough surface exposure to heat the rapidly moving air. Furthermore, eliminating the hot-air chamber reduced the complexity and the cost of the apparatus, one of the objections to it being that it cost too much for thrifty people to buy. Of course, as Franklin pointed out, after purchase there would have been a substantial saving of fuel which the iron fireplace used to adequately heat a room. It is, in this case, evident that potential long-run savings do not induce a prospective purchaser to buy an expensive commodity.

Another change is evident; the Doylestown example has a hole in the top to which a smoke pipe was attached. This was necessary because not all chimneys were suited to the down draft arrangement which Franklin used on his original model. It is probable that other improvements were gradually made until the original shell survived, which seems to have performed the function which Franklin intended.

Another version of the iron fireplace is illustrated in *An Account of the Pennsylvania Stove Grate*, published by James Sharp in London in 1781. This example is a square boxlike structure with a grate raised above the hearth, doubtless used in lieu of andirons, which were needed for Franklin's model. England's use of coal for heating by this time probably accounts for this change. The sides were squared with the back, but were later flared like Franklin's to throw more heat into the room.

An iron fireplace very similar to the one in the Bucks County Historical Society is in the Metropolitan Museum in New York City. This one has a simple flaring form without legs, because, like Franklin's original, it was designed to rest flat on the hearth. An evolutionary change is evident, however, in its decoration. The frieze is divided into

Cast-iron Franklin-type fireplace with busts of Franklin and Washington on the frieze. Made in the last quarter of the eighteenth century. *Courtesy Metropolitan Museum of Art, New York City*

three panels with draping swags, obviously influenced by the contemporary style in fireplace friezes. Additionally, busts of Franklin and Washington in the outer panels over the swags suggest the period of 1780 to 1800. At that time both Franklin and Washington had reached the apogee of their popularity in America, and were logical subjects for a decoration of this type.

Progress in the design and function of iron fireplaces continued. Near the end of the eighteenth century a model was made with an inverted funnellike top, which resembled the shape of the throat in contemporary chimneys. If there had been any tendency for them to smoke, an appendage of this sort should have minimized it. The presence of an eagle on the frieze suggests the period of the fireplace, and emphasizes the wide usage of this new symbol of the Republic. There are also columns on each side, suggesting influence from the classical patterns used on wooden mantelpieces. Brass turnings on top of the fireplace above the columns are embryonic evidence of a trend which came into full bloom at a later time. By 1820 two or three finials with brass grills between them became standard parts.

In 1816 a patent was taken out for a Franklin fireplace by an inventor named Wilson who lived in Poughkeepsie, New York. This one also bore a patriotic theme on the frieze, consisting of an eagle with thirteen stars. A later model had an inverted cone on the top with an added brass finial. This cone greatly increased the usefulness of the fireplace by providing additional surface for the radiation of heat. Later, the cone was reduced in size, but the brass finial was retained. Both of these

An attractive Franklin-type fireplace by Wilson, who is reported to have lived in Poughkeepsie, New York. Possibly the "New York" on the fireplace refers to New York City. *Courtesy Edwin Jackson, Inc., New York City*

Iron fireplace with sharp decorative details and three brass finials on the top. The curved flaring jambs and original grate make this example a particularly pleasing one. *Courtesy Edwin Jackson, Inc., New York City*

fireplaces have feet, which earlier ones lacked, suggesting that they were being used in rooms without hearths. The raising of the cast-iron hearth off the floor was an improved feature which was continued on many iron fireplaces thereafter.

A known later model, marked "H. H. Stimpson, Boston," is probably fitted with its original grate of cast iron. It is very evident that ridges were cast into the jambs of the fireplace to accommodate such a device. Thus, it could be used for burning coal with the grate, or the grate could be removed and wood burned in the traditional way. The sharp details on the parts of the fireplace suggest that it was not used very much.

One alternative to installing a Franklin-type iron fireplace was to utilize an iron frame consisting of two jambs with columns on the front and a frieze across the top. These were in the style of the Federal era (1790–1820) and were doubtless made and used at that time. This arrangement served a dubious purpose, for iron reportedly reflected less heat than masonry and, lacking the fireback which protected the back wall from deterioration, only the jambs were covered and deterioration

Franklin fire-frame of cast iron, used in lieu of a Franklin fireplace. Original examples are rarer than Franklin fireplaces, although most artifacts of this type are difficult to find today. *Courtesy Edwin Jackson, Jnc., New York City*

there from the heat was minimal. All the iron parts of this new frame were cast. The plates covering the jambs were either flat or curved. Many were ornamented with designs cast into the surface. The back wall continued to be made of brick, stone, or soapstone. Soapstone was used in areas where it was readily available, for it could be given the shape desired for the interior part of the fireplace. After heating, it became hard and glossy, and reflected heat very well. A sizeable number of fireplaces in New York state were built of this material.

Another variation from the iron fireplace was the use of three cast-iron plates to cover the two jambs and the back wall of masonry fireplaces. One of these is known to have classical motifs cast on the surface as well as the imprint of the maker or perhaps the merchant for whom it was made. The particular example seen by the writer bears the name "Mark Richards," who is listed in a *Philadelphia Trade Directory of 1811* as occupying a store at 130 N. Third Street. Samuel, George, and Thomas Richards are listed as iron merchants in the same directory; presumably, all four of them were in the same business.

Most of the iron fireplaces and auxiliary appendages observed by the writer were made in Philadelphia, New York, or Boston, or, at least, bear the names of merchants in these cities. This can probably be attributed to the fact that they were used where the supply of fuel was a critical matter, it having been pointed out by Franklin that the iron fireplace consumed much less fuel than a large masonry one. The "Blast

Plates of cast iron used to cover the jambs and back wall of a fireplace chamber. The decorative motifs are of the Federal era and are marked "Mark Richards, Philad." There is a possibility that iron front covers for the jambs were used with these plates. *Courtesy Kindig Antiques*

55

Acc of Stoves &c Sent to Bunge Souder &c

Acc of Stoves &c Sent to Bunge Souder &c

Date 1851																						
June 14	2	2	3	1	1	2													Also Sent 6 as flat by Iron crane
July 4	2	3	"	1	2	1	2	2											ditto
Aug 15	"	"	"	"	"	"	2	3	3	2	2	3	2	1					
" 30	"	"	2	1	"	"	"	"	1	1	"	"	2	1	2	2	2	
Sep 12	"	"	2	"	"	"	"	"	"	1	4	"	0	1	4	1	1	75 Bottom grate fsr
Octobr 26	"	"	2	2	"	"	"	"	"	2	2	1	"	2	"	2	1	
Nov 12	"	"	2	"	"	"	2	3	"	"	2	"	"	1	"	1	1	2	2 4 Extra bottom
Dec 6	"	"	"	1	"	"	"	1	"	1	1	2	2	"	"	"	"	1	1 D
" "	"	"	"	2	"	"	"	"	"	"	1	1	2	"	"	"	2	"	"
" 24	"	"	1	1	"	"	"	"	"	2	2	"	1	"	1	"	"	1	

Entered in Day Book Jany 5. 1832 Page 8

1832																				
Feby 18	"	Extra Sep Slide door for Coal &c		Stove Mounts	4	"	"	"	"	"	"	6	"	"	0
March 21	"	"	3	3	"	"	1	"	5	"	7	8	5	"	4	5	"	5
April 14	"	"	2	1	"	"	2	2	"	2	"	1	"	0	2	2	2
" 25	"	"	"	"	"	"	"	"	2	2	2	"	2	"	2	"	2

Entered in Day Book May 1. 1832 Page 27

Acc of Stoves &c Sent to Powell Stackhouse in Front Street Philadelphia

Date 1851																					
June 14	1	1	2	1	2	1	1	1												
July 4	1	2	"	"	2	4	4	"	1	2										
Aug 15	"	2	1	"	"	3	2	"	1	1	2	1	2							
" 30	"	"	1	1	"	"	2	"	1	2	1	"	2	"	1					
Sep 28	"	"	"	1	2	"	1	"	2	1	"	"	2	"	"	2	2	1		
Dec 6	"	"	2	2	"	1	1	"	"	"	"	1	"	2	"	"	1	1	2	

Entered in Day Book Jany 5. 1832 Page 8

1832																				
April 10	"	"	"	3	3	3	"	"	3	3	3	3	3	"	"	"	1	3	3

Entered in Day Book May 1. 1832 Page 27

Books" of Hopewell Furnace in Pennsylvania also show that city merchants supplied patterns for iron castings with their names applied, another practice more likely to be followed in big cities than small towns.

One exception, and there were probably a number of others, is a fireplace/stove made by Stafford Benedict and Co. of Albany, New York. The following extract from *Collections on the History of Albany from Its Discovery to the Present Time* pinpoints the time of its making:

> At the close of the war [of 1812] which assured fortunes of the brothers (Stafford), John left the firm and then were admitted Hallenbake, son of Mr. Stafford, and Lewis Benedict, his son-in-law. A temporary removal to 5 Hudson Street occurred while the new store was being erected, but in 1814 the firm entered their new quarters, known as 387 South Market Street, which, until 1825, was, as has been remarked, the theatre of an extensive and prosperous business.

The same source comments that "Thus was laid the foundation of a business which today exceeds the then combined trade of the city." It is evident that the business of selling stoves was very good. The picture of Mr. Stafford's residence confirms such an appraisal.

The Stafford Benedict product is a very attractive example of the period. It closely resembles earlier iron fireplaces which were built for burning wood. The easy availability of wood in the Albany region might logically explain such a continued procedure. It stands on short legs, has a semicircular hearth plate with a small rim to keep live coals from rolling onto the floor. Sunbursts were cast into the interior surfaces of the jambs and the back. A threadlike effect was cast into the corner posts at the front of the jambs, and a repoussé design, suggesting ribs of leaves, was cast into the frieze.

Although the Stafford Benedict product was in most ways an iron fireplace, it might be more logically considered a stove, because the opening in the front could be closed by doors hinged on two front corner posts. These doors controlled the draft of the fire, as well as the heat which was projected into the room. Probably the front portion of

Page from a "Blast Book" (1831) of Hopewell Furnace in Pennsylvania, showing that "Coal Grate Franklin" fireplaces were being made at that time. *Courtesy Hopewell Furnace and National Park Service* the stove extended into the room, so that heat was not only projected, but was also circulated from the heated top portion of the stove. One would think that such a device would have swept the iron fireplace into oblivion, but not so. From 1790 until 1873 inclusive, there were over one hundred patents for fireplaces filed with the patent office. The iron fireplace of E. A. Jackson was patented in the 1870s.

Of all the fireplace patents examined, the Jackson iron fireplace has been selected for a number of reasons. In the first place, after examining the specifications of many patents, it is obvious that many were impractical ideas and probably never used to any great extent. However, it should be noted that, of the total number of patents issued, the specifications of only a few have survived in the patent office. It is entirely possible that some of the missing records contained many practical ideas.

In the second place, it is possible to examine a small replica of the patent model in the possession of Edwin Jackson, Inc., in New York City, and to ascertain that it embodies a reasonably successful idea. As a matter of fact, it is not greatly unlike Franklin's initial plan for an iron

This combination iron fireplace and stove was sold by Stafford Benedict & Company in Albany, New York. Records indicate that they were in business in the first quarter of the nineteenth century. *Courtesy Willis Barsheid*

Index of patents issued from the United States Patent Office from 1790 to 1873, inclusive—Continued.

Invention.	Inventor.	Residence.	Date.	No.
Fire-kindling and fuel	I. Bicknell	Cincinnati, Ohio	Jan. 7, 1868	72, 964
Fire-kindling composition	D. B. Andrews	Fort Wayne, Ind	Jan. 22, 1867	61, 378
Fire-kindling composition	E. Bellinger	Mohawk, N. Y	Dec. 13, 1859	26, 408
Fire-kindling composition	M. Carsten	N. Y	20, 1866	
Fire-kindling composition		City	1872	
Fi				
Fir	W. Towers	Boston, Mass	Mar. 5, 1867	62, 704
Fire, ... ing the progress of	B. Taylor		Mar. 23, 1794	
Fire, Mode of protecting plastered walls and ceilings from.	P. Naylor	New York, N. Y	Feb. 22, 1839	1, 087
Fire, Mode of supplying water to buildings for the purpose of extinguishing.	I. Lowell	Pendleton, N. Y	Oct. 16, 1840	1, 489
Fire-place	T. C. Aldridge	Saint Louis, Mo	June 8, 1869	91, 059
Fire-place	A. C. Bacon and J. G. Jennings	Cleveland, Ohio	Dec. 22, 1863	40, 989
Fire-place	T. W. Baird	Bowling Green, Ky	Sept. 6, 1870	106, 985
Fire-place	T. F. Baker	Cincinnati, Ohio	June 15, 1869	91, 299
Fire-place	Bean and Skinner	Sandwich, N. H	June 12, 1835	
Fire-place	J. S. Blair	Boston, Mass	May 17, 1864	42, 739
Fire-place	P. Brecher	Louisville, Ky	June 20, 1871	116, 146
Fire-place	W. Bryant	Boston, Mass	Apr. 19, 1864	42, 342
Fire-place	R. Buck	Acton, Me	July 1, 1836	
Fire-place	W. Burgess	Middleborough, Mass	Mar. 12, 1836	
Fire-place	T. F. Card	Cincinnati, Ohio	Apr. 17, 1860	27, 886
Fire-place	A. Carson	New York, N. Y	May 22, 1860	28, 347
Fire-place	A. E. Chamberlain and J. B. Crowley.	Cincinnati, Ohio	Dec. 3, 1867	71, 698
Fire-place	G. A. Clark	Farmington, Conn	Oct. 4, 1859	25, 629
Fire-place	W. B. Coates	Philadelphia, Pa	July 28, 1868	80, 455
Fire-place	B. F. Conley	Funnelton, W. Va	Nov. 23, 1869	97, 050
Fire-place	C. D. Cooper	Albany, N. Y	June 27, 1810	
Fire-place	B. F. Cowan	Memphis, Tenn	Mar. 26, 1861	31, 785
Fire-place	J. M. Crockett	Newbern, Va	Oct. 12, 1869	95, 660
Fire-place	M. A. Cushing	Aurora, Ill	July 18, 1871	117, 053
Fire-place	A. D. Dailey	Terre Haute, Ind	Apr. 20, 1869	89, 203
Fire-place	T. C. Damborg	Philadelphia, Pa	July 16, 1872	128, 953
Fire-place	S. D. Dearman	Rock Hill, S. C	Apr. 23, 1872	125, 938
Fire-place	C. Dodge	Pittsburgh, Pa	Mar. 18, 1856	14, 447
Fire-place	J. Ervin, sr	Princeton, Ind	Nov. 3, 1868	93, 701
Fire-place	J. U. Fiester	Winchester, Ohio	June 4, 1867	65, 364
Fire-place	J. S. Ganson and C. T. Coit	Buffalo, N. Y	May 14, 1861	32, 283
Fire-place	J. L. Garlington	Snapping Shoals, Ga	July 8, 1873	140, 621
Fire-place	E. H. Gibbs	New York, N. Y	Dec. 14, 1869	97, 902
Fire-place	E. S. Greely	Dover, Me	Oct. 6, 1835	
Fire-place	C. B. Gregory	Beverly, N. J	Mar. 3, 1868	75, 155
Fire-place	C. B. Gregory	Beverly, N. J	Apr. 14, 1868	76, 750
Fire-place	G. Gridley	Newburyport, Mass	Mar. 14, 1808	
Fire-place	E. Griffiths	Philadelphia, Pa	Mar. 6, 1820	
Fire-place	W. D. Guseman	Morgantown, W. Va	Apr. 14, 1868	76, 751
Fire-place	J. Hackett	Louisville, Ky	Feb. 21, 1871	111, 929
Fire-place	J. Hackett	Louisville, Ky	July 25, 1871	117, 276
Fire-place	S. Hammond	Baltimore, Md	June 25, 1839	1, 197
Fire-place	E. Hampton	New York, N. Y	Feb. 23, 1869	87, 099
Fire-place	C. Harris and P. W. Zoiner	Cincinnati, Ohio	Apr. 16, 1867	63, 885
Fire-place	D. Hattan	Zanesville, Ohio	Aug. 4, 1868	80, 731
Fire-place	M. Haughey	Saint Louis, Mo	Aug. 13, 1872	130, 427
Fire-place	D. Hemingway	Leesburgh, Ky	Nov. 13, 1844	3, 821
Fire place	J. R. Hendrickson	McKeesport, Pa	Sept. 24, 1861	33, 349
Fire-place	W. Hoyland	Newcastle, Pa	Nov. 10, 1870	144, 675
Fire-place	W. Hoyt	Brookville, Ind	June 3, 1825	
Fire-place	J. M. Irwin	Pittsburgh, Pa	Sept. 16, 1873	142, 791
Fire-place	W. H. James	Cincinnati, Ohio	Apr. 25, 1865	47, 423
Fire-place	E. Jenks	Colebrook, Conn	Sept. 2, 1818	
Fire-place	A. B. Johnson	Washington, Ind	July 26, 1870	105, 806
Fire-place	I. Kepler	Corry, Pa	Nov. 12, 1867	70, 858
Fire-place	W. M. Keplor	Cincinnati, Ohio	Aug. 26, 1873	142, 241
Fire-place	D. F. Launy	Philadelphia, Ba	Mar. 18, 1813	
Fire-place	J. E. Layton	Pittsburgh, Pa	July 2, 1861	32, 700
Fire-place	E. Lester	Killingsworth, Conn	June 21, 1830	
Fire-place	C. A. Littlefield	Covington, Ky	Sept. 11, 1860	29, 980
Fire-place	W. Lossie	Owensborough, Ky	Aug. 19, 1873	141, 937
Fire-place	J. Maggini	Baltimore, Md	Feb. 4, 1822	
Fire-place	S. Martin	Detroit, Mich	Nov. 30, 1869	97, 307
Fire-place	T. McCleary	Blairsville, Pa	Nov. 13, 1866	59, 620
Fire-place	R. D. McDonald	Jersey City, N. J	Sept. 21, 1869	95, 030

69 P

Record of patents issued for fireplaces and fireplace accessories from 1790 until 1873. Only a small number of these patents can be examined in the Patent Office today.

Index of patents issued from the United States Patent Office from 1790 to 1873, inclusive—Continued.

Invention.	Inventor.	Residence.	Date.	No.
Fire-place	G. H. McElevey	Newcastle, Pa	Aug. 25, 1868	81, 389
Fire-place	W. T. McMillen	Cincinnati, Ohio	Dec. 4, 1866	60, 220
Fire-place	J. McMurtry	Fayette County, Ky	Jan. 22, 1861	31, 212
Fire-place	W. P. Miller	San Francisco, Cal	Feb. 12, 1867	62, 053
Fire-place	E. Mix	New Haven, Conn	Apr. 25, 1812	
Fire-place	G. Moody	Piqua, Ohio	Jan. 30, 1866	52, 375
Fire-place	A. Moon	Bethlehem, Ind	Feb. 20, 1866	52, 735
Fire-place	J. Moore	Ergineth, Ireland	Apr. 5, 1870	101, 645
Fire-place	M. Moore	Bartlett, Tenn	Jan. 16, 1872	122, 775
Fire-place	E. Nott	Schenectady, N. Y	Feb. 3, 1819	
Fire-place	C. W. Peale		Nov. 16, 1797	
Fire-place	T. Phillips	Cadiz, Ohio	Oct. 11, 1870	108, 180
Fire-place	W. R. Prescott	Hallowell, Me	Mar. 19, 1836	
Fire-place	F. Proudfoot	Toronto, Canada	June 10, 1873	139, 813
Fire-place	C. S. Rankin	Cincinnati, Ohio	Mar. 30, 1869	88, 509
Fire-place	A. G. Redway	Cincinnati, Ohio	May 7, 1867	64, 446
Fire-place	I. I. Richardson	Delaware, Ohio	Mar. 19, 1867	63, 098
Fire-place	W. D. Robb	New Philadelphia, Ohio	July 1, 1873	140, 543
Fire-place	E. Y. Robbins	Cincinnati, Ohio	July 19, 1864	43, 604
Fire-place	E. Y. Robbins	Cincinnati, Ohio	Sept. 10, 1867	68, 653
Fire-place	P. M. Roche	Cleveland, Ohio	Apr. 25, 1871	114, 045
Fire-place	F. M. Rogers	Cincinnati, Ohio	Apr. 10, 1866	53, 880
Fire-place	D. A. Ross	Cincinnati, Ohio	Sept. 8, 1863	39, 836
Fire-place	J. K. Ross	Lebanon, Ohio	Apr. 3, 1860	27, 741
Fire-place	W. Salisbury	Derby, Vt	Aug. 16, 1817	
Fire-place	H. Saxton	Eden, N. Y	July 8, 1834	
Fire-place	G. R. Scriven	Hanging Rock, Ohio	Feb. 6, 1872	123, 518
Fire-place	L. Shepherd	Northampton, Mass	Jan. 25, 1817	
Fire-place	E. A. Skeele	Saint Louis, Mo	June 23, 1863	38, 991
Fire-place	E. Skinner	Sandwich, N. H	Mar. 12, 1836	
Fire-place	H. E. Smith	Cincinnati, Ohio	Sept. 13, 1864	44, 228
Fire-place	J. Smith	Brantford, Canada	Feb. 28, 1871	112, 188
Fire-place	J. Smith	Pittsburgh, Pa	Jan. 2, 1872	122, 410
Fire-place	J. W. Smith and J. S. Gallaher, jr.	Washington, D. C	Mar. 6, 1855	12, 491
Fire-place	A. Snyder	Richmond, Va	Oct. 5, 1869	95, 529
Fire-place	S. Spalding	Colchester, Conn	Apr. 11, 1822	
Fire-place	A. J. Sprague	Springfield, Mo	Mar. 16, 1869	87, 884
Fire-place	P. Sternberg	Montgomery County, N. Y	Mar. 20, 1811	
Fire-place	P. Sternberg	Montgomery County, N. Y	Oct. 28, 1811	
Fire-place	P. Sternberg	Montgomery County, N. Y	Nov. 19, 1811	
Fire-place	D. and J. Stoner	West Overton, Pa	May 17, 1864	42, 804
Fire-place	J. C. Strong and L. C. McNeal	Buffalo, N. Y	Sept. 21, 1869	94, 984
Fire-place	R. P. Thomas	Solotoville, Ohio	Dec. 12, 1871	121, 911
Fire-place	I. H. Upton	New York, N. Y	Nov. 6, 1866	59, 484
Fire-place	W. R. Warden	Boston, Mass	Aug. 3, 1858	21, 094
Fire-place	M. D. Wellman	Pittsburgh, Pa	May 7, 1867	64, 465
Fire-place	M. D. Wellman and J. Old	Pittsburgh, Pa	July 11, 1865	48, 752
Fire-place	J. W. Wetmore	Erie, Pa	Feb. 28, 1871	112, 199
Fire-place	E. Whiting	Great Barrington, Mass	June 18, 1810	
Fire-place	A. Wilkin	Lucas County, Ohio	June 8, 1869	91, 190
Fire-place	J. E. Wood	Webster, Ohio	Apr. 25, 1871	114, 075
Fire-place and chimney	R. Bacon and E. Harris	Boston, Mass	Apr. 8, 1835	
Fire-place and chimney	C. Blood	Washington County, Md	Apr. 7, 1825	
Fire-place and chimney	D. Hemingway	Covington, Ky	July 17, 1860	29, 168
Fire-place and chimney for saving fuel	S. Morey	Philadelphia, Pa	Jan. 18, 1813	
Fire-place and chimney-stack in buildings	H. R. Sawyer	New York, N. Y	Mar. 26, 1841	2, 016
Fire-place and furnace	E. B. Wilson	London, England	Nov. 15, 1864	45, 111
Fire-place and grate	C. Lane	Hingham, Mass	Dec. 15, 1835	
Fire-place and grate, Open	R. M. Sherman	Fairfield, Conn	June 30, 1837	249
Fire-place and oven	J. Knight	Stoddard, N. H	Dec. 15, 1831	
Fire-place and stove	C. Guernsey	Poultney, Vt	July 7, 1813	
Fire-place and stove	E. Haskell	New London, Conn	June 25, 1813	
Fire-place and stove	C. Neer	Troy, N. Y	May 31, 1853	9, 756
Fire-place and stove	E. W. Newton	Middletown, Conn	Dec. 3, 1834	
Fire-place and stove	A. Pollock	Boston, Mass	Apr. 23, 1807	
Fire-place and stove	F. Stevens	Springfield, Mass	Mar. 2, 1836	
Fire-place and throat of chimney	C. W. Russell	Washington, D. C	Mar. 5, 1850	7, 149
Fire-place and warming buildings	J. Cox	Philadelphia, Pa	May 2, 1834	
Fire-place back	J. C. Bard	New Orleans, La	Feb. 15, 1870	99, 748
Fire-place back	G. W. Cummings	Franklin, Pa	Apr. 22, 1873	138, 135
Fire-place called "The defiance," Construction of	E. Bartholomew and W. Church	Boston, Mass	Aug. 18, 1815	
Fire-place, Cast-iron	A. Hayward	Easton, Mass	Sept. 25, 1834	
Fire-place, Chimney funneled	A. Gerrish	Shopleigh, Me	Jan. 23, 1835	
Fire-place, Close	H. G. Spafford	Hudson, N. Y	May 3, 1805	
Fire-place, Close and open	J. C. Brush	Washington, D. C	Aug. 19, 1819	
Fire-place, Columbia	R. Heterick		June 30, 1803	
Fire-place, Cooking and baking	J. C. Howard	Howard's Valley, Conn	Oct. 27, 1835	
Fire-place, Doric	J. Pierpont	Boston, Mass	Jan. 8, 1830	
Fire-place, Double-draft	T. Rose		Jan. 23, 1804	
Fire-place fender	C. C. Algeo	Pittsburgh, Pa	May 30, 1871	115, 265
Fire-place fender	C. C. Algeo	Pittsburgh, Pa	Nov. 21, 1871	121, 073
Fire-place fender	W. N. Hall	Springfield, Tex	Feb. 27, 1872	124, 132
Fire-place fender	E. Skinner	Sandwich, N. H	Apr. 19, 1822	
Fire-place frame-work	J. W. Truslow	Lewisburgh, Va	July 15, 1856	15, 362
Fire-place front	J. L. Henderson	Covington, Ky	Oct. 22, 1867	70, 090
Fire-place, furnace, &c	E. A. Jackson	New York, N. Y	Nov. 11, 1873	144, 459
Fire-place, Grate	J. W. Boot and W. Lyman	Boston, Mass	Dec. 29, 1826	
Fire-place, Grated	J. Snyder	Philadelphia, Pa	June 12, 1835	
Fire-place heater	A. Graham	Fredericktown, Md	Nov. 24, 1810	
Fire-place heater	B. C. Bibb	Baltimore, Md	July 20, 1869	92, 781
Fire-place heater	S. S. Benk	New York, N. Y	Oct. 1, 1861	33, 412
Fire-place heater	F. L. Hedenberg	New York, N. Y	May 21, 1861	32, 364
Fire-place heater	W. C. Lester	New York, N. Y	Jan. 29, 1867	61, 623
Fire-place heater	D. S. Quimby	Brooklyn, N. Y	Oct. 9, 1860	30, 349
Fire-place heater	D. S. Quimby, jr	Brooklyn, N. Y	June 8, 1869	90, 957
Fire-place heater	W. Sanford	Brooklyn, N. Y	Jan. 5, 1869	85, 614
Fire-place heater	W. Sanford	Brooklyn, N. Y	May 4, 1869	89, 693

Index of patents issued from the United States Patent Office from 1790 to 1873, inclusive—Continued.

Invention.	Inventor.	Residence.	Date.	No.
Fire-place heater	J. M. Thatcher	Bergen, N. J	Dec. 22, 1868	85, 255
Fire-place heater	J. M. Thatcher	Bergen, N. J	June 15, 1869	91, 287
Fire-place heater	J. M. Thatcher	Bergen, N. J	June 14, 1870	104, 376
Fire-place heater	H. H. Welch	Athens, Ohio	Aug. 8, 1865	49, 325
Fire-place heater, Base-burning	B. C. Bibb	Baltimore, Md	Sept. 14, 1869	94, 700
Fire-place heater, Base-burning	B. C. Bibb and P. Klotz	Baltimore, Md	Feb. 8, 1870	99, 525
Fire-place heater, Base-burning	J. H. Burtis	Brooklyn, N. Y	July 4, 1871	116, 680
Fire-place heater, Base-burning	E. S. Heath	Baltimore, Md	Jan. 3, 1871	110, 654
Fire-place heater, Base-burning	J. Jaeger	Tompkinsville, N. Y	Dec. 6, 1870	109, 909
Fire-place heater, Base-burning	P. Klotz	Baltimore, Md	Aug. 31, 1769	94, 320
Fire-place heater, Base-burning	P. Klotz	Baltimore, Md	Feb. 14, 1871	111, 753
Fire-place heater, Base-burning	W. Magill	Port Deposit, Md	Jan. 28, 1873	135, 278
Fire-place heater, Base-burning	J. Martino	Philadelphia, Pa	Mar. 8, 1870	100, 539
Fire-place heater, Base-burning	W. L. McDowell	Philadelphia, Pa	Nov. 21, 1871	121, 185
Fire-place heater, Base-burning	A. Murdock	Brooklyn, E. D., N. Y	Aug. 9, 1870	106, 191
Fire-place heater, Base-burning	J. S. Perry	Albany, N. Y	Jan. 14, 1873	134, 767
Fire-place heater, Base-burning	S. B. Sexton	Baltimore, Md	Dec. 14, 1869	97, 970
Fire-place heater, Base-burning	S. B. Sexton	Baltimore, Md	Mar. 19, 1872	124, 860
Fire-place heater, Base-burning	G. B. Snider	New York, N. Y	June 27, 1871	116, 365
Fire-place heater, Base-burning	J. Spear	Philadelphia, Pa	Jan. 16, 1872	122, 863
Fire-place heater, Base-burning	W. E. Wood	Baltimore, Md	Aug. 1, 1871	117, 585
Fire-place-heater fender	D. Stuart and L. Bridge	Philadelphia, Pa	Feb. 8, 1870	99, 726
Fire-place heater or furnace	O. Collins	New York, N. Y	Apr. 30, 1867	64, 284
Fire-place lining	E. A. Jackson	New York, N. Y	Nov. 11, 1873	144, 460
Fire-place lining	A. J. Redwig	Cincinnati, Ohio	Feb. 4, 1873	135, 587
Fire-place lining	C. Truesdale	Cincinnati, Ohio	June 22, 1869	91, 689
Fire-place mantel and front	D. K. Innes and W. W. Magill	Cincinnati, Ohio	Oct. 31, 1871	4, 613
Fire-place mantel and front	D. K. Innes and W. W. Magill	Cincinnati, Ohio	July 25, 1871	117, 294
Fire-place, Metallic	J. F. Snider	Culpeper County, Va	July 18, 1854	11, 340
Fire-place, Open	M. D. Wellman	Pittsburgh, Pa	Dec. 18, 1866	60, 601
Fire-place or Franklin stove	J. Peckover	Cincinnati, Ohio	May 28, 1872	127, 265
Fire-place or grate, Portable	J. Williamson	Washington, D. C	Nov. 8, 1836	74
Fire-place or open stove	J. F. Gould	Newburyport, Mass	Feb. 1, 1808	....
Fire-place or stove	J. E. Cayford	Milburn, Me	Dec. 31, 1833	....
Fire-place, Parlor	E. Backus	Brooklyn, N. Y	Sept. 25, 1847	5, 307
Fire-place, Parlor and kitchen	J. Hagerty	Monroe, Mich	Mar. 24, 1838	655
Fire-place, Portable	W. B. Johns	Georgetown, D. C	Dec. 24, 1861	33, 995
Fire-place, Reflecting	R. Jobson	Dudley, England	May 20, 1851	8, 101
Fire-place register	E. A. Tuttle	Brooklyn, N. Y	July 2, 1861	32, 728
Fire-place, Sheet-iron	J. Ingalls	Sanbornton, N. H	May 23, 1833	....
Fire-place, Sheet-iron	L. Mansfield	New Hartford, N. Y	May 29, 1833	....
Fire-place, Sheet-iron	G. Richards	Ashfield, Mass	Nov. 26, 1835	....
Fire-place, Steam	J. W. Cochran	Lowell, Mass	July 18, 1834	....
Fire-place to prevent smoking	H. Roberts	Delhi, N. Y	Apr. 30, 1840	1, 578
Fire-place warming-apparatus	C. Kalbfues	New Richmond, Ohio	Aug. 13, 1867	67, 769
Fire-place with a flat funnel	A. Fisher	Feb. 19, 1807	....
Fire-place with gridiron attachment, Movable	J. W. Wetmore	Erie, Pa	Apr. 4, 1865	47, 176
Fire-places and grates, Back-plate for	F. E. Pitts	Nashville, Tenn	Mar. 3, 1857	16, 768
Fire-places, Back-plate and chimney-throat for	J. E. Layton	Pittsburgh, Pa	Oct. 29, 1861	33, 591
Fire-places, Constructing flue of open	T. Whitson	New York, N. Y	June 14, 1838	784
Fire-places, Fire-back for	S. M. Echols	La Fayette, Ind	July 15, 1856	15, 331
Fire-places for burning coal, Building and altering	A. Terrell	Boston, Mass	Oct. 25, 1832	....
Fire-places, stoves, &c., Composition slab for lining	J. Putnam	Salem, Mass	Aug. 20, 1835	....
Fire-places, Ornamental back for	W. H. Jackson	New York, N. Y	July 27, 1869	92, 974
Fire-plug	J. W. Baker	Parkersburgh, W. Va	Sept. 24, 1867	69, 156
Fire-plug	J. P. Cummings	Newport, Ky	July 14, 1868	79, 960
Fire-plug	J. Curran	Baltimore, Md	Feb. 8, 1870	99, 646
Fire-plug	J. Fricker	Cincinnati, Ohio	Oct. 3, 1865	50, 235
Fire-plug	J. P. Gallagher	Saint Louis, Mo	July 22, 1873	141, 131
Fire-plug	R. A. Hill	Washington, D. C	May 25, 1869	90, 540
Fire-plug	F. Latta	Cincinnati, Ohio	Aug. 20, 1872	130, 726
Fire-plug	J. L. Lowry	Pittsburgh, Pa	Feb. 22, 1859	23, 034
Fire-plug	J. McClelland	Washington, D. C	Sept. 27, 1864	44, 439
Fire-plug	J. McClelland	Washington, D. C	May 30, 1871	115, 495
Fire-plug	L. Moss	Philadelphia, Pa	Nov. 10, 1857	18, 595
Fire-plug	J. H. Rhodes	Brooklyn, N. Y	May 26, 1868	78, 393
Fire-plug and cistern combined	F. Latta and W. H. Hughes	Cincinnati, Ohio	Mar. 18, 1873	137, 006
Fire-plug and hydrant	A. F. Allen	Providence, R. I	Dec. 26, 1871	122, 097
Fire-plug and hydrant	J. M. Jorden	Baltimore, Md	Sept. 8, 1838	969
Fire-plug and lamp-post, Combined	D. Y. and J. H. Johns	Cincinnati, Ohio	Nov. 19, 1872	133, 230
Fire-plugs, Casting	W. M. and J. B. Ellis	Washington, D. C	Apr. 17, 1860	27, 896
Fire-poker	G. R. Moore	Pittsburgh, Pa	July 24, 1860	29, 298
Fire-pot for coal-stoves	D. G. Littlefield	Albany, N. Y	June 25, 1861	32, 635
Fire-pot for stoves	N. O. Bond	Needham, Mass	May 24, 1864	42, 831
Fire-pot for stoves, furnaces, &c	P. P. Stewart	Troy, N. Y	Mar. 28, 1865	47, 049
Fire-pot, Tinners'	F. M. Campbell and L. W. Brown	Cleveland, Ohio	Nov. 22, 1870	109, 383
Fire-pot, Tinners'	C. W. Johnson	Neponset, Ill	Sept. 1, 1868	81, 644
Fire-pot, Tinsmiths'	W. Yapp	Cleveland, Ohio	Aug. 11, 1863	39, 521
Fire-pots, Iron lining for	E. A. Tuttle	Williamsburgh, N. Y	Nov. 8, 1870	109, 080
Fire-proof chest	J. Matthews	New York, N. Y	June 16, 1836	....
Fire-proof chest	J. Scott	Philadelphia, Pa	Nov. 12, 1830	....
Fire-proof chest or safe	D. Fitzgerald	New York, N. Y	June 1, 1843	3, 117
Fire-proof chests, Use of asbestos in manufacture of	J. Scott	Philadelphia, Pa	July 21, 1835	....
Fire-proof column, Double-cylinder	J. B. Cornell	New York, N. Y	Mar. 20, 1860	27, 528
Fire-proof composition	N. E. Blake	Almond, N. Y	Apr. 18, 1865	47, 275
Fire-proof composition for crucibles, &c	L. Held	New York, N. Y	July 12, 1864	43, 548
Fire-proof compound	R. Spencer	New York, N. Y	Nov. 17, 1868	84, 143
Fire-proof compound for coating roofs, &c	R. W. Piper	Girard, Mich	Jan. 21, 1873	135, 152
Fire-proof, Compound for rendering substances	O. A. Tooker	Green Bay, Wis	July 2, 1872	128, 678
Fire-proof houses, Construction of	W. A. Berkey	Grand Rapids, Mich	Nov. 10, 1868	84, 044
Fire-proof iron chest	J. Delano	New York, N. Y	Aug. 13, 1834	....
Fire-proof iron chest	C. A. Gayler	New York, N. Y	Apr. 12, 1833	....
Fire-proof iron chest	C. A. Gayler	New York, N. Y	Apr. 3, 1835	....
Fire-proof packing for smoke and hot-air flues	J. B. Harris	Germantown, Ky	Nov. 26, 1867	71, 300
Fire-proof paper for roofs, &c	R. W. Piper	Girard, Mich	Jan. 21, 1873	135, 153
Fire-proof store, counting-room, &c	R. D. Curtis	Erie, Pa	Feb. 15, 1848	5, 445

fireplace. It was an improvement in that the cool air entering the room from the outside was exposed to more hot metal surface and, therefore, there was less chance of cool air from the outside escaping unheated into the room.

Another point of interest is the fact that a lengthy description of the fireplace can be found in the book entitled *The Open Fireplace in All Ages* by J. Pickering Putnam, published in 1882. This discussion not only includes a description of the fireplace, and how well it functioned, but also describes the so-called scientific analysis of the efficiency of the fireplace in relation to the amount of wood it burned and heat produced.

Finally, the decorative quality of the fireplace was in keeping with the decor of the period. It is trim and shipshape; with a little modifica-

JACKSON'S VENTILATING FIREPLACE.*

We come now to a form of ventilating fireplace which combines to a remarkable extent the desiderata heretofore set forth, and at the same time presents a most pleasing external appearance. In the front elevation (Fig. 121) we see apparently nothing more than the usual open fireplace with a frame decorated in a tasteful manner. The fresh air enters the room through the openworked top of the frame at F. The section (Fig. 119) shows us the manner in which this fresh air is warmed. It enters the lower chamber B B through the register A, where it is partially warmed before it rises to the chamber surrounding the back and sides of the fireplace. Thence it enters the chamber D, where it plays around the short tubes forming the chimney-throat, and passes thence through the perforated frame above described into the apartment. Fig. 122 shows the plan of the grate and the apparatus for shutting off the fresh-air supply. This latter consists simply of a disc of iron rotated by a lever so as to close wholly or in part the mouth of the fresh-air duct shown in section at A. Fig. 120 shows the small smoke-pipes in the chimney-throat with the fresh-air chamber surrounding them.

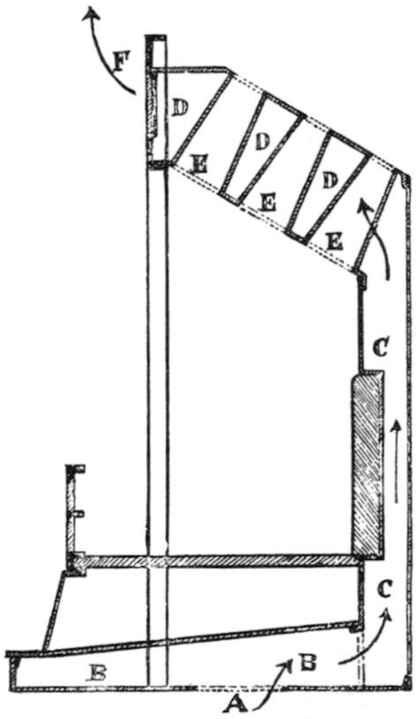

Table VII. (Appendix) shows the heating power of the Jackson Fireplace. Before lighting the fire the anemometer at the register was motionless,

Fig. 119.   Jackson's Ventilating Fireplace.

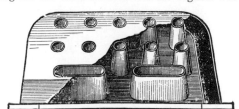

Fig. 120.   Plan of Chamber D, directly over the Fire, with Top Plate broken away, showing Flues.

showing that the air was stagnant, and the ventilation nothing, or at least imperceptible, inasmuch as the doors and windows were tightly closed.

* See appendix.

Two views of the Jackson patented iron fireplace. The side view shows the entry of the air at the bottom point A. It then rises through the rear channel C and flows outward through the channel D, which is filled with tubes for smoke disposal and heating the air.

The second view shows the small smoke pipes in channel D with the possibility of the fresh air circulating around the tubes. From *The Open Fireplace* by J. Pickering Putnam

Two other views of the Jackson iron fireplace. One view shows the attractive decorative frame around its edge, which permitted adaptation to the wall or chimney opening.

The second view shows a top view of the hearth with the opening for the air entry in the center. This opening could be closed by swinging a plate which coincided in size and shape with the opening. From *The Open Fireplace* by J. Pickering Putnam

Fig. 121.   Front View of Jackson's Ventilating Fireplace.

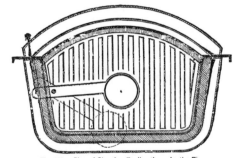

Fig 122.   Plan of Chamber B, directly under the Fire.

tion, it could be used in houses of today. This facet of the fireplace was of some importance in the mind of Putnam, who wrote:

> We come now to a form of ventilating fireplace which com-
> bines to a remarkable extent the desiderata heretofor set forth, and
> at the same time presents a most pleasing external appearance.

The function of the fireplace can be easily observed from the sectional drawing supplied for it. The fresh air enters a chamber under the hearth through a small trapdoor, which can be opened or closed. It is partially warmed there before it rises through the back and side chambers to the top. A slanting chamber across the top is filled with tubes carrying away the smoke and gas from the fireplace, and simultaneously warming the air as it moves forward around the tubes. The warmed air enters the room through an openwork grill at the top of the fireplace.

It was pointed out earlier that one of the assets of Jackson's iron fireplace was the attractive frame around the edge which fitted into the wall. Apparently a variety of designs was available, each one suited in some way to the interior decor in which it was placed. It could have been used by merely recessing the iron casting into the wall, or with the addition of a mantelpiece as the owner desired.

The ducts and channels through which the air passed to be heated can be seen in the illustration in which a part of the second or back shell of iron has been removed. The projecting studs of iron assisted the front shell in heating the air; however, their effect must have been minimal. It is claimed that the fresh air entering the room performed a double function of heating and ventilating the room, a service not rendered by an ordinary grate. A plan, not illustrated, permitted part of the heated air to be piped to a room on the second floor above the fireplace. This plan must have been quite an asset in the day when competition with hot-air furnaces in the cellar was acute and rapidly spelling doom for the open fireplace.

All the details mentioned in relation to the fireplace are especially interesting because they indicate the diligence and persistence with which inventors attempted to make the fireplace a practical device. Their pseudo-scientific experimentation, however, is possibly the most interesting aspect, particularly in the light of similar activity today concerning the same problem. The complexity of their calculations does not permit simplification or abridgement so here, complete and intact, is the record of two demonstrations, quoted from Putnam's book:

> In order to render the tests more reliable, a wooden box or flue was built around the fresh-air inlet register, to collect the air and conduct it outwards and upwards so that the thermometer placed in the current would be protected from radiation from the fireplace and other external sources. The air thus collected entered the room, of course, in a stronger current than it would otherwise have done.
>
> By the combustion of 3 kilograms of wood enough heat was saved to raise the temperature of 9,671 kilograms of air 1° Centigrade (supposing the air at 0°, 20°, 40°, 60°, 100°, weighed respectively 1.3, 1.2, 1.1, 1, and 0.9 kilograms per cubic meter). This is equivalent to 2,321 units. The wood used in the experiment contained 9 per cent., by weight, of water. Allowing for perfectly

dry wood 4,000 units, our wood would yield $.91 \times 4,000 = 3,640$ units per kilogram, and for 3 kilograms 10,920 units. But to evaporate the .09 of water contained in the wood would render latent $(531 + 75) \times 3 \times .09 = 164$ units of the heat generated. This should therefore be deducted from the 10,920 units, giving an available power of 10,756. In the above equation 531 represents, according to Despretz, the number of units rendered latent in transforming 1 kilog. of water at 100° Centigrade to vapor under ordinary atmospheric pressure, and 75 represents the number of units required to raise to the boiling-point the temperature of 1 kilogram of water from 25° Centigrade, which was the temperature of the outer air and of our fuel at the beginning of the experiment. The amount saved, 2,321 units, was therefore $^{2321}/_{10756} = 21$ per cent. of the total available heat generated. Add 6 per cent. for that obtained for direct radiation, and we have 27 per cent. utilized. Adding, as before, 5 per cent. where the upright iron flue is added, and we have a grand total of 32 per cent. obtained by the Jackson Fireplace.

Few persons realize the extent to which kiln-dried wood reabsorbs the moisture expelled by the drying. The wood used in the experiment had been kiln-dried, but had again absorbed from the atmosphere 9 per cent. of water. A portion of that used was cut up into small pieces and weighed. It was then redried and weighed again. The drying was conducted in an air bath maintained at a temperature of 150° Centigrade. Before drying the sample weighed 36.155 grams, and after drying only 33.169 grams, showing a loss of 2.986 grams, or nearly 9 per cent. of the whole; or, in other words, that the kiln-dried wood used in our experiment had reabsorbed 9 per cent. of water from the atmosphere.

In another experiment made on the Jackson Fireplace quite a strong breeze was blowing into the fresh-air duct from the outside, so that the anemometer recorded an entering current of 70 meters per minute before the fire was lighted. This outside pressure of course increased the effectiveness of the heater, and the saving amounted to about 4 per cent. more than when the air outside was still. This test was made on the very warm evening of June 25, from 9 to 12 o'clock, the thermometer outside standing at 25° C. (77° F.). In winter, when the difference between the outer air and that of the flue is lower, a greater saving of heat is realized from any of these heaters; but the experiments lose in accuracy, partly on account of the difficulty of measuring the temperature of the inflowing fresh air current at the beginning and end of the experiment. The thermometer is influenced by radiation from the surrounding objects in the room, from which it is, of course, impossible to protect it absolutely. If it were possible, it would indicate a temperature of over 100° below the freezing-point of water, the temperature of celestial space being, according to Pouillet, as low as –150° C. Only an approximate degree of accuracy can, therefore, be expected, and it is greatest when the temperature of the room is nearest that of the inflowing air currents, as is the case in summer.

The Jackson Fireplace is at present manufactured in two sizes only. The price now (1881) of the smaller size, 30 in. wide and 32 in. high, requiring a fireplace opening in brickwork 28 in. wide, 32 in. high, and 15 in. deep, is $85, in brass; $65, all nickel-plated or bronzed; or $55, black with nickeled basket. Another size, made for very large rooms, is 39 in. wide, 36 in. high (outside of frame), and requires a fireplace 32 in. wide, 35½ in. high, and 15 in. deep. They are to be obtained of Edwin A. Jackson & Brother, No. 315 East Twenty-eighth street, New York.

The manufacturers are prepared to furnish with each grate an ornamental band of metal to diminish the height of the opening at the top after the manner of a narrow blower, for cases where the draught of the chimney is not good. By means of this strip this fireplace may be used with safety even where the chimney-draught is feeble.

With any of the fireplaces mentioned herein a flue, for disposing of the ashes, may be constructed below the grate. The flue forms an ash-pit, into which the ashes fall from the grate when shaken or dumped. The ashes are then removed through the door B, in the basement, at the bottom of the flue. A "soufflet" pipe, D, has been provided, through which air may be taken from below to increase the draught, when desired, after the principle of the Winter Fireplace; but the soufflet, in a well-constructed fireplace, is unnecessary, and its use is only to be recommended when better construction is impracticable.

Although the fireplace was almost completely eclipsed by the modern furnace of the late nineteenth and early twentieth centuries, today it has been reincarnated in many forms, one of them being a round hearth and dome of sheet iron located in the center of the room. In location and function the fireplace has now gone full circle.

Chimney Doctors

The construction and ornamentation of fireplaces posed many problems. These were matters of great concern because the fireplace was the most important feature of the room, from both a functional and decorative point of view.

As regards its function, an improperly constructed fireplace was deficient on two counts. Its inadequacy as a heating device is clearly evident from the large size of the throat and flue. All authorities agree that most of the heat went up the chimney. The second problem was that many of them "smoked"; that is, for one reason or another some of the smoke escaped into the room instead of going up the chimney. This was a matter of great inconvenience and, while it is probable that many attempts to eradicate this condition were made, few successes or failures are recorded.

The best-known solutions were advanced by Benjamin Franklin in a letter to Dr. Ingenhausz, Physician to the Emperor at Vienna, while enroute from Europe to America in 1785. This letter was published by I. and J. Taylor, at the Architectural Library, London, in 1793, and was entitled *Observations on Smoky Chimneys, Their Causes and Cure; with Considerations on Fuel and Stoves*. Although the logic of his discussion was very elementary by today's standards, his treatise was published many times and throws much light on the subject of smoky chimneys, a troublesome problem at that time.

He begins with comments on the shape of the chimney flue. Some believed that it should taper inward toward the top, while others thought it should become narrow toward the bottom. Such variations were thought to influence the drawing power of the chimney, and in extreme cases it probably did. Franklin performed an experiment showing that the form of the flue was not a basic factor affecting its draft. He placed thin fibers of silk above a glass tube, and pointed out that when the tube was not heated, air did not rise in it. When heat was applied to the tube, the air rose through it, causing motion in the silk fibers above it. He concluded, therefore, that:

> In fact, no form of the funnel of a chimney has any share in its operation or effect respecting smoke, except its height.

After establishing the fact that the shape of the flue had little effect on the rising of hot air (and smoke), he proceeded to enumerate nine reasons why a fireplace might smoke. His first was, "Smoky Chimneys, in a new house, are such frequently from mere want of air." He points out that the joints of the walls, windows, and flooring are at first very tight, so that no entry is provided for fresh air into the room. As a matter of fact, every part fitted so tightly that even a drop over a keyhole was a matter of concern. He reasoned that the constant flow of air out of the chimney was much greater than the flow inward from the outside, so that eventually a vacuum was formed in the room which not only promoted smoking, but was harmful to the health of the animals (people) in the room. Cases were known to him where houses were deemed uninhabitable because fireplaces did not draw unless a door or window was left open.

In his remedy he first points out that "When you find, on trial, that opening the door or a window enables the chimney to carry up all the smoke, you may be sure that want of air *from without* was the cause of its smoking." He placed much emphasis on the air coming from the outside, for neither a large room nor air from another room solved the problem. The practical solution was to open a door while the fire was burning, and then slowly close it until smoke came into the room. By slight adjustments the exact size of the opening could be ascertained, such as a half-inch by six feet; therefore, an opening three feet by an inch had to be provided for adequate performance of the fireplace.

He then explored the various ways by which fresh air could be brought into the room. A door left ajar or a window partially open created a draft which came cold on your back and heels as you sat by the fire. Pipes conducting air into the jambs or the flue were also unsatisfactory, because the extra supply of air had to pass through the opening

Color Plate

This Romanesque styled mantlepiece is located in the back parlor of Stanton Hall in Natchez, Mississippi. The carved designs in the spandrels and side columns include roses, pears, persimmons, pomegranates, and cupids' heads. It was imported from Italy at a cost of three hundred dollars. The house contains other imports, such as silver hinges and doorknobs from England and gilt mirrors and bronze chandeliers from France.

The house was built between 1852 and 1857 by Frederick Stanton, who chartered a whole ship to bring its exotic fittings to America. It is regarded as the most palatial residence in the city and has been compared to the White House in its dimensions, decorative theme, and perfection of detail.

Courtesy Deep South Specialties, Inc.

OBSERVATIONS

ON

SMOKY CHIMNEYS,

THEIR

CAUSES AND CURE;

WITH

CONSIDERATIONS ON FUEL AND STOVES,

Illustrated with PROPER FIGURES.

BY

BENJAMIN FRANKLIN, LL. D.

LONDON:

Printed for I. and J. TAYLOR, at the Architectural Library,
No. 56, opposite Great Turnstile, Holborn.
M.DCC.XCIII.
(Price 2s)

of the fireplace. He points out that the Frenchman Gauger, provided flues under the hearth to bring in cool air, but this was not an expedient procedure in houses already built.

Franklin then observes that a body of hot air rises to the ceiling of every heated room and that by lowering the upper sash of a window, the cool air can be mixed with the hot air. If a window cannot be lowered an opening could be cut in the wall near the ceiling, and concealed by installing a shelf under the cavity. Also, a pane of glass could be removed and replaced by a sheet of metal, hinged at the bottom so that the size of the aperture could be controlled according to the demands for such ventilation. One solution he noted from England: a round hole was cut into the window light, into which a circular set of vanes was installed. The whirling vanes did disperse the air; the noise, however, was a constant annoyance.

Franklin's second cause for smoking fireplaces was, "Their openings in the room were too large." He argues that architects were concerned only with the symmetry and beauty of the opening, and had little regard for relating the size of the opening to the dimensions of the room. He contended that the size of the opening should be related to the height of the flue; therefore, the openings of the largest flues should be the largest, and those of smaller flues should be smaller. Logically, fireplaces on the first floor should have the largest openings, and those in the attic, the smallest. Those in between should have an intermediate opening.

There was also a relationship between the size of the opening and the rarefication (heating) of the air. Too large an opening permitted unheated air to get into the chimney flue over the fire and cause smoking, while small openings created a strong draft and caused fuel to burn too rapidly.

The logical solution to this problem was to change the size of the chamber opening. If too large, the proper size could be estimated by using boards to lower the lintel and reduce the width until smoke no longer seeped into the room. Then a mason could be employed to permanently reduce the size of the opening. Franklin concluded that openings in lower rooms should be about eighteen inches. Those in upper rooms could be eighteen inches square and not quite so deep. He does not present any solutions for enlarging the opening if it were too small. Apparently, all of them were too big.

Several other recommendations of Franklin are worthy of inclusion here. In large openings pieces of firewood half the length of cord wood could be used; for smaller chambers the billet could be cut into thirds. A minimum size for the flues was necessary to accommodate the activity of chimney sweeps. If large openings were deemed appropriate for a spacious room, an appearance of largeness could be obtained by using marginal bands of marble. Franklin then comments as follows:

> And there are some, I know, so bigotted to the fancy of a large noble opening, that, rather than change it, they would submit to have damaged furniture, sore eyes, and skins almost smoked to bacon.

"Another cause of smoky chimneys is *too short a funnel* (flue)." This contingency might occur in the case of a low kitchen having only one short chimney. If the chimney were extended far above the roof, there was danger of its being blown down for lack of adequate support. Franklin's solution to this situation was very simple—add another story or two to support a tall chimney. Otherwise, contract the size of the opening. If an ample fireplace opening was necessary to accommodate cooking utensils for large dinners, he advised building additional flues. In the event that all of them were not needed, extra ones could be closed by using sliding plates (dampers) which he later described in detail.

The presence of short flues was quite common in houses where flues from the second-floor rooms were cut into flues from the first floor. Conditions for a good draft were usually bad when there was no updraft in the longer flue, and the complete draft had to be generated from an angular flue with an inadequate length. The only solution, often unsatisfactory, was to place a damper in the long flue and keep it closed when there was a fire only in the second-floor fireplace.

The fourth cause of smoking chimneys is the case when two or more fires result in "their overpowering one another." In the event that fires are burning in two fireplaces in one room, the one with the stronger fire is apt to draw air down the flue of the weaker one and cause it to smoke. This condition could occur between rooms and, in rare cases, between rooms on different floors. The solution was to have an adequate supply of fresh air from the outside, so that no fireplace had to borrow from another.

Franklin continues with a fifth cause for smoking fireplaces. He states: "Another cause of smoking is when the tops of chimneys are commanded by higher buildings or by a hill." This condition causes the wind to blow down upon the chimney and force the smoke downward. His solution was to place a turncap of iron or tin on top of the chimney with a vane, so that it would swing into the wind and protect the flue from a down draft. An alternate and more costly solution was to build the chimney higher, or to place the doors of the building facing the hill, thus forcing the air to enter the doorway and facilitate the upward motion of the smoke in the chimney. An interesting example of the situation is cited where a row of city houses had one-story kitchens with low chimneys in the back. The higher front sections formed a dam and at certain times the wind forced the air down the chimneys and out the front doors. Viewed from the end of the block, this must have been a very curious sight. Low chimneys at the rear also permitted smoke to be blown into the windows of the upper stories at the front of the house.

The "improper and inconvenient situation of a door" was a significant reason for causing a fireplace to smoke. The door was sometimes located on the same wall as the fireplace. When the door was open, air skirted by the fireplace and out through the door. Thus, a draft for the fireplace was minimized and smoke came out into the room. The solution was to place a screen between the door and the fireplace, or hinge the door on the opposite side so a contributing draft was not created.

It was also known that: "A room that has no fire in its chimney is sometimes filled with smoke, which is received at the top of the funnel [flue], and descends into the room." It is evident that when the temperature of the air in the flue is the same as that in the room and outside, there is no marked movement of air in the chimney. In the evening when air on the outside becomes cool, the air from the inside ascends; on the other hand, when the air on the outside quickly becomes warm, it will press downward on the air in the chimney flue. When smoke is issuing from neighbor's chimneys, it will be drawn downward in unused flues. The remedy is to install a sliding plate (damper) which can be closed to shut off the smoke completely.

Finally: "Chimneys which generally draw well, do nevertheless sometimes give smoke into the rooms, it being driven down by strong winds passing over the tops of their funnels, though not descending from any commanding eminence." This statement simply indicates that a very strong wind blowing over a chimney is so powerful that the lesser pressure within the chimney is overcome, and the smoke is contained in the chimney flue. As a matter of fact, Franklin states that this great pressure from without sometimes enters the chimney flue at the top and further reduces the possibility of the smoke's having a proper exit.

Although many of his theories sound unreasonable, the solution to this problem is one of the most bizarre. He recommends that the top of the flue be widened to appear like a funnel, so that when the wind strikes an interior wall it will bounce outward and permit the chimney to function properly. He points out that such a procedure would create a problem if a number of flues adjoined each other, but he offers no solution.

Franklin summarizes his thesis by saying:

> I have thus gone through all the common causes of the smoking of chimneys that I can at present recollect as having fallen under my observation; communicating the remedies that I have known successfully used for different cases, together with the principles on which both the disease and the remedy depend, and confessing my ignorance wherever I have been sensible of it. . . . For many years past, I have rarely met with a case of a smoky chimney which was not solvable on these principles, and cured by these remedies, where people have been willing to apply them; which is indeed not always the case; for many have prejudices in favour of the nostrums of pretending chimney-doctors and sumists, and some have conceits and fancies of their own, which they rather choose to try, than to lengthen a funnel, alter the size of an opening, or admit air into a room, however necessary; for some are afraid of fresh air as persons in the hydrophobia are afraid of fresh water.

It is very evident that with Franklin the functioning of fireplaces and chimneys was a longstanding preoccupation, for as early as December 2, 1758, he wrote a letter to "J. B. Esq. at Boston, in New England." This letter foreshadows his comments on the subject published by the American Philosophical Society in 1793, in which, in fact, he frequently refers to this earlier letter.

The contents of his letter to "J. B." focus principally on the installation of a sliding plate which is known as a damper today, at the meeting point between the fire chamber and the throat of the fireplace. Although this idea must have been utilized by some practical builders in the eighteenth century, the writer has never found one in a chimney of the period.

Franklin begins his exposition by suggesting that the size of the fireplace opening should be reduced. This structural error must have been a very prevalent one at the time, for he is so emphatic about it. Actually, it was not an error if proper use had been made of a facility similar to his sliding plate which would have retained much of the heat in the fire chamber, and the walls reflected it into the room. He suggested the width of the opening should be reduced to about two feet between the jambs and the height brought down to three feet above the hearth. Evidently, as late as the mid-eighteenth century many fireplaces were higher than they were wide. At least, Franklin so recommended.

The improvement consisted of an iron frame installed just back of the lintel, and extended to the back wall of the fireplace. This frame had an opening with grooves on each edge into which was fitted a plate, which could be slid horizontally backward and forward, either closing or opening the entrance to the throat and ultimately the flue. When a fire was first started, the plate was drawn forward (open), permitting excessive amounts of smoke to go up the chimney. A modern damper creates such an opening at the front instead of the rear. As the heat increased and the convection of hot air became stronger and the chimney walls warmer, the opening was partially closed and more heat retained to be projected into the room. When there was no fire, the opening was closed entirely, as Franklin frequently mentioned before.

In the same letter to "J. B.," Franklin suggests a novel use for fireplaces in the summer. He pointed out that in the summer there were drafts up and down chimneys at different times of the day. This situation occurred because the temperatures inside and outside the house were rarely the same, and, for this reason, drafts were created sometimes going up the chimney, other times coming down. He comments as follows:

> This property in chimneys I imagine we might turn to some account, and render improper the old saying, *as useless as a chimney in summer*. If the opening of the chimney, from the breast down to the hearth, be closed by a slight moveable frame or two, that will let air through, but keep out flies, and another little frame set within the hearth, with hooks on which to hang joints of meat, fowls, etc., wrapt well in wet linen cloths, three or four fold; I am confident that if the linen is kept wet, by sprinkling it once a day, the meat would be so cooled by the evaporation, carried on continually by means of passing air, that it would keep a week or more in the hottest weather. Butter and milk might likewise be kept cool, in vessels or bottles covered with wet cloths. . . . I think, too, that this property of chimneys might, by means of smoke-jack vanes, be applied to some mechanical purposes, where a small but pretty constant power only is wanted.

Franklin continued his scientific wandering by saying that if a house were built against a hill with a tube to carry air through the house on the same principle he outlined for the chimney, such a house could be kept comfortable, even on a calm day and the stillest night. As a matter of fact, a chimney thirty for forty feet high built over a mine would also effect a draft which would be beneficial to the comfort and the health of miners. He further muses that a chimney protected from the north wind by the building, but exposed to the east, west, and south can be made more effective by painting the outside black.

Finally, Franklin makes some comments relevant to the location and operation of chimneys. For example, he mentions that chimneys exposed to north winds are apt not to draw well because, when rendered cold by the winds, they draw downward. Chimneys contained within walls of a house are better than those outside. Chimneys (flues) built together in stacks are apt to draw better than single flues, because a constant fire in one flue warms the others. It is obvious that Franklin thought a great deal about the functioning of fireplaces and chimneys, and while some of his hypotheses are considered valid today, modern scientific thought has put others into discard. In this writer's opinion, his iron fireplace contrivance was more innovative and important than his observations about smoking chimneys. Although the mechanics of his damper have been changed, some form of it is used in practically every modern fireplace built in America today.

A contemporary of Franklin and possibly better known for his theories about fireplaces was Count Rumford. Rumford was born in Woburn, Massachusetts, in 1753, his real name being Benjamin Thompson. In the Revolution he became a British sympathizer, and in 1776 was sent to England with important dispatches. After a brief subsequent career in America, he joined the Austrian army and campaigned against the Turks. He entered the military and civil life of Bavaria; he took beggars off the streets of Munich, and continued his scientific studies, which he had started at an earlier time. In 1791 he became a count of the Holy Roman Empire and took the title of Rumford from the American township from which his wife came. By 1798 he was back in London, and in 1804 he moved to Paris, dying in Auteuil in 1814. He was active in foreign scientific societies and founded the Rumford professorship at Harvard. His contribution of importance in this survey is a publication called *Essay IV: Of Chimney Fire-places, with proposals to save Fuel; to render Dwelling-houses more Comfortable and Salubrious, and effectually prevent Chimnies from Smoking,* which was published in London in 1796 by an unknown publisher.

Rumford's publication is an important landmark in the literature concerning the evolving form and function of the fireplace. He rambled over much ground that had already been covered, to which he made some very significant contributions, all of which he guaranteed to be beyond improvement. As far as he was concerned he had reached the millennium in the science of building and reshaping fireplaces. When his publication was presented, he claimed success in altering five hundred smoky fireplaces, and only one failed to respond to his normal procedures.

He launches his dissertation by stating that his plan was satisfactory for fireplaces which burned all fuels, such as wood, coal, or peat; that more than half the former amounts burned were saved; that fatal drafts were eliminated; that rooms were comfortably heated; and that a door or window rarely had to be opened to allow fresh air to enter. The only complaint about his plan he had heard was that rooms became too hot, and he implies that people are to be pitied who are unable to regulate the fire by placing the proper amount of fuel on it.

His essay is quite lengthy because he deals with a number of peripheral subjects and he repeats the directions for change a number of times. All of his proposals deal with the fireplace and the throat, with no recommendations for changing the chimney. He must have assumed that the size and shape of chimneys were reasonably satisfactory in most cases. His basic changes were concerned with lowering the lintel, bringing the back wall forward, and slanting the jambs. Although one might quibble about some of his suggestions, it is evident today that he produced a satisfactory efficient fireplace.

His first comments are directed toward the fact that the great fault of all open fireplaces in common use was their immensity. This was probably a valid criticism, for large fireplaces were effective only when large fires were burning in them, which was probably not the case most of the time. The exception, of course, was the large kitchen fireplace, which had to be large enough to accommodate a number of cooking vessels at one time. One must assume from Rumford's drawings and comments that he was concerned only with fireplaces used primarily for heating. Kitchen fireplaces stayed large as long as they were in use.

It should be mentioned, however, that his plan would have improved the function of a large kitchen fireplace as well as of the smaller examples. As a matter of fact, largeness was just one of the unfortunate factors in fireplaces; the fault lay principally in the fact that there were large throats above the fireplaces which expediently conducted about 90 percent of the heat up the chimney. He mentions that these large throats were built to accommodate chimney sweeps, but this is not a fact, for some throats were large enough for two or three chimney sweeps at one time. It is very obvious that little thought had been given to improving the function of the fireplace, and for centuries it remained an ineffective heating device. It should also be noted that Rumford did accommodate the chimney sweep when he reduced the size of the throat.

The first step in reducing the size of the throat and to minimize smoking was to lower the level of the lintel. (An alternative not mentioned by Rumford was to raise the hearth, a procedure which probably accounts for many of the raised hearths found in old fireplaces.) Lowering the lintel could be done in a number of ways. A large stone could be placed under the lintel, which could be supported by the wider jambs, often built to reduce the width of the fireplace. Again, several courses of brick could be laid under the lintel which could be supported by an iron bar. A number of such examples have been located in America, and the question arises as to when this action was taken. Most people think that fireplaces were originally built that way. It now appears that they were altered to minimize smoking, or to make the fireplace a more effective heating device. Rumford mentions that great care had to be exercised in this matter for if the lintel were made too low, the draft was increased and large quantities of fuel were unnecessarily burned.

The next consideration was to make the sides and the back of the fireplace conform to the best shape and size for reflecting heat into the room. The change in the back and sides really had to be made simultaneously; however, the problems of the back will be considered first. In most cases a completely new wall was built across the back of the fireplace. The formula for locating the back wall was to measure the thickness of the lintel, which could have been as small as four inches or as large as twelve or fifteen inches. Moving horizontally back from the lintel, an open space four inches wide was left for the exit of the smoke. Rumford is very precise about the size of the exit, and comments that the size might be varied as much as an inch either way, but he found that four inches was most satisfactory in most cases. This slit extended the full width of the fireplace, so that smoke from all areas could easily arise. Then he proposed that the back wall of the fireplace be built vertically from the hearth to approximately six inches above the lower level of the lintel. This procedure could not always be followed; for example, if the lintel were only four inches thick and the exit four inches wide the depth of the fireplace would be only eight inches. The solution to the problem of a narrow lintel was to drop the wall to provide an appropriate depth for the fireplace, build it vertically as high as wood burned on the andirons, and then gently cove it forward until the four-inch exit for the smoke was achieved, above the lower edge of the lintel. From this description it is evident that he arrived at the form found to be most satisfactory for the back—rarely, if ever, found on a fireplace of the eighteenth century, but universally used today.

A number of other problems remained to be solved. If the opening were too wide, additional facing had to be added to the jambs to bring the opening to the desired ratio of height to width. At the same time the shape of the covings (jambs) was changed. In the eighteenth century most jambs formed a 90-degree angle with the rear wall. This procedure was almost universal in America and, although some fireplaces of the era have slanting jambs today, a close examination will reveal that such jambs are later additions. The discrepancy can be discerned by noting that courses of brick do not match or that there is no interrelation between the jambs and the back wall. It is obvious that parallel jambs were very ineffective for reflecting heat into rooms. Rumford slanted them, and he decided that the best angle was 135 degrees, give or take a few degrees. After slanting the jambs the suggested width of the back wall should have been about one-third the width of the front opening. This formula also varied slightly depending on conditions. The jambs were built vertically and terminated in a line level with the top of the back.

The new back and jambs were built of one layer of brick, or an equal thickness of stone. The space between the new construction and the old was filled with rubble, such as broken pieces of bricks or stones. Across the top a flat course of masonry had to be laid, firmly bound with mortar, to form a smoke shelf. Rumford said:

> There the three walls which form the two covings and the back of the Fire-place all end abruptly . . . but when the throat of the chimney ends abruptly, and the ends of the new walls form a flat horizontal surface, it will be more difficult for any wind from above to find and force its way through the narrow passage of the throat of the chimney.

He points out that no attempt should be made to make the new masonry blend into the earlier form of the chimney throat.

Thus, it is evident that Rumford's plan did indeed produce a very effective form for reflecting heat into the room and, of equal importance, created a smoke shelf which has become an integral part of every fireplace built today. The addition of Franklin's sliding plate over the smoke exit would have made the device as effective as any of those built in the twentieth century.

Rumford's plan indicates that important consideration was given to the entry of the chimney sweep into the chimney. He obviously could not crawl through a crevice only four inches wide. The doorway, as he called it, consisted of a space at the center top of the back wall which was filled with loosely fitting bricks or a large stone. When needed, an opening could be created there for the chimney sweep and, after he was finished, the parts replaced without any permanent change in the contour of the back wall.

A point of interest which Rumford raises is the suitability of the material used for fireplace construction. He mentions that materials which absorb heat do not reflect it and, therefore, that the best materials are bricks and stones. These were very fortunate choices because of the cheapness of these materials and the abundance of skilled craftsmen to construct them in their proper contour. He continues his logic by saying:

> And hence it appears that iron, and, in general metals of all kinds, which are well-known to grow very hot when exposed to the rays projected by burning fuels, are reckoned among the very worst materials that it is possible to employ in the construction of Fire-places.

Rumford then states that he realizes that his opinion about the fitness of iron for fireplaces is not shared by all people, that iron is favored by many because it appears to become hotter than masonry materials. He might also have pointed out that iron was longer lasting than masonry materials. However, he fails to observe that there is little reflection of heat from iron and most of it goes up the chimney. He recognized that iron was an essential part of the fireplaces that had grates for burning coal, a common practice in England at that time. Because many of the grates were smaller than the opening of the fireplace, the surrounding area was filled with iron plates; but this was an error, for bricks were cheaper and would have been more satisfactory for the purpose.

It has been often mentioned that bricks and stones were the best materials for constructing or reshaping fireplaces. It is very important to note that when bricks were used they were usually covered with plaster, a procedure followed in most American fireplaces of the eighteenth century. Rumford does not discuss the use of plaster; however, it was probably as resistant to heat as the bricks of the day, and was easier to replace when deterioration occurred. This concept is confirmed by several contemporary writers on the subject. The plaster and the stone should have a final application of whitewash, kept as white and clean as possible. White reflects more heat and light than any color; black which reflects neither heat nor light should be avoided.

Figures and explanations of them as found in Rumford's publication (Figs 1–11) are found on pages 237–240.

Existing records indicate that the search for a perfect fireplace did not terminate with the publication of Rumford's findings. However, it is highly probable that they did not become known immediately in America. In 1796 the American Philosophical Society in Philadelphia offered a prize of sixty dollars for improvements of stoves or fireplaces. The intent was to find improvements which could be used by poorer classes, because the plans then known were too expensive for them to implement. The Franklin stove was obviously too expensive for them. Little is known about the winner because he did not identify himself, but called his plan "Oeconomy."

Two models were later submitted (March 17, 1797) by Charles Willison and Raphaelle Peale which are exhibited by the Society today. They

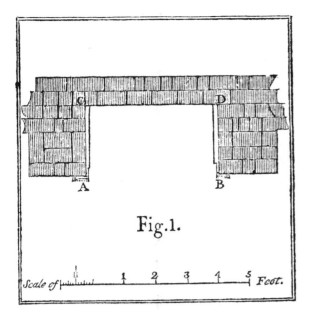

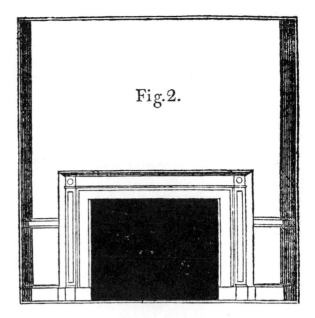

Fig. 1: The plan of a fireplace on the common construction. AB, the opening of the fireplace in front; CD, the back of the fireplace; AC and BD, the covings. *Fig. 2:* This figure shows the elevation, or front view of a fireplace on the common construction. From *Essay IV. Of Chimney Fire-places* by Count Rumford

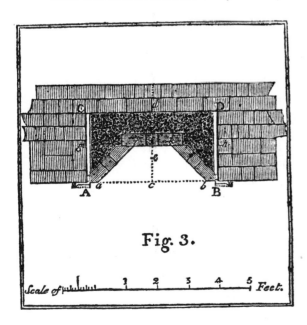

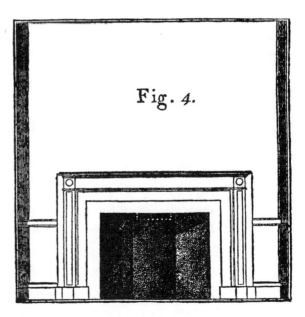

Fig. 3: This figure shows how the fireplace represented by Fig. 1 is to be altered in order to improve it. AB is the opening in front; CD the back; AC and BD the covings of the fireplace in its original state. *ab* is the opening in front; *ik* the back; *ai* and *bk* the covings after it has been altered; *e* is a point upon the hearth

upon which a plumb suspended from the middle of the upper part of the chimney falls. The situation for the new back is ascertained by taking the line *ef* equal to four inches. The new back and covings are represented as being built of bricks; and the space between these and the old back and covings as being filled with rubbish. *Fig. 4:* This figure represents the elevation or front view of the fireplace shown in Fig. 3 after it has been altered. The lower part of the doorway left for the chimney sweeper is shown in this figure by white dotted lines. From *Essay IV. Of Chimney Fire-places* by Count Rumford

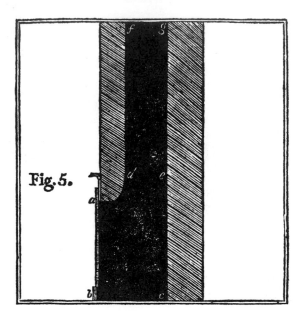
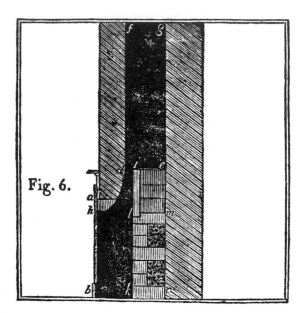

Fig. 5: This figure shows the section of a chimney fireplace and of a part of the canal of the chimney, on the common construction (sections of the same chimney represented in Figs. 1–4). *ab* is the opening in front; *bc*, the depth of the fireplace at the hearth; *d* the breast of the chimney. *de* is the throat of the chimney; *df*, *ge* is a part of the open canal of the chimney. *Fig. 6:* Shows a section of the same chimney as shown in Fig. 5, after it has been altered. *kl* is the new back; *li* the tile or stone which closes the doorway for the chimney sweeper; *di* the throat of the chimney, narrow to four inches; *a* the mantel; *h* the new wall made under the mantel to diminish the height of the opening of the fireplace in front. From *Essay IV. Of Chimney Fire-places* by Count Rumford

are less than a foot high and are built of white pine and paper. They are unmarked, but both models are decorated with ink sketches.

In a paper read before the Society at the time they were submitted, the Peales offered an arrangement designed to minimize smoking and heat loss. Their invention was the first United States patent for improving fireplaces and was granted to the Peales in 1802. The specifica-

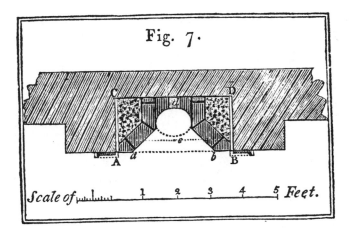

Fig. 7.

Scale of ———— 1 2 3 4 5 *Feet.*

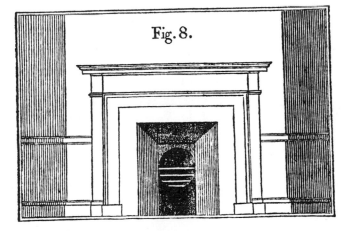

Fig. 8.

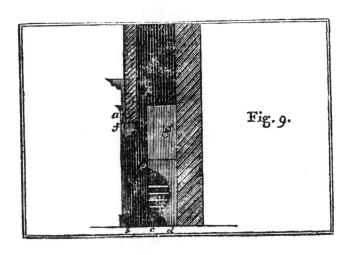

Fig. 9.

Fig. 7: This figure represents the ground plan of a chimney fireplace in which the grate is placed in a niche, and in which the original width AB of the fireplace is considerably diminished. *ab* is the opening of the fireplace in front after it had been altered; *d* is the back of the niche in which the grate is placed. *Fig. 8:* A front view of the fireplace shown in Fig. 7 after it had been altered, where may be seen the grate and the doorway for the chimney sweeper. *Fig. 9:* Shows a section of the fireplace as in Fig. 7. *cd* a section of the niche; *g* the doorway for the chimney sweeper, closed by a piece of firestone; and *f* the new wall under the mantel by which the height of the opening of the fireplace in front is diminished. From *Essay IV. Of Chimney Fire-places* by Count Rumford

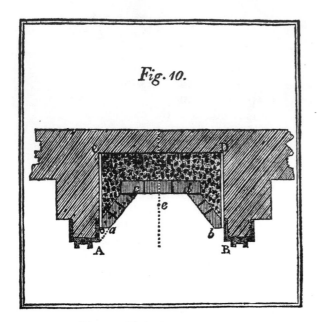

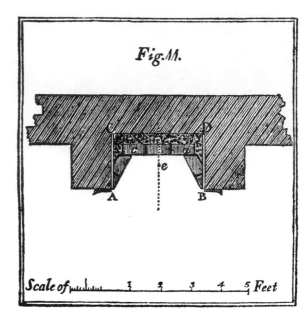

Fig. 10: This figure shows how the covings are to be placed when the front of the covings (*a* and *b*) do not come as far forward as the front of the opening of the fireplace or the jambs (A and B). *Fig. 11:* This shows how the width and obliquity of the covings are to be accommodated to the width of the back of the fireplace in cases where it is necessary to make the back very wide. From *Essay IV. Of Chimney Fire-places* by Count Rumford

tions as they were submitted to the Patent Office were lost in the fire of 1836. A description of one of the models was printed in Volume 5 of the old series of *Transactions* (of the Society).

Like their predecessors, the Peales thought they had solved the major problems of fireplace construction, namely, the elimination of smoke and an improvement in heating. They concurred with Rumford in his design of the jambs, to which they added a sliding mantel and a damper. They claimed that their additions would make a fireplace comfortable, safe, and economical. The matter of safety was a new concept and, although there was little demand for this feature, it probably worked.

In their illustration, Figure A is a sliding mantelpiece made of sheet iron, or of copper or brass if a more decorative effect was desired. One end of the cords was attached to the arms *a a*, while the other end dropped over the pulleys and held the weights. Grooves were cut in the brick-work in which the sliding mantel moved up and down. The grooves were covered with wood or marble depending on the wishes of the owner. There is a suggestion of marble in the inventors' drawing. The dotted line on Figure B shows the arms, the pullies, and the weights, with the sliding mantel positioned half way down to the hearth. The sliding mantel might more accurately be called a blind.

For convenience the mantelpiece and the overmantel should have been made in two separate pieces. This plan permitted the hollow overmantel to be removed when the cords had to be replaced. The recommended use of cords (rather than chains), for this critical function near the heat of the fire, suggests that this was an experimental model. The life span of a cord in such a situation would have been very short.

Although all facets of the Peale invention are important, the function of the so-called valve or damper was the most significant. It was fitted in the throat of the chimney about ten or twelve inches above the

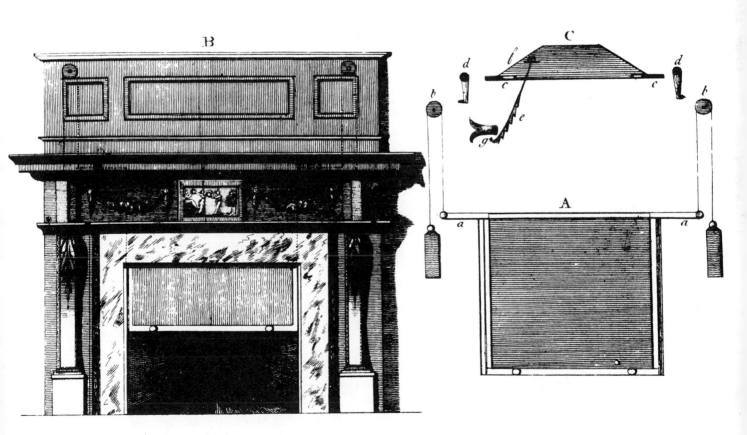

Photograph of the fireplace mantel plan proposed by Willison and Raphaelle Peale to the American Philosophical Society for solving the problems concerned with the functions of the various parts. It was obviously in the popular Federal style of the time. *Courtesy American Philosophical Society*

Advertistment of A. H. Read of Montrose, Susquehanna County, Pennsylvania, which appeared in the *Standard of Liberty* (Lancaster, Pennsylvania) on September 23, 1831. *Courtesy Lancaster County Historical Society* lower edge of the lintel, and fitted to close flush with the top of the brickwork, normally called the smoke shelf. The pivots *c c* fitted into the sleeves *d d*, which in turn were fastened into the masonry as bearing points for the moving damper. The damper was hinged at the front of the throat on the premise that the smoke and heat could more safely pass up the chimney at the back against a masonry wall than in the front where wood from the mantelpiece was apt to be exposed by a careless workman. The position of the damper was controlled by the lever *e* which could be positioned on the iron hook *g*. Small notches on the lever permitted sensitive control of the damper positions. One of the real uses of the damper was to create a large opening when the fire was started, and to reduce the size of the opening as the fire burned freely. By contracting the size of the opening greater amounts of heat could be withheld and effectively projected into the room.

The safety feature of the apparatus is described as follows:

> But the safety from the dangers of fire with this fireplace is not of the least importance, for whatever fire is left in the place at night, with the valve close shut, and the sliding mantle lowered to join the hearth, the fire will be smothered. In like manner if by accident the soot takes fire in the flue of the chimney, no alarm follows, as it may be instantly extinguished.

It is also pointed out that if the chimney smoked it was a simple procedure to lower the sliding mantelpiece, thus increasing the draft.

The last improvement was concerned with the problem of smoke passing between the sliding mantelpiece and the parts into which it loosely fitted to permit smooth operation in raising and lowering it. A hole was cut into the brickwork above the opening of the fireplace, forming a small flue to let in external air and thus forcing the smoke up the chimney instead of out into the room. This procedure seems to have been more a theory than a practical way for increasing the draft.

There is no doubt that many other plans were devised for improving the function and appearance of the fireplace. The intent here is to give a cross-sectional view of plans which were introduced over a span of about one hundred years. One would think that the ingenious Americans would have solved this important matter in much less time, but the last proposal presented here indicates that when fireplaces were replaced by other modes of heating in the mid-nineteenth century the problem was not completely solved.

It is interesting to note that each man who advanced a theory or practice was sure that his was not only the best solution, but virtually the only one. On September 23, 1831, an announcement appeared in the newspaper *Standard of Liberty* (Lancaster, Pennsylvania) by A. H. Read of Montrose, Susquehanna County, Pennsylvania. In that year one of the residents of that small community laid claim to solving a problem which had defied the best brains of the world. His entire notice is included here. However, the certainty of his results are expressed in the following sentence:

> The progress recently made in that science (Chemical science) has enabled the subscriber to reduce the art of building chimneys to a system, *invariably* producing the desirable result with respect to smoke, and at the same time making a saving of fuel.

The final discussion in regard to perfecting heating and ventilation in a room with a fireplace is of the solutions given by A. J. Downing in his book *The Architecture of Country Homes*. The focus of his attention is toward fixing the chimney to circulate pure air throughout the room in which the fireplace is located. The urgency for this action is evident in the second paragraph of his chapter about "Heating and Ventilating" where he says:

> The want of attention to ventilation arises from the fact that the poison of breathing bad air is a slow one, and though its effects are as certain as those which follow from taking doses of prussic acid, yet they are only observed remotely, and little by little. Nature does not immediately protest against slightly impure air as against want of food and water, and, therefore, we go from day to day, suffering the accumulated evils resulting from our ignorance, and only wondering at our want of physical health and spirits. . . .
>
> We are forced also to attribute the general want of health of women in America, and the paleness, delicacy, and want of color and bloom upon the cheek after the first few years of youth are past, to their voluntary in-door life, and sedentary habits, in rooms always close, and always badly ventilated, for at least five months of the year.

Downing then goes on to explain how the rooms become virtually filled with foul air with the results described above. He notes that the only exit of air is through a fireplace. The air enters the room around the cracks in the windows and doors and, because of the draft of the fireplace, it never rises in the room but is drawn to the height of the lintel, usually at about thirty to forty inches. Thus the rest, or upper part, of the room is filled with air which has been inhaled and exhaled by the occupants many times. His conclusion is: "Hence, the heads of persons in such a room as this, in a winter's day, are almost always in a stratum of bad air."

Downing's solution to this serious problem was to insert a chimney-valve or register in the wall or the chimney-breast near the ceiling. He maintains that through this opening the foul air would pass slowly and effect a complete circulation of pure air in the room. The action of the valve was facilitated by a strong upward current in the chimney; as a matter of fact, this current could be so strong that the egress of the air from the room had to be controlled by some means. For this he recommended Arnott's Chimney-valve (invented by Dr. Arnott of London), which served a double function. (However, Downing does not explain how.) Not only could the quantity of air be controlled which left the room, but it also prevented smoke from the chimney from entering the room. This valve could be easily built into the chimney wall, and if deemed an undesirable sight, it could be covered by hanging a picture over it.

Finally, Downing points out that, to make the ventilation of a room perfect, some means had to be provided for the intake of fresh air from the outside, particularly if houses were new and well built. (Obviously a repetition of Franklin's comment a hundred years earlier.) Downing describes the arrangement:

> In a room arranged in this way, the fresh air would enter from the outside, become slightly warmed in the brick air-chamber, at the side or the back of the fireplace, and pass into the room through the opening at the side. On the other hand, the air, rendered impure by respiration, the exhalations from the skin, etc., would rise and pass out of the chimney-valve at the top.

It is interesting to note that Downing expresses his belief that the open fireplace was the most satisfactory way to heat and ventilate a room—of course with the addition of a chimney-valve. He mentions that all who can afford a fireplace should never be persuaded to use a stove of any kind. However, by 1850 the fireplace had "run its race" and chimney doctors soon became unwanted and unemployed experts.

The Bye from Bake-house, she had brought / Thus if it fall for want of thought

The ACCIDENT in LOMBARD-STREET / PHILADA 1787 *inspired & engraved by CW Peale*

And laughing Sweeps collect around / The bye that's scatter'd on the ground

No. 1

Chimney Sweeps

*A*lthough the trade of chimney sweeping has been recognized as a traditional one in Europe, little is known about its practice in America. It is a fact, however, that it was followed here from the middle of the seventeenth century until modern times, particularly in the big cities of the eastern seacoast area. Modern building technology and a humane attitude toward the welfare of workers have almost eliminated this horrible pursuit; forever, it is hoped.

It was an entirely natural procedure for the chimney sweep to take up his trade in America. It has been pointed out that the first colonies were merely transplants of European culture in America, and he was needed here as much as in Europe. The American chimney flue was possibly less tortuous than those of old London; nevertheless, the danger of fire in the chimney was ever-present. There was danger because the daub inevitably became dry and fell off the walls of wooden chimneys, thus creating a fire hazard which needed prompt attention. In addition, there were some twists and long horizontal flats in chimney flues which not only were fire hazards but also resulted in inefficient operation of the chimney when undue amounts of soot collected in these areas.

Engraving by Charles Willison Peale showing chimney sweeps on a Philadelphia, Pennsylvania, street. It is labeled "The Accident in Lombard Street Philadᵃ 1787 designed & engraved by C.W. Peale." The accompanying verse is as follows:

> The pye from Bake-house she had brought
> But let it fall for want of thought
> And laughing sweeps collect around
> The pye that's scatter'd on the ground.

Courtesy Henry Francis du Pont Winterthur Museum, gift of Caroline Clendenin Ryan Foundation, 1962

There was also the constant problem of birds' nests and other debris collecting in the chimney, which at best did not improve the function of the air passage.

An associate who shared the responsibility of the chimney sweep was the chimney viewer. He was appointed in the colonies in the seventeenth and eighteenth centuries to make periodic checks of chimneys and hearths to determine if they were fouled (full of soot) or needed repairs. Because his appearance at the door of a house always presaged the prospect of expenditures for the owner, he was a very unpopular person. Often he had the authority to fine the property owner if his directions were not followed, an act which further decreased his popularity. Sometimes the onus of the job was too great for the viewer, in which case he himself had to be fined for not carrying out his duties. As a matter of fact, the situation became so bad in one area that a man was fined because he refused to accept the appointment to this disagreeable position.

One of the major hazards the viewer tried to control was the blazing of chimneys at the top. This condition was bona fide evidence that the chimney not only needed cleaning, but also that the potential for nearby destruction by fire was great. The thatched roofs of most villages were first-class prospects for sparks and whole villages are known to have been destroyed because of faulty or fouled chimneys.

The reluctant house owners obviously had to be prodded to employ a sweep. In 1683 the fine for a chimney which spewed forth flames was fifteen shillings. This sum was increased in 1697 to forty shillings. In different towns and cities the rates varied from ten to forty shillings. A rebate was allowed sometimes for those who took action promptly, but the inertia with respect to cleaning and paying fines was great, particularly if important persons of the community were involved in the action.

The poor and the penurious were inclined to clean their own chimneys, particularly if the house was a low one, as most early houses are

Advertisement of Joseph Scarlett's Chimney Office, 40 Brattle Street, Boston, Massachusetts. It is undated, but Scarlett was in business at that address as early as 1855 and as late as 1892. Its thirty-six lines of poetry are an unusual part of such an advertisement. *Courtesy Baker Library, Harvard University*

JOSEPH SCARLETT'S

My boy never falls, like **this** one, but he stays until the chimney is well cleaned, and then comes down the same as any one would.

CHIMNEY OFFICE.

Having devoted years to the study, philosophy and cure of Smoky Flues, the subscriber feels confident that he understands and can remedy the evil in most instances, and is willing to warrant them to work well, or no pay, even after others have tried and failed. Office hours for advice, at 8 o'clock, A. M., and 2 P. M.

JOSEPH SCARLETT.

As sparks fly upward, oft 'tis said,
So man to evil turns his head ;
Not that he's *always* false to duty,
But keeps his *Chimney awful sooty!*

Now private peace and health demand
The *magic* stroke of SCARLETT'S hand ;
'Twill make a Paradise of home.
And sweeten life for years to come.

The man who keeps his chimney dirty,
Will not be wise at three times thirty ;
He'll always by the fair be cursed,
And never gain a public trust.

Sure he who'd keep his conscience clear,
Will look to his chimney year by year ;
And he who'll aid him to be neat,
Is SCARLETT, 40 *Brattle Street.*

A smoky house, a crabbed, scolding wife,
Are little evils, and of old complaint ;
They make poor souls a-weary of this life,
Provoke the curses of a very saint.

But smoky chimneys cured can always be.
For SCARLETT'S sweep-boys can clean out the flues ;
Then fires in kitchen, parlor, hall, burn free,
And none, with scolds, will longer have the blues.

On top of chimney hear the song so clear,
When "Sweep O" mounts aloft in airy seat,
Chanting *Sweet Home*, sung out like chanticleer,
From *gloom* to *glory* bursting out so sweet.

The flue all clear, sounds like an organ pipe,
The smoke mounts up, and leaves the room all free
The fire burns bright, the hearth has got a wipe,
And children smile once more on papa's knee.

Then call on SCARLETT, he can comfort bring,
Make smoke and smother leave the palace hall ;
Without his aid, the life of e'en a king
Will be uneasy, wrapped in smoky pall.

Persons having Smoky Chimneys, Ovens, Boilers, Ranges, or Furnace Flues, will do well to give us a call.

known to have been. Brooms or long poles could easily be poked into the aperture from either end to loosen the unwanted debris. Doubtless, some discovered that a swirling chain dropped from the roof functioned quite well, but the most bizarre method was to tie a rope around the neck of a goose and drop it down the chimney. After the goose had made several trips through the chimney flue, its powerful wings flapping en route, it was very likely that the chimney was clean. Perfect cleanliness was usually determined by the fact that soot no longer fell on the hearth. These procedures were poor substitutes for the work of the sweep, for only he could find loose bits of masonry or accumulations of soot in ledges or corners which might eventually ignite and cause trouble.

An attractive array of chimney shapes on the Carter-Moir House in Williamsburg, Virginia. One is inside the wall of the house, the near one is outside. *Courtesy Colonial Williamsburg*

Sometimes chimneys were cleaned by deliberately setting fire to them. This was an ancient custom followed in Europe where chimneys were built of brick or stone. There was inherent danger to the property involved in such a procedure. However, if the authorities approved the practice when sweeps were not available, it had to be done on damp days. The unfortunate aspects of this firing finally became so evident that in the end people were fined for burning their chimneys. All of these make-shift operations played into the hands of the sweep, who was the "pro" when it came to cleaning chimneys.

In America as in Europe, the lowly stature of the sweep caused him to be despised and consequently ill-treated. Every aspect of his life was ridiculed; the lowest appraisal one could make of another's character or habits was to compare them with those of a chimney sweep. Scornful poems were written about sweeps, they were called disgraceful names, and they were the butt of many jokes which ridiculed their calling. Children were quickly tamed into submission when threatened with the prospect of facing the chimney sweep.

There were many reasons for the wretched status of the sweep. In the first place, to be successful he had to have a small, emaciated body so that he could climb within the confined flues of the chimneys. A sickly rather than a robust child was best suited to the work. Most of them were apprenticed at the ages of eight to ten years, when they were small and agile. Apprentices for the work were solicited from poor families who could not afford to raise all of their children, and the orphanages were scoured for recalcitrant children, who were then turned over to the master sweep until they were approximately fifteen years old. At that age, when they could no longer crawl through the chimney apertures, they were discarded for younger prospects. With a body and a mind that had been discredited by society, his chances for learning another trade were minimal.

The young sweep became the property of the master sweep, who had an unwholesome reputation for cruel and wanton mistreatment of his charges. He provided them with tattered clothing, usually the castoffs of more prosperous boys. However, they are usually pictured wearing an incongruous high silk hat along with their sundry disarray of clothing. The inadequacy of their apparel was quite significant, for they usually went to work in the morning before fires were lighted, when it was cold and chilly, particularly in the northern cities.

One of the most unfortunate conditions of the sweep's life was the fact that he received no education or moral training. He worked when most boys were normally in school, and he had free time in the afternoon to get into all kinds of mischief. Many of them took a cue from their masters and trod the streets in a rowdy-like manner when they were not working. One might suspect many of them of thievery and gambling with the proceeds from the sale of their stolen booty. The general public in America took no pity on these waifs, and somehow expected that God would direct their lives into proper channels. Some of them were commended for unusual acts of honesty, but these were probably the exception rather than the rule.

Most of them were poorly housed in the cellar of the master sweep. They slept on heaps of straw or old blankets, neither the sweeper nor the blankets having been washed for weeks on end. There was little reason to wash the blanket for it was in daily use to cover the fireplace opening so that the dislodged soot did not fall into the room. The sweep was treated with equal indifference; if cleaned he merely became dirty again. The lack of sanitation combined with other hazards of the work created an unwholesome environment and many died at an early age. The following excerpt from *American Chimney Sweeps* by George Lewis Philips focuses attention on the inhuman practices of the master sweep:

> Masters had unenviable reputations for brutality arising from the methods they employed to teach their boys the art and mystery of the chimney-sweeping trade. To force a terrified child into the dark, winding flue, stinking of the acrid odor of soot, a man would apply to the infantile posteriors a few smacks of his brush, or some well aimed kicks. If the boys refused to budge once he was coerced into the flue, his master might resort to such tactics as pinching the calves of his legs, sticking pins into the bottom of his feet, or puncturing his rump with an awl. If the urchin complained that he was jammed and could not move, his instructor sometimes helped him to extricate himself by starting a straw fire on the hearth. Frightened by the thought of being burned to death, the child usually found enough strength to free himself. Of course, by depending upon his elbows and knees for leverage in flue climbing, the new sweep boy developed bloody sores, often ulcerous,

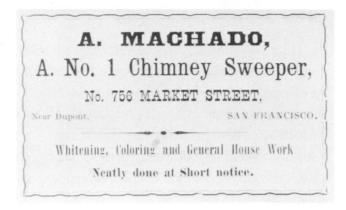

Trade card of a chimney sweeper who was not shy about the quality of his service. He obviously added other trades to his major work. *Courtesy Baker Library, Harvard University*

which the master rubbed with saltpeter until they hardened within six months or so. To break a lad properly, the masters agreed, there could be no soft-heartedness, no sympathy shown him.

At another point Philips states that:

> Just as there were accidents incidental to the trade, so there were diseases more serious than the usual bleared eyes caused by fine particles of soot lodged under the eyelids. Consumption was more prevalent; chimney-sweepers' cancer, the more dreaded because of greater pain. By inhaling the fine soot particles, chimney sweeps often acquired tuberculosis which shortened the lives of many; by not scrubbing the soot out of the folds of their scrotums, they became troubled with ulcerous sores, resulting from the tar irritant, which gradually hardened into lumps, known in the trade as "sooty-warts." If they sought a surgeon's advice, they learned they had two choices, to be operated upon and live the rest of their lives as eunuchs, or continue to suffer until death brought relief.

The business procedures of the trade were controlled by the master sweep, who owned his charges. He coralled them from various sources from which they could be obtained, he supplied them with food and equipment, and he took most of the money they earned. Sometimes the master sweep had an established "office," where he could be contacted when his services were needed. He posted hand bills, advertised in newspapers, and on rare occasions was listed as a master sweep in the business directories published in some of the major cities, such as Boston, New York, and Philadelphia. The names of two sweeps are listed in the business directory of Boston, published in 1789; and the 1811 directory of Philadelphia includes the names of two sweeps and six master sweeps.

The common advertising image with which we are all familiar is that of the little blackened urchin, wandering the streets soliciting work by yelling "sweep-Ho." Before sunrise these boys were herded into the streets, eating a dry crust of bread, if they were lucky. This stingy procedure was probably an attempt to have the prospective customer supply breakfast before the sweep went to work. Some of them went directly to the homes of people who had engaged their services, but were then left standing, in snow or rain, until landlords or servants were prepared to let them indoors.

After entering the house, the sweep first fastened his blanket over the fireplace, so that the soot would not blacken the furniture or the rugs. If the flues were narrow, he removed all his clothing down to his underwear, to minimize the chances that rumpled clothing would jam him in a flue, or catch on a ledge. Next, he pulled a coarse cloth cap over his head to keep soot from getting into his eyes, grasped a brush and scraper, and began his ascent of the chimney. In England chimneys were built to accommodate a sweep, but such a kindness has never been reported for American sweeps.

SOLOMON,
(*Not improperly Sirnamed* GUNDY)
CHIMNEY-SWEEPER, *in* Annapolis,

HAVING acquired that ART in his Youth, with painful Study and Application, and not juſt *taken up the Trade* as a certain Perſon has done, Hereby gives Notice, That he can ſweep Chimneys as well as, if not better than, *Peter Wilſon*, and that he can climb up Chimneys, without either Ladder or Rope, of any Height, and not do as he is inform'd a *certain Perſon* ſome Times does, that is, only *come down them*, as indeed any Body might do if they were but to go up a Ladder and *fling themſelves in at Top*; but he *goes up* and *comes down*, and makes *clean Work*, with Care and Expedition, and waits upon Gentlemen [or Others], for Six Pence a Funnel, *ready Money*.

N. B. I may be ſpoke with in my Maſter's Kitchen in *Church-Street*, facing *Conduit-Street*.
                                        SOLOMON GUNDY.

An eye-witness account of a sweep is recorded by Philips in *American Chimney Sweeps:*

> Mute, the little fellow stood while his chief removed from the fireplace the oven in which bread was baked, pushed back the "crane" where swung the pots and kettles, then feeling the chimney to see if sufficiently cool, fastened across the front, by means of two forked sticks, the aforesaid blanket, behind which disappeared the pajama-clad midget. After a minute or two of fluttering, suggestive of a chimney swallow, came a silence proportionate to the height of the chimney, when with a "Sweep-Ho"! he emerged from the top and poured forth his reassuring song, telling his master the faithfulness of his trust, and the public generally of the woes of the poor little sweep. . . . Resting awhile in the upper air he slowly began his descent, and as the scrape, scrape was heard the showers of soot fell behind the blanket until at last, the little ebony figure appeared, with a cone shaped cap drawn down over his eyes, and held out a grimy hand for the big round penny which awaited him below as his personal prerequisite.

The distasteful working conditions, the contempt of society for sweeps, and the callous indifference of the master must have goaded many into the thought of running away. Run away they did, and their masters inserted advertisements in the press informing the public of their departure, as well as offering a reward for their return. The following advertisement appeared in the *Boston Gazette* on November 14, 1752:

> Chimney sweep.— Ran away on Thursday last, from his master James Fairservice, of Boston. A Servant Lad, named W. Thomas, about 17 years old, small of his age, short black Hair, black Eyes, (he often brings the same to the grief and damage of His Master), was bred a Chimney-sweeper, and went away in an with his Sweeper's Gears, had on two dark jackets pretty sotty: chews tobacco plentifully, and chuses the best sort. Whoever shall take him up and bring him to his Master shall have two dollars, and necessary charges.

A more respectable species of sweep was the adult who seems to have operated a more reputable business "on his own." Sometimes a man would have an assistant or a partner. These were probably men who had been apprenticed as sweeps in their youth, and, having found it difficult to pursue another trade, continued their work in chimneys which a single adult could handle. He is described as one who cleaned chimneys principally by using a ladder and brushes or brooms. His procedures were best suited to low houses with ample flues, which could be easily reached. An examination of many early chimneys verifies that his equipment was well-suited to the work at hand.

By placing his ladder on the hearth and up the chimney, he could reach at least the lower half of it, although he was doubtless begrimed by the falling soot. With the ladder he could also reach the eaves of the house and crawl to the chimney top to repeat his cleaning operations. If the chimney was very long and too narrow to permit entrance, a different cleaning technique was employed. He dropped a strong bag filled with bricks through the flue until it was reasonably well cleaned. He, or his assistant, might have tied a rope to a bundle of brushwood and pulled it up and down until a clean flue was the result.

Such work was usually performed in the morning, after which the sweep took the soot in a bag to his place of business, and screened out the cinders before offering the soot for sale as a fertilizer or insecticide. His limited income as a sweep was enhanced by doing odd jobs such as beating carpets, whitewashing, emptying cesspools, and cutting down trees. Possibly, he received double pay when he was allowed to take the wood home and sell it to his neighbors.

The intolerable conditions under which the boys worked went unnoticed in England and America for many years. Parliament did nothing to alleviate the unbearable conditions until 1788, when laws were passed limiting the number of sweeps under each master, fixing a minimum age at eight years, as well as regulating the number of hours of work each day. In 1833 the minimum age was raised to ten years, and in 1840 the age was raised to twenty-one. Finally in 1875 a law was passed requiring master sweeps to be licensed and thus control was finally brought to a trade that had maimed and killed children for centuries.

In America the more humane treatment of sweeps resulted from the presence of machines to do their work rather than from any belated sympathy for the boys. One of the first machines was invented by John Smart in London in 1893. Smart's machine is described as follows in *American Chimney Sweeps:*

> Constructed of jointed rods of cane or ash, fashioned to fit together like a fishing rod, Smart's machine supported on the topmost joint a whalebone brush which, in being pushed up the

Color Plate

A very wide range of fireplace facilities compatible with contemporary architecture are available today. Many are designed to be used against a wall, which is somewhat a compromise with tradition, while others are "free-standing" and can be installed at any desired place. Wood, gas, and electricity can be used for fuel. Many are finished in bright enameled colors, one company offering units in ten different colors.
Courtesy The Majestic Company

chimney, remained furled like an umbrella but on reaching the chimney top was opened by the operator pulling a cord. When it was hauled down the flue, the stiff bristles loosened the soot which fell behind a green baize curtain hanging before the hearth and having in its center a hole through which the operator manipulated the apparatus. As the rods could not reach around sharp elbows of a flue, chimneys had to have soot-doors installed at these right angles to permit the machine to function. Doubtless Philadelphians complained about the expenses and bother of having these doors hung. Londoners certainly protested, even while admitting that machines prevented the sacrifice of children.

Two adult chimney sweeps carrying the tools of their trade. One has a ladder, a ball on a rope, and a "sweep" under his arm. The other has his blanket thrown over his shoulders.
Courtesy Baker Library, Harvard University

THIS certifies, that Mr. _West_

had _Store_ chimney fwept,

on _Decem_ — 10 — 180_7_,

by a fweep belonging to JOHN VINTON.

D.   C.

Receiv'd — 50 — for the fame. _J. Vinton_

☞ Please to apply for sweeps at the Chimney-Office, No. 100, Orange-Street, or at the Office of the Clerk of the Market, under Faneuil-Hall.

Receipt for the work of a chimney sweep belonging to John Vinton of Boston, Massachusetts. The directions for service suggest a mode of operation comparable to a more respectable business. *Courtesy Baker Library, Harvard University*

The relevance of Smart's machine to the Philadelphia scene came about because the Society of Friends in England shipped a number of his mechanisms to Philadelphia in 1818. A Philadelphia Quaker, Robert Vaux, held high hopes for the use of the machine in America, but it was regarded as inefficient in American chimneys and was never widely accepted here.

The spirit of invention being rife in England and America in the early nineteenth century, six men applied here for patents for chimney-sweeping apparatus between 1817 and 1821. Later, other men made devices to clean chimneys, but none seemed so successful as William Hall of Boston. Hall received permission to set up in business and had

JOHN WALLIS, Chimney-Sweeper,
Who ferved his Time to that Bufinefs in London, *and underftands it as well as any Man in* America.

LIVES now in *Annapolis*, and will fweep Chimneys in the beft Manner, fo that there fhall be no Danger of their firing (which often happens when they are pretendedly fwept with long Broom), and cleans them, for one Shilling a Chimney. Any Gentlemen, or others, who fhall be pleafed to employ him, may depend on being faithfully ferv'd by
Their humble Servant, JOHN WALLIS.

a service charge fixed by law. In 1820 a man named Harding opened an office for such work in Providence, Rhode Island. He inserted the following advertisement in the March 17, 1820, issue of the *Rhode Island American and General Advertiser:*

> The subscriber, agent to William Hall, a patentee of a Machine for Sweeping Chimnies and Stove Pipes, which has been proved useful in this and other towns, and a number of gentlemen having subscribed to have such Machine introduced into general use in this town, now gives notice, that a suitable person will attend the calls of such persons in this town and its vicinity as shall desire to have their Chimnies cleaned by said Machine, which can be effectually done by it, without the danger attending the burning of them, and the inconvenience of sweeping by climbing.

An Associated Press Report from New Orleans, Louisiana, on August 14, 1970, provides a final word regarding sweeping chimneys. It reports that a man named Tillman, 67, has been sweeping chimneys in New Orleans since 1923. He used to cry "R-r-ramoney!" on the streets because it is derived from "ramoneur" the French word for chimney sweeper. Recently he has gotten all his business by word of mouth among the citizens of the city. He has had some customers for as long as 35 years. Instead of walking, he now uses an automobile.

He carries a ladder to get to the roof tops where he uses tools such as a small shovel, a hand brush, a flashlight, and a sheaf of palmetto straw fastened to the end of a rope. December and the spring months are his two busiest times. The clue to his identity is a high silk hat. Maybe times haven't really changed very much.

No legislative action was ever taken in America to control or eliminate the sweeping boys, so competition between humans and mechanical sweeps has obviously continued until the present. What really decided the issue was the gradual conversion to central heating, reducing flues in size so that mechanical devices had to take over. The common method now is to use a vacuum device with a large bag which works quickly and efficiently. But the operators *do charge* higher prices than that which the boys received.

Andirons

*B*ecause the word "andirons" hardly ever appears in the day-to-day communications of contemporary society, it seems appropriate to provide a definition of the term. The natural procedure for supplying a definition would be to refer to a prestigious source, the *Oxford English Dictionary* (*O.E.D.*) for example:

> A horizontal bar, one of a pair sustained on short feet, with an upright pillar, usually ornamented at front, placed at each side of the hearth, to support burning wood.

It is probably poor judgment to quarrel with a definition from the *O.E.D.*; however, if such a definition were perfect and complete, there would be no need for this survey. Some of its errors can be corrected at once. In the first place, it has been noted from research that there was not always a pair. When the need for a contrivance of this sort was first realized, logically it consisted of one horizontal bar upon which wood was stacked from each side. This procedure was probably quite satisfactory when the hearth was in the center of the room. Again, although many of the earliest examples were ornamented only on the front, probably the greatest number of andirons were decorated with pillars or columns, which were turned on a lathe, and thus presented the same appearance when viewed from any angle. Finally, they were not used exclusively for the burning of wood. One would expect an English dictionary to inform the reader that by the eighteenth century

One of the earliest andirons extant. The two parallel horizontal bars are probably unique. There is much evidence of deterioration on the surface of the metal. *Courtesy Colchester and Essex Museum, Colchester, England* the products of England's woodlands had been virtually consumed by its iron furnaces and that sea-coal had become the major fuel of the country, particularly in the large cities.

Being somewhat aroused by the limitations of definitions, the writer pursued the subject of andirons in Chambers' *Cyclopedia, or an Universal Dictionary of Arts and Sciences* (London, 1741), only to find that neither andiron nor firedog (as it was sometimes called) is included in its entries. This omission is unexplainable, for at that time these objects were found in every English household, and should have received considerable notice in a publication of this type.

It might also be noted that Dobson's *Encyclopedia* (Philadelphia, 1798) does not include an entry "andiron"; however, an earlier one called the *Encyclopedia Parthensis*, published (no date) at Perth, Scotland, makes the following contribution to the subject:

> ANDIRON. (Supposed by Skinner to be corrupted from Hand-iron; an iron that may be moved by hand, or may supply the place of the hand). Irons at the end of a fire grate, in which the spit turns; or irons on which wood is laid to burn.— If you strike an entire body, as an andiron of brass, at the top, it maketh a trebel sound, and at the bottom a baser.

Possibly the most accurate definition is found in Ure's *A Dictionary of Arts, Manufactures, and Mines* (New York, 1856); however, it is evident that all the important details are not included:

> Andirons, or Hand-irons, also called firedogs. Before the introduction of the raised and closed fireplace stoves these articles were in general use. Strytt, in 1775 says, "The Hand-irons are used this day and are called cob-irons; they stand on the hearth, where they burn wood, to lay it upon, their fronts are usually carved, with a round knob at the top; some are polished and bright. Anciently many were embellished with a variety of ornaments."

The image of the andiron is pretty well rounded out with the addition of the definition found in the fourteenth edition of the *Encyclopaedia Britannica*, published in 1929. The comment there follows:

> ANDIRON (older form *anderne*), one of a pair of horizontal iron bars upon which logs are laid for burning in an open fireplace. Andirons stand upon short legs and are usually connected with an upright guard, giving the grotesque appearance of a dog (hence

Andiron showing the earliest type of legs used. The column is split into halves and the separate parts are bent outward to form the legs. Examples of this type are very rare. *Courtesy Quentin Bowers*

fire-dogs, q.v.). This guard, being a very conspicuous fixture, is often elaborately designed with figures, grotesque animals, emblems and the like. Andirons with little or no ornament were also used in the kitchens, with ratcheted uprights for the spits.

It may not be evident to the reader (but it is to the writer) that the facts included in these definitions do not cover all the important aspects of the subject. For example, they do not suggest the vast array of styles in which they were made, the various materials of which they were fabricated (some were of silver, others of cast iron), nor do they define their real function, which was to lift fuel off the flat hearth so that the increased draft would help the fuel burn brighter and thus create more heat. A great many other details of andirons and their history remain to be discussed.

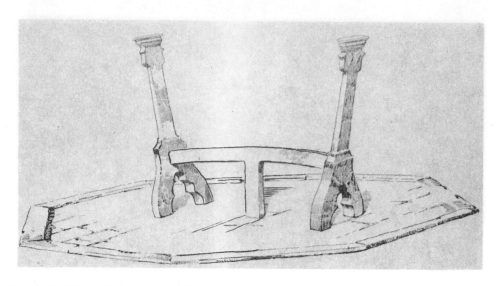

Large double-ended andiron of cast iron. The extra leg in the center of the billet bar supported the bar and kept it from bending when it became very hot. *Courtesy Alec Tiranti, Ltd.*

It should be noted that at least two special types of andirons eventually evolved—one for a fireplace used for heating and for the preparation of food, usually in the kitchen, and the other for fireplaces in living rooms and bed chambers, used principally for heating. The major difference between the two types was that the kitchen variety had a minimum of ornamentation and often was equipped with spit hooks to hold a rotating spit. Those for the living room were very ornamental and were styled to be compatible with the decor and architecture of the room in which they were used. Of course, in the earliest times there was little difference between the two.

It is extremely difficult, or virtually impossible, to determine when man first discovered that raising the fuel above the level of the hearth provided increased draft and generated more heat. It seems logical to assume that this principle was accidentally discovered by primitive societies, and that the practice was continued until fireplaces were completely replaced by other devices for heating a room. It is important to recognize that the American Indian, although living in essentially a Stone Age culture, used a primitive type of andiron. Presumably, groups in other parts of the world had made the same discovery. It is reported in *Fire as an Agent in Human Culture*, by Walter Hough, that:

> Almost all of the primitive fireplaces had an early addition, perhaps a bordering circle of stones which, among other things,

facilitated the keeping of the fire and protected it in a measure from winds. At a later stage we see three stones or bosses of mud placed in the fire as a rest for the cooking pot. Trivet bosses of baked clay in one piece, forming a fireplace, have been uncovered in ruins of both cliff and open-air type (quarters) in New Mexico and Arizona by the writer.

These primitive andirons are suggestive, and it is allowable to see in them the rude beginnings of the stove and an approach to the idea of draft.

It is very likely that andirons were used centuries before the refined form of the eighteenth century had been invented. It is probable that early crude types were improved for utility and durability, but a sizeable gap of time and information exists between those used by primitive peoples and the surviving specimens of metal. It should be noted that,

Massive andiron excavated at Jamestown, Virginia, with a depressed panel and a cherub's head on the front surface. Examples similar to this one can be seen at the Victoria and Albert Museum in London.
Courtesy National Park Service

despite the sophistication of domestic heating at the height of Roman civilization, there is no evidence that they used andirons of any type. This omission can be easily explained by the fact that they did not have fireplaces; excavations at Pompeii and Herculaneum have not brought any to light. However, at least one Romano-British andiron does survive, which was found at Colchester, England, and it is thought to be of the third century A.D.

This rare specimen is made of wrought iron, and a few comments about that metal might logically be made here. In the first place, it is not made of cast iron like many later examples, for at that time technologists could not generate enough heat to melt iron out of the ore, and cast it into a desired shape. They could, however, find high-grade

Andirons of wrought iron, late seventeenth or early eighteenth century. Half circles form the front legs which probably had feet at the ends at one time. Striations in the metal of the vertical columns are due to impurities in the metal. *Courtesy Henry Francis du Pont Winterthur Museum*

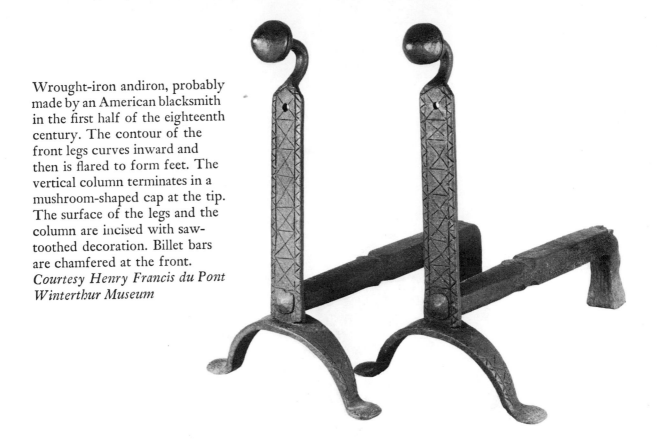

Wrought-iron andiron, probably made by an American blacksmith in the first half of the eighteenth century. The contour of the front legs curves inward and then is flared to form feet. The vertical column terminates in a mushroom-shaped cap at the tip. The surface of the legs and the column are incised with saw-toothed decoration. Billet bars are chamfered at the front. *Courtesy Henry Francis du Pont Winterthur Museum*

iron ore on or near the surface of the ground which could be converted in forges or bloomeries into impure but usable pieces of iron. By numerous heatings and poundings most of the impurities could be excluded, and possibly a number of small pieces could be welded together; finally, a useful piece of iron was obtained in this way. The fact that billet bars (the horizontal bar holding the wood) were most frequently made of wrought iron attests to the fact that it was well-suited for this purpose. Subsequently, the object took its name from the material of which the earliest metal ones were made.

The Colchester example consists of two vertical bars and two horizontal bars. The top portions of the vertical bars bend outward into a pair of simulated horns, attached in an arrangement that seems to resemble the heads of two animals, possibly bulls. The lower ends are split for eight or ten inches and spread apart, forming two bowed legs with no feet attached. Immediately above the juncture of the legs with the vertical bar, a single horizontal bar is attached to keep the vertical bars upright. Several inches above this bar another larger horizontal bar is attached to give rigidity to the arrangement and provide a substantial support for the burning logs as well. This was a single double-ended andiron,

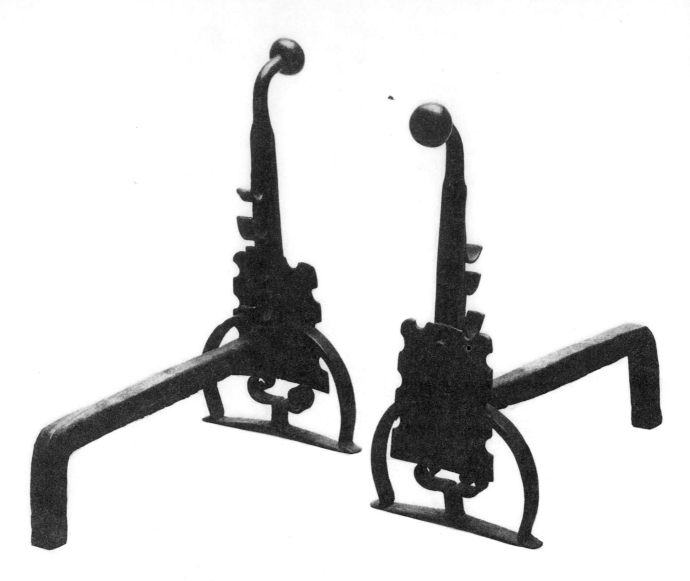

Iron andirons of the early eighteenth century showing considerable ornamentation by the use of a decorative plate on the front and a scrolled centerpiece between the legs. *Courtesy Henry Francis du Pont Winterthur Museum*

used when the fire was burning on a central hearth in a room, the smoke finding its way out through unglazed windows, cracks in the masonry, or a smoke hole in the roof. Although no writer, in describing these famous andirons, has suggested the utility of the horns, it is entirely possible that their decorative quality was supplemented by a function such as holding a spit. As a matter of fact, their arrangement suggests a similar one used outdoors, where forked sticks are driven into the ground and a horizontal bar is placed in the forks to support a kettle or to hold a cut of meat for roasting.

The next English example is located at Penshurst Place, Kent. It is similar in form to the Colchester example, but it is much heavier and made of cast iron. This andiron is believed to be of the sixteenth century. By that time the blast furnace had been invented, and reasonably large metal pieces could be formed on the casting floor of sand adjoining the tap hole of the furnace. The vertical sections of this single double-ended andiron are 44 inches high, and the billet bar possibly 50 inches long. The dimensions of this andiron were dictated by the fact that it was used in the center of a large room. Andirons of this size not only were appropriate for an area of large proportions, but also accommodated bulky timbers, with a resulting hotter and longer-lasting fire.

There were doubtless some overlapping of styles in andirons, and one must step backward at this point to pick up a new form, which probably predates the large single-ended cast-iron examples which follow. Undoubtedly, the advantage of using two andirons occurred to a practical innovator along the way and the first of these examples closely resembled the single double-ended pieces. The move toward using a pair was probably motivated by the fact that two provided a better draft for the fire, and with the addition of newly invented spit hooks,

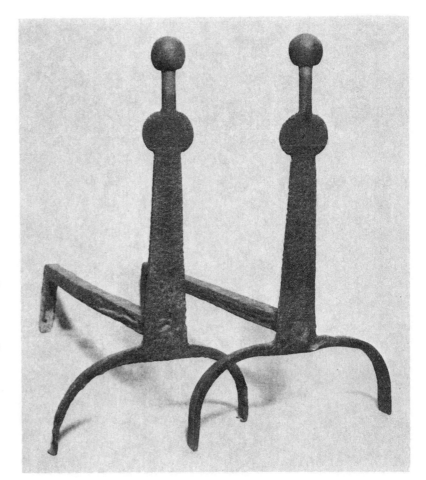

Small all-iron andirons used in small-chamber fireplaces or in conjunction with larger andirons in a large fireplace. When used with larger andirons they were called fire-dogs or creepers. These were probably made to be used alone in a small fireplace. *Courtesy Bucks County (Pennsylvania) Historical Society*

allowed meats to be slowly roasted beside the fire instead of directly over it. Thus to the technological properties of the andiron was added the culinary function. The example in the author's collection has low bowed legs, which were made separately and attached by welding to the billet bar. It was logical to have used a pair of andirons when the fire was on the hearth in the center of the room; it became almost imperative when the hearth was moved to an outside wall.

The process of refinement and improvement continued in the course of which drastic alterations in size and substance were achieved, and by the seventeenth century the form of the andiron as it is known today had evolved. The fragility of the earlier wrought-iron varieties probably resulted in considerable overheating of the billet bar and other parts, with some deterioration of the metal, if the damaged condition of later

Pair of late eighteenth-century knife-blade andirons (lacking finials) made by N. Starr, a well-known arms manufacturer of Middletown, Connecticut. Although the finials were screwed onto these columns, earlier finials were fastened by riveting. The name is impressed near the top of the column. *Courtesy Mr. and Mrs. William Ball*

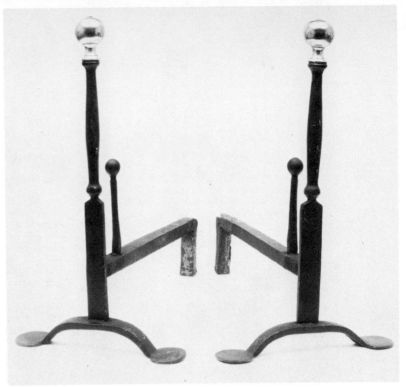

Iron andirons with brass finials marked by the maker, Turle, who is thought to have worked in New England about the middle of the eighteenth century. Such early signed andirons are extremely rare. *Courtesy Henry Francis du Pont Winterhur Museum*

billet bars is taken as evidence. As a matter of fact, the early surviving examples of andirons show so much scaling and deterioration caused by heat that often only their skeletons remain.

Goaded by the necessity to create a product which could better withstand the great heat of large burning timbers, and stimulated by the vast possibilities in the use of cast iron produced by the blast furnaces, the technologists turned to the production of massive examples of cast iron. This new style was single-ended, and had three legs instead of the earlier four legs. The front side of the vertical column was often profusely decorated with geometric designs or human figures. In a few cases dates were added, which is a great convenience to anyone who studies the subject today. Surviving examples of this type are seen in English museums and private collections; one of the most massive has been excavated at Jamestown. It seems fairly safe to assume that the Jamestown example was cast in England, one of the first of many instances of the reliance on English technology which was destined to persist for a century or more.

By mid-seventeenth century conditions in America had improved. One of the most important single improvements came about with the erection of a blast furnace at Saugus, Massachusetts, which could produce andirons such as those being used in England. Patterns, carved from wood, were pressed into the sand of the casting floor in front of the

Single example of andiron made
entirely of iron, almost matching
the pair at Winterthur, which
is located in the Victoria and
Albert Museum, London,
England. *Courtesy Victoria and
Albert Museum*

furnace. Molten iron flowed from the furnace into the molds to the
desired shape. Since one pattern could be used many times it is probable
that a sizeable number of cast-iron andirons were produced in America.
This is simply a hypothetical statement, for none of that era has survived; nevertheless, it is obvious they were badly needed.

Toward the end of the seventeenth century, wrought iron began to
supplant cast iron as a medium for andirons. The whim for change, the
great weight of cast-iron andirons (some examples weighed as much as
fifty pounds), the ready availability of wrought iron, and the growing
number of blacksmiths in the colonies—all were contributing factors.
Also a forged, single-ended type with three legs was developed at this
time. The front vertical column was made of a bar of forged iron
approximately two inches wide, about three-eighths of an inch thick,
and about 30 inches high. The height was dictated by the dimensions
of the large fireplace openings used at the time, as well as by the size
of the fire required to adequately heat the far reaches of the rooms.

The smith split one end of the bar in the middle of its width for about eight inches and reshaped the prongs into bowed legs. The top end was shaped into a ball or an appropriate scroll to make an attractive finial. The billet bar, possibly an inch square, was bent at a right angle to create the third leg at the back of the andiron. The other end of the billet bar was inserted in a hole punched in the vertical column above the jointure of the legs. There it was riveted into place, with a small rosette appearing on the front side of the column. These were made in pairs and positioned on the hearth to accommodate the length of billets prepared for them.

The upright bar or column was made functional for kitchen use by attaching a series of spit hooks on the front or back side. The number varied from three to six. In some cases, the hooks were individually welded to the vertical bar; in others, the hooks were welded together into a single unit and were then attached to the column with a rivet.

Andirons with large brass finials indicating a trend toward andirons with columns made completely of brass. It is interesting to note that columns of the matching creepers are made entirely of brass. *Courtesy Henry Francis du Pont Winterthur Museum*

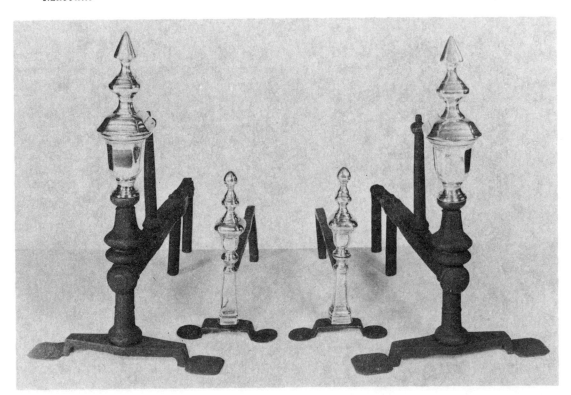

One example is known with a hole near the top of the column, indicating that at one time spit hooks were attached but were removed when no longer needed.

Although the form of these wrought-iron andirons was pleasing, and some thought was given toward making them attractive, the earliest ones were more functional than decorative. The next step was to introduce elements which were ornamental. One of the first procedures was to chisel or chase designs into the plain surfaces of the column and the legs. The blacksmith ordinarily decorated some of his products in this manner and it was not unusual that he adapted it to andirons. In a different vein, one example is known which has the billet bar chamfered on the corners for about a foot back from the column. Extending the decoration further would have been useless for it would not have been

New hollowed pattern for top half of a hollow brass andiron. This procedure eliminated the use of a core and was very economical in the quantity of brass used.

Brass andirons of the first half of the eighteenth century. The billet bars, of course, are made of iron. The low bow of the legs and the penny feet suggest that the style was influenced by earlier examples of iron. *Courtesy Kindig Antiques*

seen, and it finally would have been impaired by the scaling effects of the fire on the iron. Another procedure was to make the legs of a separate piece of metal and fabricate a number of scrolls, which seem to evolve from the bar of which the legs were made.

Another advance, possibly simultaneous with other decorative treatments, was the use of brass in making andirons; this was a step toward the final and almost complete fabrication of andirons of brass. It is likely that brass was used sparingly at first, pieces being applied to iron. For example, in the 1692 inventory of Capt. Samuel Ruggles of Roxbury, Massachusetts, the following entry appears: "A pr. of small Cob-

irons brassed." A 1695 inventory of John Hayward, Merchant, of Roxbury, Massachusetts, lists "A pr. of brass andirons." Similar entries are found in other inventories. It is impossible to determine if these andirons were made in England or America. However, the scarcity of brass and the undeveloped brass industry at that time in America would suggest English production.

Before embarking on a discussion of brass andirons in the eighteenth century, it is important to give further consideration to those made of iron. The tall wrought-iron examples common in the kitchen were used throughout the colonies. A small chamber type seems to have been popular in New England, judging from the great number of surviving examples found there. Most of them were made completely of iron and consisted of three pieces of metal: a column, a billet bar, and a bowed piece forming two legs. The legs had small delicate circular feet, frequently called "penny feet." The columns terminated at the top in a variety of shapes, such as balls, scrolls, or faceted cubes. They were about eighteen inches high, and the length of the billet bar was suited to the shallow chamber of the fireplaces in which they were used. Some examples have simple finials of brass, which the blacksmith probably bought from a nearby brass founder or from a "city" hardware store.

In the first half of the century some rather elegant baluster types were made of iron; they have a round shaft with a bulbous section near the base of the column. These were either turned on a lathe or forged by a clever blacksmith. The balance of the andiron consisted of conventional parts of the period, but they usually have turned finials, possibly done by a whitesmith who specialized in turning and polishing metal parts. This style is very attractive and rarely comes upon the market today; however, ones with a flat column and an enlarged section near the base of the column are reasonably easy to obtain. Most of the latter type show evidence of having been forged by a blacksmith. They invariably have brass finials and may have a flat plate of brass at the

Brass andirons of the third quarter of the eighteenth century, believed to have been made in New York. The legs are unusually heavy and clumsily attached to a heavy plate under the plinth, which is very short. The faceted cube (sometimes called a diamond) and the flame finial are attractive parts of the elegant columns. Andirons of this style are very rare. *Courtesy Quentin Bowers* base of the column which conceals the riveted joint of the billet bar with the column. A number of this type, called "knife-blade" andirons, have the initials "I. C." stamped on the brass plate, and their occurrence here suggests that they were made by an unidentified American craftsman. The shape of the finials on these andirons suggest that they were made throughout most of the eighteenth century.

The substitution of brass for iron in andirons was attended by some important changes in the technology of their manufacture. As a matter of fact, the replacement never was complete, for the writer has never seen a billet bar made of any metal other than iron. It is evident that the first step toward creating an all-brass andiron was to make a brass finial, or face one with brass. The result proved to be so attractive and popular that the next logical move was to use more brass in the making of the column. One has been called to the writer's attention which has a brass finial and brass legs with a column of iron. In most cases the finial was enlarged to form a part of the column, with the result that the column became half brass and half iron.

A number of reasons could be advanced for the penurious use of brass. The advertisements of the founders indicate that brass was a scarce commodity, and every bit of scrap metal had value to a brass founder. This scarcity promoted the habit of using it sparingly. It is also known that blacksmiths outnumbered other metal craftsmen; for this reason one might logically conclude that their products were inexpensive and reasonably easy to obtain. It is also known that styles changed slowly and no one was apt to discard a pair of good iron andirons for ones made of brass. Finally, houses were a primitive type in the first half of the eighteenth century, and for most of the people iron andirons were considered a luxury rather than an eyesore to be replaced by a more glamorous accessory.

There could have been, however, a deeper motive underlying the slow transition from iron to brass. Those of iron were made by a smith who rarely, if ever, made two pairs alike. The lack of identical pairs

Photostat of a bill rendered by Daniel King to John Cadwalader for a variety of his products. The most important item is "fier Dogs With Corinthen coloms." The final item, three pounds of rotten stone, was for polishing the brass objects. *Courtesy Historical Society of Pennsylvania*

1770 John Cadwalater Esqr to Dand King Dr

Sepr 4th to a Large Brass knocker of the new Conseruation — 1 - 14 - 0
         to a Scugin & Drop for the frunt Door 3/6 — 0 - 3 - 6
         to 8 Dove tale hinges at 25/ Each — 10 - 0 - 0
         to 4 hinges for Blank Door at 15/ Each — 3 - 0 - 0
         to 2 Scugings & Drops for the Blank Door 0 - 7 - 6
         to one Pare of the Best Rote fier Dogs

With Crinthen Coloms £25 — 25 - 0 - 0
         to a Pare of the Best fluted Do With
Cunter fluts £10 — 10 - 0 - 0
         to one Pare Do Plane fluted £9 — 9 - 0 - 0
         to one Pare of the Best Plane Chamber Dogs - 6 - 0 - 0
         to one Pare of Chamber Dogs £5 — 5 - 0 - 0
         to one Park of Chamber Dogs £4 — 4 - 0 - 0
         to 3 Pare of the Best Brass tongs & Shovel
                  at £2 - 10 pr Pare — 7 - 10 - 0
         to 3 Pars of tongs & Shovel With Stell Legs
                  at £2 - 10 pr Pare — 7 - 10 - 0
         to 3 Pound of Roting Stone at 2/6 pr Pound 0 - 7 - 6
                                          £89 - 12 - 6

              Cash Recd £45 — 45 - - -
                        Ball: due £ 44 - 12 - 6

Recd 13th Novem: 1770 of John Cadwalader
forty four Pounds 12/6 in full of the
above acct   pr me Dand King

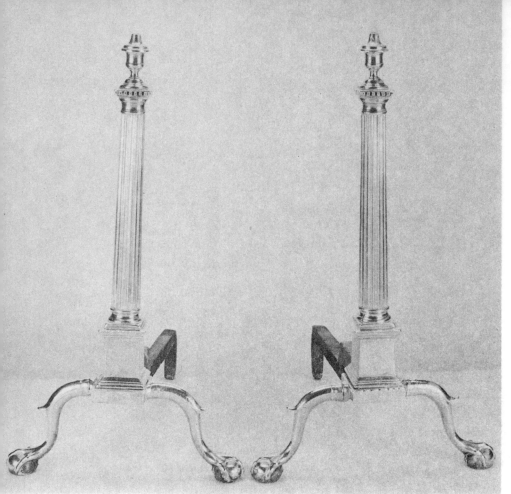

Brass andirons made and signed by Daniel King of Philadelphia, Pennsylvania. These are an example of the "Corinthen colom" [Corinthian column] type he made for John Cadwalader. They are made of many parts fastened together. The plinth has a skirt around its edge to which the legs are attractively fastened. There is a single small spur below the knee. The signature is on the plate at the top of the column. *Courtesy Henry Francis du Pont Winterthur Museum*

in the furnishings of the period suggests that people preferred unique custom-made objects, and encouraged craftsmen to follow such a procedure. The word probably got around that a pattern was used to cast andirons of brass, which meant that an endless number of duplicate pairs could be made. It would have been obviously wasteful to make a pattern and discard it after casting only one pair. Some variation in details could be introduced by the craftsman as he turned them on the lathe, but such work had limitations, and some craftsmen might not have tried to vary their products in such a way. But the pattern maker knew that there was finality and permanence in the pattern which he made, and in most cases his design and workmanship are commendable, particularly when compared to similar pursuits in the nineteenth century.

It is likely that by mid-century andirons with brass columns and legs were being made, although no examples known to the writer can be attributed to a particular American craftsman working in the period. Brass founding, like most other metalworking trades, was the responsibility of men; however, the earliest advertisement mentioning andirons found in making this survey is that of a woman. It is very possible that her husband had been a brass founder and, with the assistance of apprentices and journeymen, she was able to carry on the work. Her advertisement appeared in the *Boston Gazette* in 1736.

> Braziers' Wares.— Mary Jackson, at the Brazen-head, in Cornhill, makes and sells all sorts of Brass and Founders Ware, as Hearths, Fenders, Shovels and Tongs, Hand-irons, Candlesticks, Brasses for Chaises and Saddles, of the newest Fashion; all sorts of Mill Brasses; Mortars, Cocks, large and small; all sorts of polished Brazier's Ware, at reasonable rates. A quantity of Large brown Paper fit for sheathing ships, to be sold: Likewise buys old Copper, Brass, Pewter, Lead, and Iron.

Considering the scarcity of brass and the production problems involved in making andirons, one would naturally expect that those of the first half of the eighteenth century were small and simply styled.

Brass andirons made and signed by J. Davis, Boston, Massachusetts, who probably made them in the last decade of the eighteenth century. The style is usually called "steeple-top," and was made by a number of craftsmen who worked in that area. The name is stamped in block letters on the brass plate on the top of the billet bar, and to the rear of the small brass log stops. The design and workmanship of these andirons is of good quality. *Kauffman collection*

The brass portions of the andirons were made in separate parts, the legs (one or two parts), the plinth, the column, and the finial. Possibly the most striking element of design was the low arch of the legs. This shape was doubtless a carry-over from the style of some earlier models of iron. As furniture styles seem to have slowly invaded the area of andirons, the legs became more bowed until they resembled the cabriole legs used on furniture.

The legs and billet bar were held together by the inner shaft of iron, which rose through the assembly and held the entire unit together. A hollow square plinth was mounted on top of the legs, a turned column was placed above this, and a finial topped the whole assembly. The earliest brass andirons were held together by turning a rivet on top of the inner bar, and over the finial. Close inspection of the various parts reveals that the plinth, column, and finial were cast in halves and

Pair of brass andirons signed by T. Brooks who worked in Philadelphia, Pennsylvania, in the last decade of the eighteenth century. This is the only pair known to the writer which is signed on the plate holding the plinth. The rings around the legs next to the plinth suggest production in the Philadelphia area. *Courtesy Quentin Bowers*

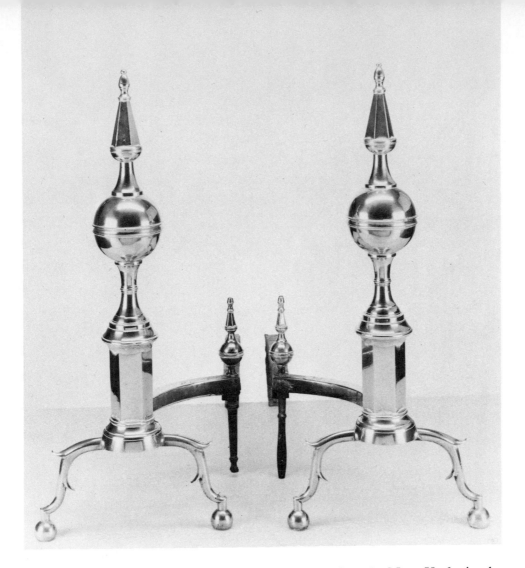

"Right and left" brass andirons made by R. Wittingham in New York, in the early nineteenth century. S-scrolled legs with "spurs" on the ball feet support six-sided plinths. The ball and cone on the top of the column suggest they are of the "steeple-top" style. "R WITTINGHAM / N. York" is stamped on the back panel of each plinth. *Courtesy Henry Francis du Pont Winterthur Museum*

soldered together with spelter, a substance similar to the silver solder used today. The heated joints were kept clean by a flux, the cleaned surfaces being evident on some andirons after two hundred years of exposure.

After mid-century, economic and technological changes occurred which affected the style of brass andirons. A more affluent society built more extravagant houses, which required new and larger styles in andirons. The legs became true cabriole types with spurs and penny feet. Plinths became massive, columns became tall and round, and finials were shaped like acorns, lemons, or flames. The simultaneous appear-

ance of ball and claw feet tended to emphasize the fact that the age of Chippendale had arrived.

The advent of the Chippendale style created a unique relationship between furniture and andirons. Cabriole legs with ball and claw feet have been mentioned, but other similarities appeared. Hairy feet so rarely found on furniture were repeated on the feet of andirons. A pointed tab was cast on the knees of some legs, while others have a series of rings at the point where the knees join the base of the plinth. The pedestal of Philadelphia tea tables has a plain area at the bottom comparable to the plinth, both have a turned ball above the plinth, and there is similarity in the style and proportions of the pedestal and the column. On the turned balls of some tables are swirled reeds which can also be found on andirons. The andirons with swirled reeds on the ball also have a faceted cube topped with a twisted flame. The profusion of details on the finest Chippendale andirons is comparable to the best used on the furniture of the period.

About 1770, a new architectural style—called "Adam" or "Classical" —was brought to the attention of architects and craftsmen in England and America by the Adam brothers. In this new concept there was an attentuation of forms which was adapted to mantels, furniture, andirons, and so forth. The tall column of the Chippendale era was made more slender, it was either round or square with fluting or reeding, and it was often topped with an urn which became the bench mark of a piece made in the Classical era.

The documented proof of the existence of this Classical style in America is found in the bill which Daniel King, a famous Philadelphia brass founder, rendered to John Cadwalader of the same city on September 4, 1770. The invoice lists among other objects sold to Cadwalader, "one Pare of the Best Rote fier Dogs With Corinthen Coloms, £25." The sum of £25 for one pair of andirons seems exhorbitant today. It is quite evident that Cadwalader wanted the best in andirons. (He paid the cabinet maker, Thomas Affleck, only £10 each for his great sofa and mahogany desk.)

A typical pair of brass andirons made by Hunneman of Boston, Massachusetts, and a set of fire tools with matching finials, marked "Boston." It is very likely that Hunneman also made the fire tools. *Courtesy Teina Baumstone*

These tall andirons are very attractive and quite practical for use in the fireplaces of the eighteenth century, some of which were as tall as wide. (A great height of fireplace was needed to clear the andirons with the logs as they were placed upon the fire.) Wide acceptance of the tall andirons is attested by the fact that they continued to be used in the later Federal period, usually fitted with an urn finial, as previously mentioned. John Bailey, a brass founder of New York City used such a design on his bill-head dated 1792, and Richard Wittingham is also known to have made some of this style during the last decade of the eighteenth century.

Styles inevitably change, however, and the trend toward lower lintels and smaller fireplaces created a demand for shorter andirons, unfortunately, of a less graceful style. In New England (principally Boston) the plinth became longer and assumed a circular or hexagonal shape, sometimes bowed at the sides like a tall slender barrel. Ball, lemon, and steeple finials became popular. Legs retained their cabriole form and were supported by Dutch (snake) feet matching the style of contemporary firescreens, tea tables, and candlestands. The base plate, on which the earlier plinths were set and held in position by pins, disappeared and the plinth rested on the knee of the legs. The fact that a number of brass founders stamped their names on their products has made the task of identifying the period and place where they worked easier. Andirons with makers' names were produced principally in Boston and New York, with the exception of Thomas Brooks of Philadelphia, William Webb in Warren, Maine, Barnabas Edmands at Charlestown, Massachusetts, the firm of Noyes & Cummings in Salem, Massachusetts, and Charles Weir of Baltimore.

A new design of the Federal period, a double lemon pattern mounted on reasonably high andirons, is associated with men who worked in New York City. A ball and steeple design similar to the Boston pattern was also used there. Cabriole legs had no ornament at the knee near the plinth, and the plinth base rested on the knees of the legs as previously described. Legs had as many as three spurs, and feet were generally small brass balls cast as an integral part of the leg. Here, as in Boston, a few founders marked their andirons with their name and city (John Bailey omitted "New York").

Since there frequently were no brass log stops except in the case of

Typical pair of brass Empire andirons which were made in many sizes, very very small to very large. *Courtesy Bradley Antiques*

right and left designs, there was no brass plate on the top of the billet bar, and the maker stamped his name on the back of the plinth. Of course, many unsigned examples have been found which can be attributed to certain makers, because of the similarities to a number of their products which they had signed.

By 1820 most of the famous makers of andirons had died, retired, or turned to other work. The Hunneman family continued, however, to make andirons of a turned column without feet, and topped with a single round ball. A second leg was obtained on the single-column type by curving the billet bar at the rear of the front column for about six

Pair of American cast-iron andirons, probably made between 1780 and 1820. Each column is in the form of a Hessian soldier in uniform facing right. Billet bar, rectangular in cross-section, is bent at right angle to form back leg. *Courtesy Henry Francis du Pont Winterthur Museum*

Pair of short cast-iron andirons similar to a pair illustrated on the trade card of Joseph Webb, a Boston, Massachusetts, iron merchant of the late eighteenth century. His trade card was engraved by Paul Revere. These diminutive figures are very charming. Only a few pairs of this type are known to the author. *Courtesy John P. Remensnyder*

inches, forming an intersection with the straight rear portion. A second foot was installed at the intersection. The third leg was formed by turning the back end of the billet bar downward to the hearth floor. The Hunnemans made examples in a more traditional pattern than those just described, but they became famous principally because they signed so many of their products.

Surviving examples of andirons from the nineteenth century suggest that their style continued to be influenced by fashions in furniture and architecture. The beautifully balanced elegance of the eighteenth century was lost. The mode of fabrication was improved, but this advance was not reflected in the quality of the finished product.

The last important form of brass andiron made in America, with a few exceptions, utilized a long cabriole-type leg terminating in a ball foot. On top of the thin legs was mounted a massive profusion of turnings with little character, seemingly much too heavy for their underpinning. These were made in different sizes ranging from 10 to 25 inches in height. Most of this style seem to have been cored for casting, and thus were cast in one piece. They were skimmed on the lathe in the traditional way, and given a high polish by using reasonably modern abrasive materials. This style is commonly known as Empire.

The great number of brass andirons surviving from the eighteenth and nineteenth centuries, and the scarcity of cast-iron ones suggests the ratio in which they were probably made. Comparing the quality of both types, there appears to have been little reason to make them of cast iron beyond the fact that some people preferred them, or could not afford to buy those of brass. Whatever the reason, it is evident that at least two patterns in cast iron were made, and curiously, both patterns were of human figures.

The best-known pattern is that of Hessian soldiers, presumably inspired by the mercenary troops brought here by the British in the American Revolution. These men seem to have struck a note of sympathy and are mentioned in a number of matters subsequent to the Revolution. The legs of the soldiers form the two front legs of the andirons, the turned-down back end of the billet bar providing the third leg. (A word of caution must be included here: It is very easy to make reproductions of cast-iron objects and the buyer should make sure of the age of his purchase.)

The second example of cast-iron andiron was sold (and possibly made) by Joseph Webb, a hardware merchant in Boston. At the top of his trade card is illustrated a short pair of andirons, the front column portraying a man dressed in a Colonial costume. The period of this example is known by the fact that Paul Revere engraved the trade card. The trade card also illustrates a variety of cooking utensils of the period which were made of cast iron.

Doubtless patterns other than these were made, but examples have not survived or have not been identified as products of this era.

Possibly the last distinctive type of andirons made in the nineteenth century in America were in the Victorian (Gothic) style. These were cast in iron from patterns of wood with a profusion of design elements typical of the period. At least one pair is known to have been made by a foundryman named Savery in New York. Doubtless many other examples of this era have survived.

Makers of Brass Andirons

Name	Location	Working Date
Allison, Peter	New York, N.Y.	1804
Bailey, John	New York, N.Y.	1778
Brooks, Thomas	Philadelphia, Pa.	1797
Carr, Robert	New York, N.Y.	1820
Clark, John	Boston, Mass.	1789
Davis, James	Boston, Mass.	1803
Edmands, Barnabas	Charlestown, Mass.	1799
Griffiths & Morgans	New York, N.Y.	1832
Hunneman, William C.	Boston, Mass.	1797
King, Daniel	Philadelphia, Pa.	1770
Molineux, John	Boston, Mass.	1806
Norton, T.	unknown	unknown
Noyes & Cummings	Salem, Mass.	unknown
Noyes, John	Bangor, Maine	unknown
Phillips, David	New York, N.Y.	1815
Smylie, F.	unknown	unknown
Stickney, John	Boston, Mass.	1820
Stimson, John	Boston, Mass.	1830

Tuston, W.	Philadelphia, Pa.	1811
Wallace, Robert	New York, N.Y.	1802
Webb, William Holmes	Warren, Maine	1799
Weir, Charles	Baltimore, Md.	1796
Wittingham, Richard	New York, N.Y.	1794

Advertisers Who Made Brass Andirons

Name	*Location*	*Working Date*
Baker, Joseph	New York, N.Y.	1801
Baxter, Isaac	Philadelphia, Pa.	1831
Belcher, Joseph	Newport, R.I.	unknown
Caustin, Isaac	Philadelphia, Pa.	1791
Geddy, David & William	Williamsburg, Pa.	1751
Gregory, Thomas	Philadelphia, Pa.	1819
Hedderly, Richard	Philadelphia, Pa.	1819
Jackson, Mary	Boston, Mass.	1736

Cast-iron andiron signed "Savery & Sons, N. Y." The company is known to have been in business in New York in the middle of the nineteenth century. The Victorian style of this andiron is very evident. *Courtesy Mr. and Mrs. Reginald French*

Kip, James	Fishkill, N.Y.	1782
Leaycraft, Richard	Fishkill, N.Y.	1793
Servoss, C. K.	Philadelphia, Pa.	1831
Smith, James	Philadelphia, Pa.	1753
Syng, Philip	Annapolis, Md.	1759
Wareham, John	New York, N.Y.	1793
Zane & Chapman	Philadelphia, Pa.	1792

Makers of Iron Andirons

Name	Location	Working Date
Ball, L.	unknown	unknown
C. I.	unknown	unknown
Crammer, H. D.	unknown	unknown
Starr, N.	Middletown, Conn.	1800
Steel, John	Philadelphia, Pa.	1818
Turle, I.	unknown	unknown
Webb, Joseph *	Boston, Mass.	late 18th century

* Webb's products are identified from illustrations on his trade card.

Accessories

BELLOWS

These devices are for creating a draft by producing a stream of air under pressure, particularly convenient when a fire is being started. Their form and function were completely established as early as the sixteenth century; since then they have undergone little change. The earliest types were up to 24 inches in length and were not decorated. In the eighteenth century some were carved, while others were overlaid with sheets of metal. In the nineteenth century many were painted, and a parlor type were decorated with arrangements of leaves and flowers. On some of the latter type, the name of the American manufacturer is stamped on the flap of leather attached to the inner side of the bottom board.

The parts of a bellows are: the boards, the head, the nozzle, two bows, and leather. Two boards make up the main part of the device. They are attached in the form of a "V" to the head, into which the nozzle is inserted. Special large-headed nails are used to fasten the leather to the two boards so as to form an air chamber between them. The bows are made of hazel twigs, which keep the leather taut. A hinged flap within the air chamber covers a hole in the bottom board. This flap acts as a valve, permitting air to enter but not to escape, the only egress being through the nozzle.

BRAZIER

A brazier is a small circular or square metal pan, used on the hearth for holding coals or charcoal over which to cook or heat small quantities of food or drink. Examples are known having a bowl of copper, while others have a square arrangement. Because of their small size and

Bellows, "fancy and common," were important commodities to advertise as late as June 11, 1830, in the New Holland (Lancaster County), Pennsylvania, *Anti-Masonic Herald*.

Brazier with pan made of copper and with legs of iron. Such articles obviously served as small stoves, possibly in a bedroom fireplace or in a military camp. *Courtesy The Metropolitan Museum of Art, gift of Mrs. Robert W. de Forest, 1931*

great utility they have been on occasion called "camp stoves." Both types are mounted on legs of wrought iron, and both usually have handles.

BROILER

An appliance used on the hearth to prepare meat by scorching its outer surfaces. It consists of two gridirons about 10 inches square mounted in a vertical position. One of the gridirons is hinged to the stand so that it can be lowered for installing or removing meat. These objects were probably never very plentiful, and they are quite rare today.

Broiler for preparing meat before the fire on the hearth. This one was formed by the traditional forging techniques of the blacksmith in the eighteenth or early nineteenth century. *Courtesy Bucks County (Pennsylvania) Historical Society*

CANDLE BOX

A cylindrical container about fifteen inches long with a diameter of four inches. Examples made of sheet iron or tinplate have a hinged lid and two straps attached to the back of the cylinder for hanging on nails on the face of the chimney jamb. Some American examples are decorated by a punching technique similar to the one used on coffee pots, chandeliers, lamps, etc. European examples were sometimes made of sheet brass and decorated by the repoussé technique.

A cylindrical box for candle storage is mounted on the wall above the right end of the fireplace in the dining room of the Vermont House, at Shelburne Museum, Shelburne, Vermont. These were an essential part of every household; however, they were most frequently found at a kitchen fireplace. *Courtesy Shelburne Museum*

Rectangular wooden candle boxes were also used. Most of them are beautifully proportioned and some are attractively decorated.

CALDRON

A very old type of cooking pot used on the hearth for preparing stews, etc. American examples are very rare, but usually can be identified because many times the founder cast his name on the top side of the handle. Most examples are made of bronze or brass. They stand on three short legs which are cast as an integral part of the vessel. Probably none were cast after the eighteenth century.

CHIMNEY CRANE

A bracket of iron installed in the corner of a kitchen fireplace from which pots and kettles were suspended over the fire. It could also be swung over the hearth so that utensils could be removed without the housewife being dangerously near the fire.

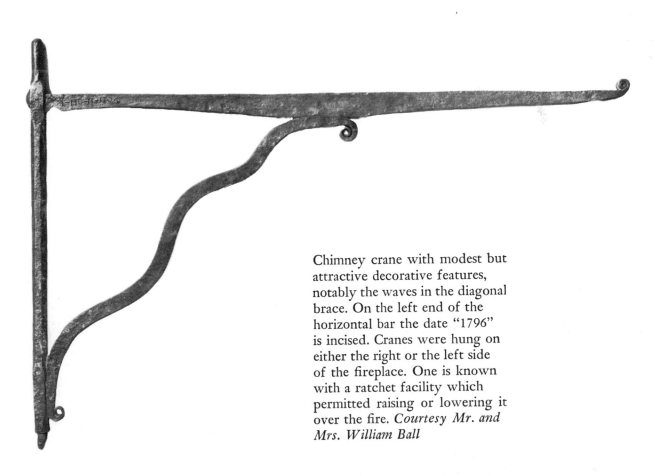

Chimney crane with modest but attractive decorative features, notably the waves in the diagonal brace. On the left end of the horizontal bar the date "1796" is incised. Cranes were hung on either the right or the left side of the fireplace. One is known with a ratchet facility which permitted raising or lowering it over the fire. *Courtesy Mr. and Mrs. William Ball*

They were forged of wrought iron by a blacksmith. A long arm was welded to a short one with a diagonal brace between them for reinforcment. The short bar had rounded ends which were fitted into eyes held firmly in the masonry wall of the fireplace. Parts were sometimes ornamented by twisting or adding scrolls.

COAL CONTAINERS

These articles were used extensively and for a long period of time in England, where coal was first widely used in fireplaces in the sixteenth century. Because of hard usage, very few old ones have survived; however, reproductions are plentiful. A very small number of American examples exist which were made by Hunneman, a coppersmith working in Boston in the late eighteenth century. His products are deep cylindrical containers, standing on end, with a handle or bail on the top. A few attractive examples were made for railroad use in the nineteenth century.

CREEPERS

Miniature andirons used between large andirons, usually repeating the design of the larger. They kept parts of large partially burned timbers from dropping onto the hearth, thus increasing the draft for the fire. Examples are very rare today. (A pair is illustrated in the chapter on andirons.)

Brass curfew highly ornamented with repoussé designs of the seventeenth or eighteenth century. Originally there was a handle on the top surface to lift it from the smouldering coals. *Courtesy Rowland Antiques*

CURFEW

A quarter-sphere of metal or ceramic material used to cover a small quantity of coals to keep them alive overnight. Metal ones are known to have been made of copper or brass; however, examples of any material are scarce. The custom of clearing the streets of a town or city at the time when the fires were banked accounts for the use of the word for that social practice.

DOWN-HEARTH

Now commonly called the hearth. Usually this area on the floor of the fireplace was made of a fire-resistant substance, such as bricks, tiles, or stones, and rarely raised slightly above the level of the floor. Most American fireplaces have hearths built even with the floor.

FENDER

The earliest fenders were simply bent pieces of sheet iron, placed on the edge of the hearth, to prevent live coals from rolling off the hearth onto the wooden floor. The decorative quality of these objects was soon established and many were polished, blackened, or painted, depending on the taste of the purchaser and the decor of the room in which they were to be used.

In the eighteenth century, after brass founding was developed into a stable industry, a number of attractive fenders were cast in brass. A solid band of metal provided a firm edge at the top and bottom of the band, while an inner panel was decorated with appropriate motifs. These were shaped in the form of a long bow to keep them upright on their edge. These cast bands of brass were mounted on flat heavy sheets of metal to increase the stability of the fender.

Advances in the metal technology of the nineteenth century made possible another mode of producing fenders of brass or steel. The metals could then be rolled into thin sheets, after which a pattern was laid out to be punched on a fly-press. Dies were prepared in exactly the shape and size of the desired openings. These were installed in a press with a long vertical spindle, on top of which was a handle (horizontal) with a heavy ball on each end. The sheet metal was inserted

This fender is made of brass wire and rods instead of sheet or cast metal. The earlier serpentine form has been dropped for the straight front and ends turned inward to keep it in an upright position. Late eighteenth or early nineteenth century. *Courtesy Metropolitan Museum of Art*

between the two parted dies, the heavy handle spun, and the meshing dies removed small bits of metal. This procedure was repeated until the entire design was created. The slightly distorted sheet was then levelled with a hammer, after which it was polished with sand on a leather-covered wheel. The upper and lower edges were made rigid by riveting a bar to them. The ends were turned inward to keep the form erect, and sometimes feet were added to make them more stable and attractive.

FIRE BACK

The rapid deterioration of masonry walls in the back of the fireplace required that a protective sheet of iron be placed there, which added a decorative as well as a functional quality to the fireplace. They were first used in England in the seventeenth century and some quite early American examples are known to have survived.

Interest in them is heightened by knowing just how they were made. Patterns of wood were carved, the earliest ones having only a simple molding around the edge. They were then pressed into the bed of sand before the iron furnace; and molten metal was allowed to flow into this prepared cavity. Some early examples were decorated by pressing objects into the sand which were not part of the pattern. Later, attractive designs were carved on the pattern itself, from which very elegant fire backs were made.

They were always an evidence of luxury, and very few American examples have survived. They were used principally in New England and Virginia, but rarely in Pennsylvania.

Fire back cast at Aetna Furnace, Burlington County, New Jersey, about 1775. The bottom portion shows some deterioration from the fire, while the top is virtually intact and perfect. *Courtesy Metropolitan Museum of Art, Rogers Fund, 1936*

FIRE CARRIER

These rectangular boxes of sheet iron were possibly six by six inches and ten inches long. On one end was a hinged lid for filling and emptying live coals, on the other end a handle for carrying. Because of the difficulty in lighting a fire before the time of matches, such boxes were used to carry hot coals from one fireplace to another.

Fire carrier of sheet iron. This one is simply made and has holes in the lid for ventilating the live coals. *Kauffman collection*

FIRE BOARD

The function of this device was to conceal the fireplace chamber when not in use, to prevent drafts from the chimney, to keep soot from blowing onto rugs and furniture, and even to prevent the possibility of birds entering a room. These were in service before dampers became generally used to close the chimney flue. They were fitted snugly into the framework of the mantelpiece. Some were painted and decorated with an intent to make an esthetic addition to the decor of the room.

FIRE SCREEN

An ancient device which stood between the fire and a person seated near the fireplace to minimize draft and the glow of flickering flames. The base of a pole screen resembled that of a tea table, having three legs, an ornamental pedestal, a turned pole, and a shield.

Their importance warranted the craftsmen of the eighteenth century to lavish their finest skills on them. They were frequently made of mahogany; the pedestals and feet were sometimes profusely carved, a

Fire board, neatly paneled and fitted into a fireplace of the early nineteenth century. The house in which it is located is in Sumneytown, Pennsylvania. *Courtesy Mr. and Mrs. John Hoy*

few having ball-and-claw hairy-paw feet. The latter detail is considered the apogee of workmanship in the trade of cabinetmaking.

The shields were covered with a variety of textiles, such as patterned silk, plain fabric with crewel work, and silk-and-metal brocade.

FIRE TOOLS

In the earliest times fire tools were very simple and functional, made completely of iron. They consisted of tongs, shovel, and brushes; however, virtually no old brushes have survived. The later fire tools were also made of iron, but had brass "knobs" or handles. Philip Syng, a brass founder from Philadelphia who relocated in Annapolis, Maryland, advertised in the *Maryland Gazette* that he "Makes (or Repairs) all Sorts of Brass-Work, such as Candlesticks, Heads or Knobs of all Sizes for Shovels, Dogs, etc." These brass fittings sometimes matched the designs used for the finials of andirons. The most desirable shovels have a "key-hole" shape and are much rarer than later models with a rectangular form. Although American craftsmen advertised the fact that they made fire tools, only a few bear the name of the craftsman who made them.

Brass-knobbed fire tools of the eighteenth century. The style of these is particularly pleasing. *Courtesy Schiffer Antiques*

FOOTMAN

A four-legged stand of brass or iron with two straight legs and two cabriole legs. About fifteen inches high, they stood before the fireplace on the hearth to hold an object, such as a copper teakettle, when it was not in use.

GRATE

A framework of bars, parallel to or angled toward each other for holding coal. The grates for fireplaces were first used in Europe, probably in England, because of the scarcity and high cost of wood. Although a grate can be used for burning either coal or wood, the fuel most often burned was coal.

The first ones were naturally experimental and were formed of wrought iron in the shape of a basket by a blacksmith. These baskets were supported on the billet bars of andirons. A transitional style utilized the front columns of andirons, but otherwise stood on back legs to keep the whole grate off the hearth. Finally, any resemblance to andirons disappeared, and massive grates of cast iron replaced the earlier examples. Small openings were made for grates instead of the earlier large fireplaces, or the edges around the grates were filled in with masonry or metal plates.

Combination grate and andiron assembly installed in a fireplace of the late eighteenth or early nineteenth century. The mantel is by McIntire and Lemon. *Courtesy Museum of Fine Arts, Boston, Massachusetts*

GRIDDLE

A heavy plate of cast iron, usually round, supported by a half-round handle with a loop for suspension from a crane or a chimney bar. They were used for frying foods, particularly pancakes (griddle cakes) over a hearth fire. A few have short legs.

GRIDIRON

A low framework of wrought or cast iron, mounted on short legs, and used on the hearth in a horizontal position to prepare food over

Cast-iron griddles, probably of the nineteenth century. The one with the legs stood on the hearth, the one with a ring hung from a pot hook or a crane. *Courtesy Bucks County (Pennsylvania) Historical Society*

glowing coals—really a horizontal broiler. Most of them have a handle for convenient use. A late type had channeled grids which carried the fat to a main trough from which it could be emptied.

JAMB HOOK

A small hook or open loop, attached to the frame of wood around the fireplace opening, to support standing fireplace tools. Considerable variety exists among the earliest type for they were individually forged from iron by a blacksmith. Of course, they were made in reasonably identical pairs. Later examples were made of cast brass. A few jamb hooks have finials which match those of fire tools and andirons.

Crudely forged gridiron with channels in the grids to carry the fat to the trough at the low end. Signed "B B" and dated "1822."

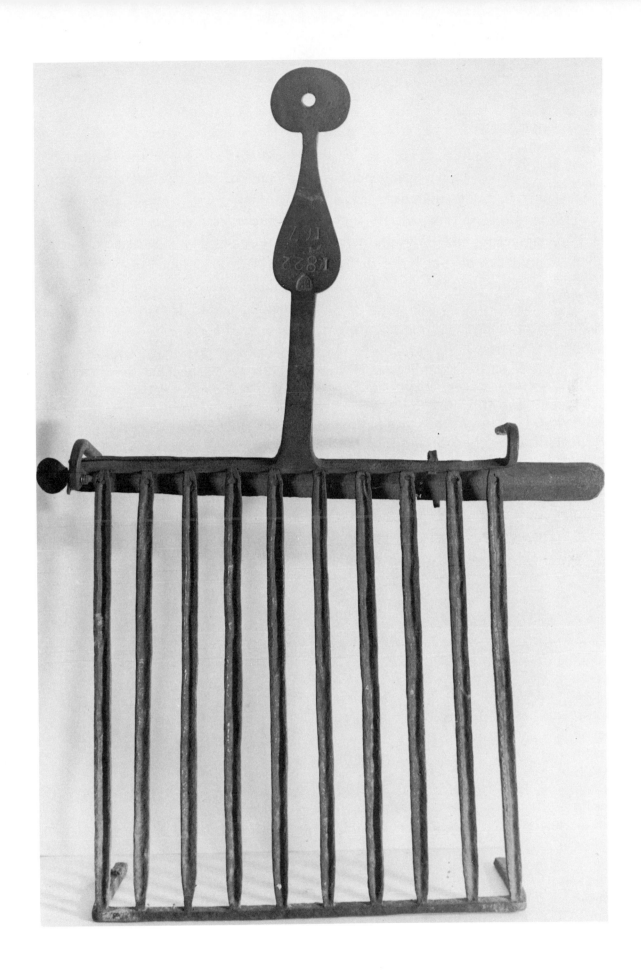

KETTLE

A container in a variety of shapes and sizes for use at the fireplace. These vessels were suspended from a crane or chimney bar above the fire by using trammels or pot hooks. Many were made of cast iron in the blast furnaces and foundries of the eastern seacoast in the late eighteenth and early nineteenth centuries. A few have the name of the producer on the outer surface. A considerable number of teakettles were made of cast iron. Most of these objects were heavy and required considerable heat to bring food to a boiling point. They also retained heat a long time after they were removed from the fire.

Cast-iron kettle with the makers' names, "Sampson & Tisdale," and "New York" on the side. They are listed as foundrymen in New York City in the first half of the nineteenth century. *Kauffman collection*

Cast-iron teakettle made by J. Savery & Son, 113 Beekman Street, New York City, in the first half of the nineteenth century. Although cast-iron teakettles are not very rare, few can be identified as positively as this one. *Courtesy Shelburne Museum, Shelburne, Vermont*

Two copper teakettles by Pennsylvania craftsmen showing the range of sizes in which they were made. The larger one is signed by John Getz, the small one is unsigned. *McMurtrie collection; courtesy The Magazine Antiques*

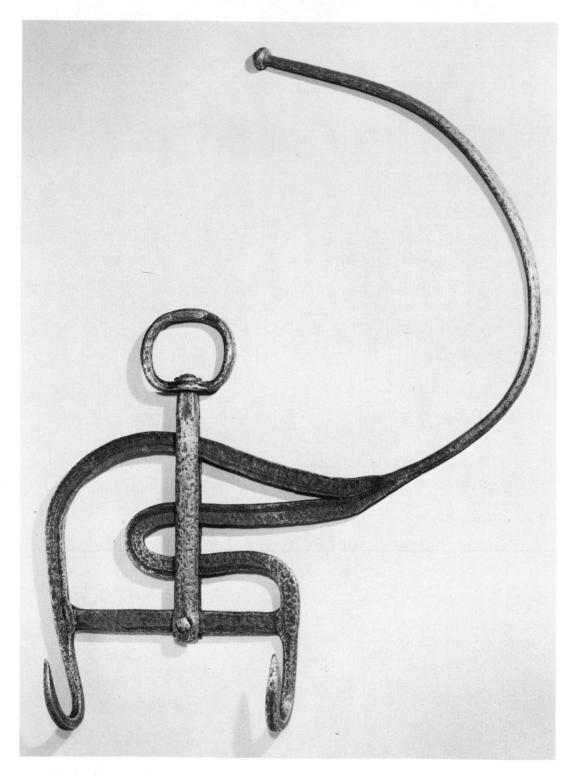

Kettle tilter used to tilt a heavy iron teakettle without removing it from its support in the fireplace. The handle of the teakettle was supported by the two hooks at the bottom of the tilter. *Courtesy Mr. and Mrs. James A. Keillor*

Probably the most attractive kettles were teakettles made of copper or brass (extremely few were made of brass). They were made principally by coppersmiths working in Pennsylvania, and by a few craftsmen working in various localities from Virginia, through New York, and into New England. Some craftsmen imprinted their names on the top surface of the handle.

KETTLE-TILTER

A pivoting device used for tilting a heavy teakettle without removing it from the crane. This device not only saved lifting the heavy kettle, but also provided a clean, cool handle for tilting. Most examples are made of a number of parts; however, some teakettles are fitted with a bar attached between the handle and the spout, a substitute arrangement for tilting which is quite simple and functional.

PIPE RACK

A device consisting of three rings of iron about four inches in diameter, connected by two or three horizontal bars, with legs on the bottom and a ring handle on the top. The exact use of this piece of equipment is not known precisely, but it is frequently mentioned as an accessory for the hearth.

PLATE WARMER

Two types of plate warmers were used on the hearth before the fire. One had a three-legged base with a platform on which four vertical prongs were installed to hold a stack of plates for warming. The other type closely resembled a vertical tin oven with a semicircular body, open on one side, and mounted on iron legs. Some of the latter type were painted and decorated.

POTHOOK

A chain with a hook on the end for suspending a pot over the fire at a desired level. One end of the chain was attached to the crane or chimney bar; the other end had a double-ended hook which held the pot and could be hooked into any link to provide the needed level.

POSNETS

Cast bronze or brass skillets, called "posnets," were widely used in Europe in the sixteenth and seventeenth centuries. The opening was greater in diameter, to make the inside more accessible, than in the earlier caldrons and they were mounted on three short legs. They have straight tapering handles with the name of the maker frequently cast into the top surface, and sometimes a date.

A later type was made of iron by the blacksmith, a few of which also bear the name of the maker.

Cast-iron posnet or skillet by John Taylor, Richmond, Virginia, about 1793. This is of an earlier European form, not frequently made and signed by American craftsmen. Their heavy weight suggests that they were used for simmering food on the hearth rather than for regular cooking purposes. *Courtesy Old Salem, Inc., Winston-Salem, North Carolina*

Iron skillet on three legs, made by a blacksmith named G. W. Ibach. The number of these found in Pennsylvania suggest that they were made there. It is a common form, but signed examples are rare. *Kauffman collection*

SKEWER

A large pinlike object used to fasten meat to a spit. Although these usually lack any outstanding quality, the holders from which they were suspended when not in use are often very attractive and eagerly sought by antiquarians.

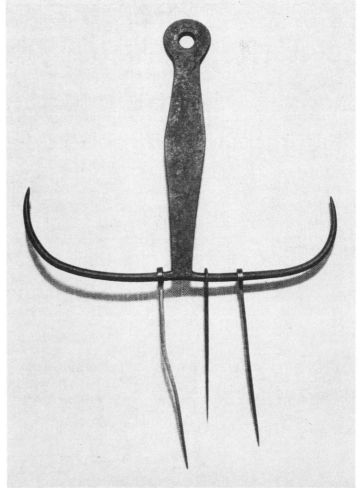

Skewer holder with three skewers. The holder was usually placed near the fireplace where unused skewers could be easily stored. They were forged of iron by a blacksmith. *Courtesy Bucks County (Pennsylvania) Historical Society*

SPIT

Sharp rods of wood or metal used for piercing a piece of meat for roasting. Many kinds of spits were used in the seventeenth and eighteenth centuries, the most common being a long rod of metal which was suspended from the spit hooks of the andirons. Near the center of these rods a portion was often flattened, through which holes were punched so that skewers could go through the meat and the spit, thereby holding the roast firmly in place as it rotated before the fire. Another arrangement was to affix to the main spit small parallel bars which gripped the meat and prevented it from slipping.

Spits were made to rotate by a number of methods; one was to have a slave or a small boy turn them by means of a handle on the end. Other spits had a grooved wheel on the end which was attached to a mechanical device by a belt. The most common apparatus used to spin the spit was a clocklike movement, mounted on the side of the fireplace, and activated by weights or a heavy stone suspended from it. This mechanism looks much like the one for a grandfather's clock, and it was wound with a key. There were also rotary dog treadmills, mounted on the wall above the spit, which utilized dogs trained particularly for such work.

Another device was the smoke-jack, also called "clock-jack" or "lazy-jack." This was a wind-wheel mounted in the chimney flue and rotated by the upward movement of hot air in the chimney. The importance of the smoke-jack is obvious from the description and illustrations of it found in Dobson's *Encyclopedia*, Philadelphia, 1798.

> *Smoke-Jack.* This ingenious machine is of German extraction; and Messinger, in his *Collection of Mechanical Performances*, says it is very ancient, being represented in a painting at Nurenberg, which is known to be older than the year 1350.
>
> Its construction is abundantly simple. An upright spindle GA (fig 5), placed in the narrow part of the kitchen chimney, turns round on two pivots H and I. The upper one H passes through an iron bar, which is built across the chimney: and the lower pivot I is of tempered steel, and is conical or pointed resting in a conical bell-metal socket fixed on another cross bar. On the upper end of the spindle is a circular fly G, consisting of 4, 6, 8, or more iron plates, set obliquely on the spindle like the sails on a windmill, as

Steam-jack for turning spits on the hearth, invented by John Bailey of New York City in 1792–93. It was advertised in the newspapers of New York and was exhibited there in Baker's New Museum. Steam was generated in the container on the left and transferred through a series of gears to a rotary motion. The disc with the two slots motivated the spit. *Courtesy John P. Remensnyder*

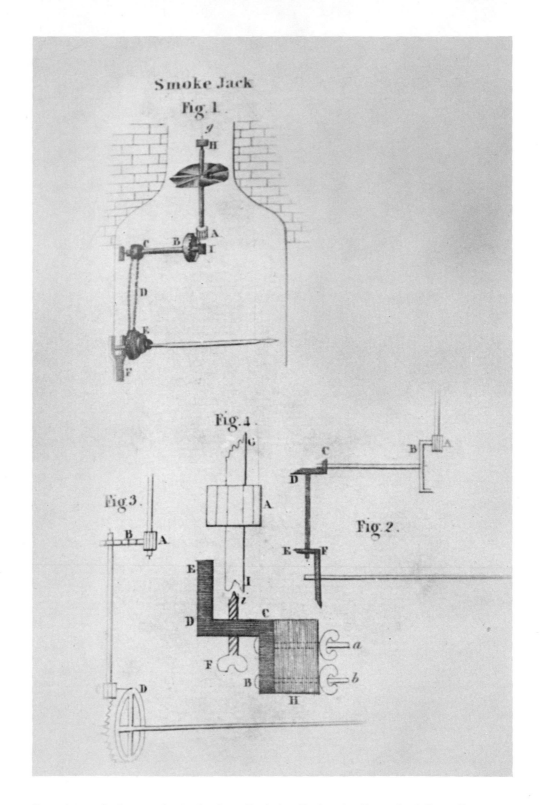

Drawing of the smoke-jack described in *Dobson's Encyclopedia*. The technologists of the time seem to have taken such delight in making the function of a reasonably simple mechanism sound very complicated.

we shall describe more particularly by and by. Near the lower end of the spindle is a pinion A, which works in the teeth of a contrate or face wheel B, turning on a horizontal axis BC. One pivot of this axis turns in a cock fixed on the cross bar, which supports the lower end of the upright spindle HI, and the other pivot turns in a cock fixed on the side wall of the chimney; so this axle is parallel to the front of the chimney. On the remote end of this horizontal axle there is a small pulley C, having a deep angular groove. Over this pulley there passes a chain CDE, in the lower bight of which hangs the large pulley E of the spit. This end of the spit turns loosely between the branches of the fork of the rack F, but without resting on it. This is on the top of a moveable stand, which can be shifted nearer to or farther from the fire. The other end turns in one of the notches of another rack. The number of teeth in the pinion A and the wheel B, and the diameters of the pulleys C and E, are so proportioned that the fly G makes from 12 to 20 turns for one turn of the spit.

The manner of operation of this useful machine is easily understood. The air which contributed to the burning of the fuel, and passes through the midst of it, is greatly heated, and expanded prodigiously in bulk, becomes lighter than the neighboring air, and is therefore pushed up the chimney. In like manner all the air which comes near the fire is heated, expanded, becomes lighter and is driven up the chimney. This is called the *draught* or *suction*, but would with greater propriety be termed the drift of the chimney. As the chimney gradually contracts in its dimensions, and as the same quantity of heated air passes through every section of it, it is plain that the rapidity of its ascent must be greatest in the narrowest place. There the fly G should be placed, because it will there be exposed to the greatest current. The air striking the fly vanes obliquely, pushes them aside, and thus turns them round with a considerable force. If the joint of meat is exactly balanced on the spit, it is plain that the only resistance to the motion of the fly is what arises from the friction of the pivots of the upright spindle, the friction of the pinion and the wheel, the friction of the pivots of the horizontal axis, the friction of the small end of the spit, and the friction of the chain in the two pulleys. The whole of this is but a mere trifle. But there is frequently a considerable superiority in the weight of the meat on different sides of the spit; there must therefore be a sufficient overplus of force in the impulse of the ascending air on the vanes of the fly, to overcome this want of equilibrium occasioned by the unskillfulness or negligence of the cook. There is, however, commonly enough power when this machine is properly constructed. The utility of this machine will,

Clock-jack for turning spits, without its crank, chain, and weight. Its rotary mechanism was connected to a spit with a pulley to transfer the power from one device to the other. The holes in the brackets on the rear end were for attaching the jack to or over the heavy lintel used in kitchen fireplaces. *Courtesy Gertrude Weber*

we hope, procure us the indulgence of some of our readers, while we point the circumstances on which its performance depends, and the maxims which should be followed in its construction. . . .

With respect to the manner of applying this force (air and smoke), it is evident that the best construction of windmill sails will be nearly the best for the fly. According to the usual theory of impulse of fluids, the greatest effective impulse (that is, in the direction of the fly's motion) will be produced if the plane of the vane be inclined, to the axis in an angle of 54 degrees 46 minutes. But since we have pronounced this theory to be so very defective, we had better take a determination founded on the experiments on the impulse of fluids made by the academy of Paris. These authorize us to say, that 49½ or 50 degrees will be the best angle to give the vane; but this must be understood only of the part of it which is close adjoining the axis. The vane itself must be twisted, or *weathered* as the millwrights term it, and must be much more oblique at its outer extremity. . . .

It is easy to see that an increase of the surface of the vanes will increase power: therefore they should occupy the whole space of the circle, and not consist of four narrow arms like the sails of a windmill. It is better to make many narrow vanes than a few broad ones; as will appear plain to one well acquainted with the mode of impulse of fluids acting obliquely. . . .

Vertical rotating jack device used for roasting meat in the nineteenth century. The shell and framework above were expertly made of sheet tin. The door in the rear could be conveniently used to examine the progress of the roasting procedure. *Courtesy Schiffer Antiques*

It is an important question where the fly should be placed. If in a wide part of the vent, it will have a great surface, and act by a long lever; but the current in that place is slow, and the impulse weak. . . . It appears that it is of particular importance to place the fly in an elevated portion of the vent, where the area must be contracted. In order still farther to increase the power of the machine, it would very proper to lengthen the spindle still more, and to put another fly on it at a considerable distance above the first, and a third above this, etc.

In the eighteenth century there were also small stationary spits, mounted on short legs, with hooks on which small fowl or fruit were mounted to broil before the fire. These were attractively shaped by a blacksmith of iron and usually have survived in excellent condition. In the nineteenth century a clocklike mechanism was encased in a container from which dropped a chain or rope. This devise was suspended within a half-round form of sheet metal, standing vertically before the fire, and rotated the suspended meat as long as torque was supplied by the spring mechanism. The case around the rotating mechanism was often made of brass, and some have a plate bearing the maker's name.

Common form of toaster for slices of bread widely used in the eighteenth century. However, the arrangement was so successful that it continued in use into the nineteenth century. Most of them are made entirely of iron, and all of them are attractively decorated. *Courtesy Gertrude Weber*

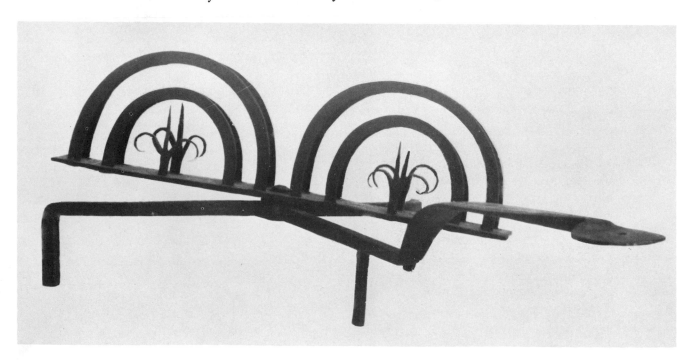

TOASTER

A variety of toaster forms exists, but most consist of a handle, with legs, on which is mounted a rotating bar, and several half-round loops to hold the pieces of bread in a vertical position. The rotating plate or bar permits the toaster to be swung 180 degrees, thus exposing each side of the bread.

A simpler form resembled a large fork with tines turned at a right angle to the long handle. To the tines were added upturned arms to hold the toast in a vertical position as it browned before the fire on the hearth.

TRIVET

Most old trivets were three-legged objects of wrought or cast iron on which utensils were supported over a bed of live coals on the hearth. It is unlikely that many of the seventeenth-century trivets have survived in America although a sizeable number of the eighteenth-century ones are found in museums and private collections. The earliest examples were made of wrought iron by blacksmiths. Many are round, others are triangular, while some are in fanciful shapes, such as hearts, stars, and the like. A few have long handles with a tang, fitted with a hand-grip of wood.

In the nineteenth century some were made of cast iron. A foundryman in Baltimore, named Rimby, made some very attractive ones with motifs

Iron trivet with three legs and a handle. The hole in the handle was used to hang it by the fireside when not in use. The joints were usually welded or riveted together. Virtually no trivets have been identified as products of American craftsmen. *Courtesy Bucks County (Pennsylvania) Historical Society*

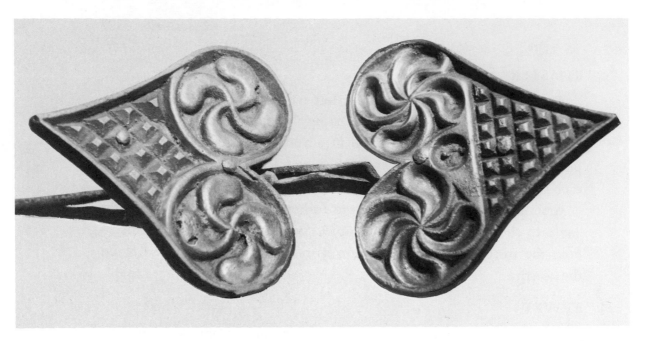

Waffle iron in the shape of a heart, consisting of two depressed cavities attached to two handles by rivets. One side was filled with batter which expanded while being baked to fill the second side. The designs were impressed on both sides. The mechanism of the handle worked like a pinchers or blacksmith's tongs. *Courtesy Mr. and Mrs. Walter Himmelreich*

of Pennsylvania folk art. The motifs were very thoughtfully interlaced with the result that his trivets were not only useful but also very attractive. In addition to his motifs, his products are also distinguished by the fact that some are signed and dated. Most of them were made in the 1840s.

WAFER IRON

Two heavy plates of metal, usually round or elliptical, and about three-eighths of an inch thick, were mounted on scissorlike handles. The thick dough, placed between the two slabs of metal, was baked until brittle, making the crisp cakelike wafers.

WAFFLE IRON

Waffles are batter-cakes baked in an enclosed waffle iron. The device consists of two shallow open-sided rectangular boxes, with the open sides facing each other. They, like the wafer iron, are mounted on scissorlike handles so the assemble could be open or closed. The cavity could be conveniently opened to put in batter, and then closed for baking.

Warming pans were used in England in the seventeenth century, the earliest type having iron handles and highly ornamented lids. They were also made in America in the eighteenth century. However, few examples can be attributed to production by a particular craftsman. This one is signed "I W" on the hinge but the name of the maker is not positively known. It has been tentatively attributed to Joshua Witherle, a coppersmith working in Boston, Massachusetts, late in the eighteenth century. The ornamentation on the lid is very simple when compared to other examples. *Kauffman collection*

WARMING PAN

A circular dish with a diameter of from 10 to 12 inches and a depth of about 4 inches. It had a slightly domed lid and a long handle. Although these warming pans did not function at the fireplace, they were filled with hot embers there and carried into a bedroom, where they were passed between sheets or blankets to reduce the chill before retiring.

Most of the seventeenth-century examples were made of brass, and have long handles of iron with a loop in the end for hanging. Holes were punched in the hinged lid, and some motifs formed by repoussé or chasing. Examples of the eighteenth century were made of copper or brass, and have long handles of wood, formed by turning on a lathe. Holes were also punched in the lids of these although most of the decorating was done with a chasing tool, or occasionally engraving tools. Very few examples were signed by the makers, and only a handful can be identified as the products of American craftsmen.

Fireplace Cookery

by Leland Rickard Meyer

*I*n this chapter we will try to re-create the atmosphere of the early American kitchen, its activity centered about the cooking fireplace. We envision the bustle, the warmth, and the conviviality. The fragrant aromas from the bake ovens and from the stew pots on the hearth envelop us. What meats went into the iron kettles? How was the bread baked? How hot should the fire be? These and other details to satisfy the curious will be touched upon, including some recipes handed down through generations of good old-fashioned cooks. It must be remembered that, although stoves and ranges began to come into use about 1840, the use of fireplaces for both heating and cooking continued for many years, in some communities until near the close of the nineteenth century.

Cooking fireplaces were large: high and wide, but sometimes not very deep. The opening of one that can be regarded as typical is about 5 feet high, 6 feet wide at the front, and 24 to 30 inches deep. It is wide enough so that one can have two fires going at the same time, one blazing, the other glowing coals. It also has two cranes. Some fireplace cooking was done on a high trivet over hot coals on the hearth. Besides cooking in the fireplace, baking was done in the beehive or Dutch ovens. Roasting was done on either spits or in a reflector oven, often called a "tin kitchen."

In 1813, a writer suggested that a young couple start out with at least the following utensils: a pair of andirons, several pot hooks, a pot, a teakettle, a medium-sized kettle, a frying pan, a bake pan (all of cast iron), and several bowls. At that time these would have cost about

10 to 12 shillings, or about $2.50. As the family increased in size and affluence, many other utensils would be added. Some of the later utensils were of tin, brass, or copper.

In addition to the articles mentioned above one might also have, all of cast iron: a Dutch oven, several sizes of kettles with lids, a number of different sizes of frying pans, a number of various sizes of stew pots on long legs, a pancake griddle, dripping pans, a hanging revolving spit, a bird roaster, several gridirons, several trivets, a toasting fork, a toaster, waffle and wafer irons, a boat spice grinder, and a mortar and pestle. Other articles, made of tin, were two reflector ovens, one for roasting meat, the other for baking biscuits.

At this point it would be well to consider what foods were available in the days of fireplace cooking. Natural foods were used whenever they could be found: butternuts and other native nuts, strawberries, blackberries, thimble berries, huckleberries, mulberries, and grapes; and from Indian orchards, plums, peaches, crabapples, and cherries. A great variety of what we call weeds were used as vegetables: dandelions, cowslips, milkweed, chickweed, marsh marigold, sorrel, glasswort, pusley (or purslane), as well as wild onions, leek, wild rice, and root artichokes. Then, of course, fish and the flesh of wild animals were used, both fresh, smoked, and salted: rabbits, squirrels, coons, muskrats, and woodchucks. Of the wild birds, those commonly used were passenger pigeons, doves, robins, blackbirds, blue jays, pheasants, partridges, grouse, ducks, geese, and turkeys. Bees were not native to America but were brought from Europe about 1630 and allowed to go wild, so honey was obtained from the bee trees. In the North and especially the Northeast, maple sugar was used extensively. In kitchen gardens were grown several kinds of beans, peas, cabbage, squash, pumpkins, turnips, carrots, and sunflower seeds. In fields were found maize (Indian corn), potatoes, sweet potatoes, wheat, rye, oats, barley, and by 1830 buckwheat. New varieties of orchard fruit trees were imported from

Interior view of the kitchen at the Brush Everard House at Williamsburg, Virginia. The spit rack mounted on the wall over the fireplace is rarely seen in restorations today. The bake oven is built outside the wall of the kitchen and can be seen on the exterior of the building. Attention is called to the location of the bake oven by having the door ajar. *Courtesy Colonial Williamsburg*

Europe or developed from wild stock, as well as currants (red, white, and black), gooseberries, and black and red raspberries.

The easiest way to cook over an open fire was in kettles hung from a crane or trammel. Trammels seem to be older, or at least used earlier than cranes. A trammel was adjustable and hung from a lug pole high up in the chimney. The advantage of the crane over a trammel was that more than one kettle could be hung over the fire at a time. When cooking in kettles over an open fire, one had to have plenty of hot water available to replenish that in the kettle, since the pot was liable to boil dry sooner than on a stove. Lids for kettles were also necessary, since ashes might fall into an open kettle. Perhaps it is safe to say that most fireplace cooking in the early days was done in kettles. So most of the foods used in those days were boiled or stewed.

A popular stew or ragout was made of numerous kinds of vegetables and four kinds of meat. The raw meat was cut in cubes in these proportions; 1 pound beef, ¾ pound lean pork, ½ pound veal, and ¼ pound lamb. The meat was cooked in one kettle and the vegetables in another, the contents of both kettles being put together at the end. The choice of vegetables was an individual matter, but certainly potatoes, carrots, onions, and celery were most frequently chosen. The vegetables that needed to cook the longest were put in first to start them cooking. The others were added later. If all were put in at one time, the faster cooking ones would fall apart before the cooking was completed.

There were numerous variations for stew. One used in Holland Dutch sections was parsnip stew. Salt pork was diced and fried in a kettle; when the fat melted, minced onion was sauteed in it. In the meantime in another kettle, diced parsnips, potatoes, and a few carrots were stewed. When both were cooked, the vegetables were added to the pork and onions. These needed to have hot water added.

Of course, any vegetable or meat can be cooked in kettles. Sometimes in large families, several vegetables were cooked together in a very large kettle, each being hung in a separate wire basket in the kettle. Then, when cooked, the baskets were removed and each food was separate from the other. The liquid left in the kettle made an excellent and nourishing soup.

Another method of cooking over an open fire was the hearth method. If the fireplace was broad enough, this was done at one side of the main fire. If there was insufficient space in the fireplace proper, it was done on the hearth in front of the fire. The utensils used in this method were high-standing trivets (8 to 10 inches), stewing pots on high legs, and gridirons. It was also handy to have a "down-hearth" bench. This was a bench varying in length, which stood about 5 or 6 inches from the floor. If one had to kneel and get up and down frequently to attend to cooking, this was much easier on the cook than kneeling

This massive fireplace from the house of the "Miller at Millbach," near Lebanon, Pennsylvania, is now located in the Philadelphia Museum of Art. The large mantel shelf with its supporting molding is very striking and attractive. An unusually large crane was required for kitchen facility. *Courtesy Philadelphia Museum of Art*

on the hearth. Glowing coals were removed from the fire by the use of tongs or a shovel, or both, and placed on the hearth. Over these coals were set the trivet and the stewing pot or gridiron, depending on which utensil was best suited for one's purpose. A gridiron would have been used for broiling steaks or chops. If one did not have a stewing pot on high legs, a small kettle or pot on a trivet could be used. Sauces, gravies, and bastings were cooked by this method.

The Plough Tavern in York, Pennsylvania, built in an ancient medieval style, belies its construction in the middle of the eighteenth century. Its reconstructed fireplace has a raised hearth, and the shape of the throat is exposed in an earlier European tradition. The absence of andirons might be explained by the fact that some experts believe they were sparingly used by the German residents of early Pennsylvania. *Courtesy York County (Pennsylvania) Historical Society*

Meats were roasted in several ways, by using a hanging revolving spit, a reflector oven, or by the older method of utilizing andirons with hooks in front or back on which a spit could be placed. This older method required almost constant attention, since the spit must be turned so that the meat could be roasted on all sides. Later, clock-jacks or lazy-jacks were used to turn the spit. Except when using the reflector oven, a dripping pan was necessary to catch drippings from the meat as it roasted. These drippings with water added were used to baste the meat. Later, the bastings made excellent gravy.

The reflector oven, or "tin kitchen," was a later invention, coming about 1830 or 40. As indicated, this was made of tin. It was generally half cylindrical in shape with short legs, one side being open. The meat was fastened on a spit inside the cylinder by means of skewers. The spit was so arranged that the meat could be turned. There was a door at the back so that one could look at the meat from time to time to check its progress. The juices dropped to the bottom, where they collected and could be used for basting. The whole thing was placed in front of the fire, where the meat roasted both by direct and reflected heat.

Meats that must be thoroughly cooked would be placed further from the fire than those requiring only little cooking. The closer to the fire the oven was placed, the more crusty the outside of the meat would be. Thus, pork and veal would be placed farther from the fire because of the length of time required for roasting. If beef was to be rare, the oven would be placed near the fire for fast roasting on the outside, leaving the center rare. When the meat had been sufficiently roasted, the skewers were taken out and the meat removed from the spit. On one end of the cylinder was a spout, through which the drippings could be poured into a skillet or pot to be used for gravy.

For roasting birds and small fowl, a bird roaster was used. These were of two kinds. The earlier one of iron consisted of an upright rod held erect by a tripod foot; on the upright rod was a sliding circle or escutcheon, on which were several spikes. The whole roaster was then placed in a dripping pan in front of the fire. The circle could be raised or lowered or turned around to adjust the birds to the proper amount of heat. Another type of bird roaster was made of tin. This consisted of an L-shaped piece of tin about 12 inches high and 8 inches wide. The horizontal leg of the L formed a shallow pan to catch the drippings and to form a foot to keep the roaster erect. On the upright portion of the roaster were four to six hooks on which the birds were hung.

Frying was also done over the fire. As with kettles, skillets or frying pans came in many sizes. The old ones were made of iron. One example measures 13 inches in diameter and has a handle 33 inches long. This was used directly over the fire, the long handle resting on the crane. The long iron handle enabled the cook to stand away from the fire. Earlier skillets were made of cast iron and stood on three legs, three or four inches high. These were used on the hearth over glowing coals.

Baking was done either on a griddle, in a Dutch oven, in a beehive oven, or in a reflector oven. A cast-iron griddle hanging from the crane over the fire was used to make griddle cakes or pancakes. On many a farm in the early days pancakes were made for breakfast every day of the year—wheat cakes in summer and buckwheat cakes in winter.

An oldtime recipe for wheat cakes called for 1 quart sweet milk, 1 pint Indian meal (corn meal), 4 eggs, 4 tablespoons white flour, and salt. All the ingredients were beaten together and baked on a hot greased griddle. Buckwheat cakes took one cup boiling water, ½ teaspoon salt, 1 tablespoon molasses, ¼ cup lukewarm water in which ½ yeastcake was dissolved, 1 cup buckwheat flour, ¼ cup white flour, and 1 teaspoon soda. Mix boiling water, salt, and molasses; when lukewarm, add the dissolved yeastcake. Gradually add the flour and soda; beat well. Let stand over night. Beat again; bake on a hot griddle. If the plan was to serve buckwheat cakes morning after morning, a little of this batter was saved each day as a starter for the next day. The cakes tasted better after this holding over. With pancakes were served gravy, or butter and maple syrup. In addition to the cakes fried salt pork, ham, bacon, or liverwurst and fried potatoes were served. If eggs were plentiful they might be served, too. Breakfast was served about seven o'clock, but the men had usually been working in the barn for three hours before that.

A Dutch oven in the old days, as now, was a heavy cast-iron kettle on three or four legs, with a tightly fitting lid. Anything that required baking could be baked in a Dutch oven—bread or cake or pie. The food to be baked was placed in the oven on a very low trivet so as to allow for the circulation of hot air. Then, the tight fitting lid was put in place and the whole oven buried in hot coals. Thus the oven received heat from all sides, including the top. Of course, baking in a Dutch oven required experience, which perhaps came through trial and error or from watching an experienced baker. Too long or too short exposure to the heat was disastrous. Failure to keep the proper amount of heat around the oven also invited unfortunate results.

A tin reflector oven, somewhat similar to the one described above for roasting meat, was used for baking muffins or biscuits. Instead of being cylindrical in shape, it was angular. Instead of a spit, a shallow oblong pan was slid on a rack provided for it in about the middle of the front opening. There was no rear door through which to observe the baking. Since the most heat was on the fire side, it was necessary to remove the pan on which the biscuits were baking and turn it around so that the biscuits to the rear were now in front.

Tavern biscuits were a favorite baked in an oven of this type. To 1 pound of flour, add ¼ pound sugar, ½ pound of butter, some powdered mace and nutmeg, and a glass of brandy or wine; wet it with milk and when kneaded, roll it thin, cut into shapes and bake quickly.

Perhaps the real test of successful fireplace cooking was the use of the beehive oven. The oven got its name from its shape—like an oldtime beehive or skip; that is, domed shaped. The floor or base of the oven was usually circular. The sizes of the ovens differed. One in upstate New York (Mohawk Valley) was large and could hold many loaves of bread, pies, and/or pots of beans. Another example is smaller, measuring about 3½ feet in diameter and 2½ feet from its floor to the top of the dome. The opening or door to the earlier beehive ovens was placed on one side at the back of the fireplace. In earlier ovens, there was no opening other than this, so that the smoke came out of the door and rose up the chimney. Later, beehive ovens were built at one side of and quite separate from the fireplace proper. The opening into the room was closed by an iron door. Beehive ovens usually were deeper than outside chimneys and so projected beyond the chimney on the outside of the house. In New England houses with a huge central chimney, the oven simply extended into the depth of the huge square.

A fire was built directly on the floor of the oven. It took several hours to heat the oven, depending on its size. Various methods are suggested for testing if the oven is sufficiently hot or cool: 1. If the carbon is entirely burned off the inside dome it is just right. 2. Sprinkle flour on the cleaned oven floor. If it burns quickly, it is too hot. If it is overheated, you must let it cool before using. 3. If you cannot hold your hand in the oven to count twenty moderately fast, it is too hot. Since it would be necessary to rebuild a fire if the oven is not hot enough, it is wise to overheat it. When the oven was heated sufficiently, the unburned wood, coals, and ashes were removed with an oven rake. The ashes were carefully kept to be used in the making of lye, which was one of the necessary ingredients in the making of soap. After the ashes were removed, the floor of the oven was swabbed with a wet cloth on a stick.

At last one was ready to do the actual baking. Of course, the foods to be baked had to be prepared while the oven was heating. In some cases, as in the baking of bread, preparations began the night before. Items which took the least time to bake were placed in the front. Articles to be baked were put into the oven on a peel—a flat, long-handled shovel. When everything had been placed in the oven, the opening into the flue had to be closed to keep the heat from being lost in the chimney. Experience by trial and error was the best teacher as to how long each article had to be baked.

In addition to beans and bread, pies, cakes, and meats were baked in the beehive oven. (Cookies were not developed until after the advent of the iron range and its oven). This recipe was used for making white bread: 1 quart warm milk, 1 quart warm water, 1½ cakes of yeast, 1 level tablespoon salt, 2 level tablespoons sugar, 2 level tablespoons melted butter, 7 quarts flour. (This makes four large loaves and one pan of biscuits.) Dissolve yeast in a pint of warm water at about 4 p.m. Mix in enough flour to about medium thickness. Set in a warm place to let rise. Then at about 7 p.m. the yeast mixture and all the other ingredients were put together and worked (kneaded) so as to form a ball; this was covered and allowed to rise over night. In the morning the dough was again worked down; let rise again; and then molded into loaves, covered, and let rise again. Then baked.

A recipe for baked beans: 3 cups dried pea beans, ½ pound salt pork, ⅓ cup molasses, 2 tablespoons salt, 1 teaspoon dry mustard. Soak the beans overnight in cold water. In the morning, drain off the water, cover with fresh water and parboil until the skins split when you blow on them. Divide the pork into two pieces. Slash deeply several times and place the pieces in the bottom of a large bean pot. Pour in the beans. Mix molasses, salt and mustard together; add to the beans with enough hot water to cover the beans. Cover and bake at least six to eight hours, adding more water as is necessary.

A little more fancy cooking was done on waffle and wafer irons. These were introduced by the Dutch. Both were made of iron and consisted of two parts hinged together like pinchers. The baking parts of the waffle iron were very similar to modern ones. A favorite recipe for waffles is as follows: 1 ¾ cups flour, 1 cup milk, 2 eggs, 3 tablespoons baking powder, ½ teaspoon salt, 1 tablespoon melted butter. Mix the dry ingredients. Beat the eggs and the milk together; add melted butter. Add the liquid to the flour combination gradually, beating with a whisk until smooth. Bake on preheated waffle iron. Serve with butter and maple syrup.

Wafers were very thin and pliable when first removed from the baking. They were then usually sprinkled with powdered sugar on one side and rolled into either a cylinder or cone. As soon as they cooled, they become crisp and brittle. If rolled into a cone, they could be filled with whipped cream or any stiff filling desired. The following recipe is for wafers: 4 eggs, 1 cup sugar, pinch salt, 1 ¼ cups graham flour, ¼ pound butter, 1 teaspoon mace or nutmeg. Bake on a preheated wafer iron until light brown.

Other Favorite Recipes

CORN CHOWDER

3 slices salt pork, cubed
1 large onion, sliced
4 large potatoes, diced
2 cups water
1 cup milk

2 cups sweet corn, removed
  from the cob
1 teaspoon salt
6 large soda crackers
dash of pepper

Fry the salt pork in a kettle until crisp and lightly browned. Stir in onion and cook until golden, then add the potatoes and water. Continue cooking until potatoes are tender. Crumble soda crackers in a bowl, pour on the milk and soak. Add to the cooked potatoes; then add corn, salt, and pepper. Simmer for 8 or 10 minutes.

BEAN PORRIDGE HOT

1½ cups dried beans
⅓ cup Indian meal

3 or 4 lbs. lean corned beef
salt and pepper to taste

Soak the beans overnight in cold water. Drain. Cook the corned beef in unsalted water until it falls apart. Remove beef from water; cool and shred it. Cook the beans in the beef stock until tender. Add Indian meal and stir until porridge is thickened. Then add the meat shreds and taste it before seasoning. Serve hot. This will be rather thick. Hot water may be added if a thinner porridge is desired.

SCRAPPLE (Mohawk Valley, N.Y.)

1½ lb. shoulder pork
2 ts. salt
  dash of ground cloves
1 ts. dried marjoram
½ lb. pork liver

½ cup onions, chopped fine
¼ ts. dried thyme
½ ts. freshly ground pepper
1 cup Indian Meal
1 ts. dried sage

Combine pork and liver in a sauce pan with 1 qt. water and cook over moderate heat for an hour. Drain, reserving the broth. Discard all bones and chop meat and liver fine. Blend Indian meal, salt with 1 cup water and 2 cups of broth in a kettle. Cook, stirring constantly, until thick. Stir in meat and liver, onions, all the spices and herbs. Cover and simmer gently for about an hour over low heat. Pour into an 8 × 5 × 3 inch loaf pan and chill until firm. Cut into slices about ½ to ¾ inch thick. Dust lightly with flour. Fry in a little heated fat over moderate heat until crisp on both sides. Serve hot. (Scrapple was originally a thrifty way to use scraps of pork after hogs had been butchered, and *especially* to use the "cracklings" after the trying out of leaf lard.)

BUELING (Catherine Getman)

Let the following come to a boil:

2 qts. water   2 cups molasses   2 tbs. butter
   spices to taste: cinnamon, allspice, mace, nutmeg, salt.

Then stir in buckwheat flour slowly and continuously until very thick. Then stomp with a wooden spoon until unable to stir and all flour lumps are smooth. Put in greased pans. When cold, slice and fry in butter. Serve with maple syrup.

SUCCOTASH Indian recipe

3 tbs. butter   ½ cup rich milk
3 cups fresh sweet corn   3 cups shell beans
   scraped from the cob   salt and pepper to taste
   water to cover

Cook the beans in water until soft. Add the corn. Cook until water is nearly gone, then stir in milk and butter. Heat thoroughly, but do not boil, before serving.

GREEN CORN PUDDING (Frances Phillips Rickard)

2 cups sweet corn,   8 soda crackers, broken
   removed from the cob   salt and pepper to taste
2 cups milk   1 tbs. grated onion
1 egg, beaten   3 tbs. butter

Break the crackers in a well-buttered baking dish. Pour the milk mixed with the egg over them. Add the corn fresh cut and pressed from the cob. Season to taste with salt, pepper and grated onion. Let stand together until the crackers are well soaked through. Dot pieces of butter over the top of the pudding and bake in a moderate oven until set like a custard. 50-60 minutes.

PUMPKIN BREAD Old Dutch recipe

3 cups cooked pumpkin   3 tbs. molasses   1 ts. salt

Add buckwheat flour until when dropped from a spoon it does not spread. Bake in pan in slow oven until it leaves the sides of the pan. When cold, remove from the pan, slice and brown on a greased griddle. Serve hot.

SUET PUDDING

This recipe was used by my great grandmother, Catharine Nellis Rickard. Served steaming hot with a cornstarch lemon sauce, it was delicious.

½ cup suet,   ½ ts. cinnamon
   chopped fine   ½ ts. nutmeg
½ cup molasses   2 ts. baking powder
1½ cups flour   ½ cup seeded raisins
½ ts. salt   or mixed chopped fruits
½ ts. soda   milk

Mix together the suet, molasses and milk. Sift flour with the salt and spices. Combine the two mixtures with the fruit. Pour into a well-greased mold. Steam for two hours.

The sauce was made of water thickened with cornstarch, sugar and a bit of salt. Season with the juice of lemon and grated lemon peel. Cook until thick enough.

BAKED INDIAN PUDDING (Catharine Nellis Rickard)

Cut a ¼ lb. butter into 1 pt. of molasses and warm together until the butter melts. Boil a quart of milk and when scalding hot, pour it slowly over 1 pt. of Indian meal. Put this into the molasses and butter. Cover and let steep for an hour. Take off the cover and set to cool and when cold beat in 6 eggs. Stir in gradually. Add grated nutmeg. Stir hard. Put in buttered dish. Bake 2 hours.

MINCE-MEAT FOR PIE (Kathrine Rickard Meyer)

6 cups finely chopped cooked beef	1 qt. boiled cider
3 cups finely chopped suet	4 packages of seeded raisins
10 cups chopped apples	4 packages of seeded white raisins
2 cups molasses	2 cups citron, diced small

Cook together, then add:

2 oranges, juice and grated rind	1 ts. ground cloves
2 lemons, juice and grated rind	2 ts. ground cinnamon
1 ts. salt	2 ts. ground allspice
2 ts. grated nutmeg	1 ts. almond flavoring

PAN DOWDY An old upstate New York desert (Carrie Loomis)

Cover a deep pie plate with crust. Put in a layer of sliced apple, then a thin layer of shavings of salt pork, then more apple, then more pork. Bake with an upper crust. When done rake off the upper crust and turn it over on a plate. Season the mixture with sugar, molasses and allspice. Put upper crust back on. Serve hot.

JERSEY MILK PIE (Mrs. Herman Terhune)

1 qt. milk	3½ tbs. flour
½ ts. salt	½ cup sugar
2 eggs, beaten slightly	nutmeg

Mix a small amount of the milk with the sugar, flour and salt. Scald the remainder of the milk in a double boiler. Add to the above. Cool slightly, add the eggs. Pour into an unbaked pie shell, grate nutmeg over the top. Bake in a moderate oven for about an hour.

OLYKOEKS

This recipe has been handed down from Polly Snell Rickard (1793-1825). It is of Dutch origin. The original in her handwriting says it was from her grandmother. Here it is in her own words:

"About 12 o'clock set a little yeast to rise, so as to be ready at 5, to mix with the following ingredients: 3¾ lbs. flour, 1 lb. sugar, ½ lb. butter and lard mixed, 1½ pints milk, 6 eggs, 1 pt. raised yeast. Warm in the flour, add eggs last. Place in a warm place to rise. If quite light at bedtime, work down. At 9 next morning, make it into small balls with the hand and place in the center of each ball a bit of raisin, citron and apple, chopped fine. Lay on well floured pie-board and allow to rise again. They are frequently ready to boil in hot fat by 2 o'clock. In removing from the board, use a knife, well floured and just give them a little roll with the hand to make them round. Boil about 5 minutes. When drained and cool, roll in sifted sugar."

JOHNNY CAKE (Amanda Phillips)

1 scant cup Indian meal	2 cups flour
3 tbs. melted butter	1⅓ cups sour milk
2 tbs. sugar	1 or 2 eggs
1 ts. soda	2 ts. baking powder
salt	

Bake in moderate oven.

BISCUIT DOUGH SHORT CAKE (Edith Henry Pultz)

1 qt. flour	salt
3 ts. baking powder	enough milk to make a
6 tbs. shortening	fairly wet dough

Bake in a round cake pan. While still hot split it from side to side. Spread the bottom half with butter. Spoon on crushed sweetened berries or sliced peaches. Put on top half. Spoon on more berries. Serve hot. A topping of whipped cream may be added.

PLAIN FRITTERS (Katrine Rickard Meyer)

4 eggs, beaten   1½ pints milk
2 ts. baking powder   1 ts. salt

Flour to make a stiff enough batter to drop into deep hot fat. Serve hot with maple syrup.

DOED KOECKS Old Dutch recipe

14 lbs. flour   1 oz. caraway seed   5 lbs. butter
1 qt. water   6 lbs. sugar   2 ts. salt
                   2 ts. pearlash

Roll out to about 1½ inches thick, cut in circles about 4 inches in diameter. Bake.
These were served with wine at funerals.

MAPLE SUGAR CANDY (Mrs. Catherine Van Cortlandt)

Boil together 1 lb. maple sugar and 1 cup of cream and milk mixed, until it will harden in cold water. Have ready 1 cup hickory nuts and stir these in lightly before dropping on buttered paper from a spoon to cool.

Bibliography

Allen, Lewis F. *Rural Architecture*. New York: C. M. Saxton, 1852.

Benjamin, Asher. *The Practical Home Carpenter*. Boston: published by the author, R. P. and C. Williams, and Annin Smith, 1830.

Brumbaugh, G. Edwin. *Colonial Architecture of Pennsylvania*. Lancaster: Pennsylvania German Society, 1933.

The Buttolph-Williams House. Hartford: The Antiquarian & Landmark Society of Connecticut, 1956.

Chamberlain, Samuel and Narcissa. *Southern Interiors at Charleston*. New York: Hastings House, 1956.

Chambers, E. *Cyclopedia or, an Universal Dictionary of Arts and Sciences*. London: printed for W. Innys, J. & P. Knapton, D. Browne, T. Longman, R. Hett, C. Hitch, and L. Hawes, J. Hodges, J. Shuckbruck, A. Millar, J. & J. Rivington, J. Ward, M. Senex, and the Executors of J. Darby, 1751.

Collections on the History of Albany from Its Discovery to the Present Time. Albany, N.Y.: J. Munsell, 1870.

Cotter, John L., and Hudson, J. Paul. *New Discoveries at Jamestown*. Washington, D.C.: The National Park Service, 1956.

Cousins, Frank, and Riley, Phil M. *The Colonial Architecture of Salem*. Boston: Little, Brown, and Company, 1919.

Dillard, Maud Esther. *An Album of New Netherlands*. New York: Bramhall House, 1963.

Downing, A. J. *The Architecture of Country Houses*. New York: Dover Publications, Inc., 1969.

Downing, A. J. *A Treatise on the Theory and Practice of Landscape Gardening Adapted to North America*. New York and London: Wiley and Putnam, 1844.

Eberlein, Harold Donaldson, and Hubbard, Cortlandt Van Dyke. *American Georgian Architecture*. London: Pleiades Books Ltd., 1952.

Encyclopedia; or, a Dictionary of Arts and Sciences, and Miscellaneous Literature. Philadelphia: printed for Thomas Dobson, 1798.

Encyclopedia Perthensis, or a Dictionary of Knowledge. Perth, Scotland: printed for C. Mitchell & Co., no date.

Fireplaces. Huntington, Ind.: The Majestic Company, no date.

Forman, Henry Chandler. *The Architecture of the Old South*. New York: Russell & Russell, 1948.

343

Franklin, Benjamin. *Observations on Smoky Chimneys, Their Causes and Cures; with Considerations on Fuel and Stoves.* London: printed for I. and J. Taylor at the Architectural Library, 1793.

Halsey, R. T. H., and Cornelius, C. O. *A Handbook of the American Wing.* New York: printed and sold by the Metropolitan Museum of Art, 1924.

Hamlin, Talbot. *Greek Revival Architecture in America.* New York: Dover Publications, Inc., 1944.

Hough, Walter. *Fire as an Agent in Human Culture.* Washington, D.C.: Government Printing Office, 1926.

Isham, Norman M., and Brown, Albert F. *Early Connecticut Houses.* New York: Dover Publications, Inc., 1965.

Johnson, Amandus. *The Swedes on the Delaware, 1638–1664.* Philadelphia: International Printing Co., 1927.

Kelly, J. Frederick. *Early Domestic Architecture of Connecticut.* New York: Dover Publications, Inc., 1963.

Kettell, Russell Hawes. *Early American Rooms, 1650–1858.* New York: Dover Publications, Inc., 1967.

Kimball, Fiske. *Mr. Samuel McIntire, Carver, The Architect of Salem* (Salem, Mass.). Gloucester, Mass.: The Essex Institute, 1940; reprinted by Peter Smith, 1966.

Kimball, Fiske. *Domestic Architecture of the American Colonies and of the Early Republic.* New York: Dover Publications, Inc. 1966.

Kocher, A. Lawrence and Dearstyne, Howard. *Colonial Williamsburg, Its Buildings and Gardens.* Williamsburg, Va.: Colonial Williamsburg, Inc., 1966.

Labaree, Leonard W., and Whitfield, J. Bell (eds.). *The Papers of Benjamin Franklin.* New Haven, Conn.: Yale University Press; vol. 2, 1960; vol. 8, 1965; vol. 10, 1966.

Maass, John. *The Gingerbread Age: A View of Victorian America.* New York: Holt, Rinehart, and Winston, 1957.

Michaux, F. A. *Travels to the West of the Allegheny Mountains.* Cleveland, Ohio: publisher unknown, 1904.

Morrison, Hugh. *Early American Architecture, from the First Colonial Settlements to the National Period.* New York: Oxford University Press, 1952.

Nonemaker, James A. *The New York Town House 1815–1840.* Unpublished thesis, University of Delaware, Newark, Del., 1958.

Norris, Mrs. Howes. *Sketches of Old Homes in Our Village.* Martha's Vineyard, Mass.: reproduced in *The Dukes County Intelligencer*, vol. 9, no. 1.

Sharp, James. *Pennsylvania Stove Grate, An Account of the.* London: publisher unknown, 1781.

Philips, George Lewis. *American Chimney Sweeps.* Trenton, N.J.: Past Times Press, 1957.

Pierce, Josephine H. *Fire on the Hearth.* Springfield, Mass.: The Pond-Ekberg Company, 1951.

Pierson, William H., Jr. *American Buildings and Their Architects.* New York: Doubleday & Company, 1970.

Pratt, Dorothy and Richard. *A Guide to Early American Homes North and South.* New York: Bonanza Books, 1956.

Putnam, J. Pickering. *The Open Fireplace in All Ages*. Boston: James R. Osgood and Company, 1882.

Raymond, Eleanor. *Early Domestic Architecture of Pennsylvania*. New York: William Helpburn Inc., 1931.

Reference Guide to Salem, 1630, A. Salem, Mass.: Board of Park Commissioners City of Salem, 1959.

Reynolds, Helen Wilkinson. *Dutch Houses in the Hudson Valley Before 1766*. New York: Dover Publications, Inc., 1965.

Robinson, James. *The Philadelphia Directory for 1811*. Philadelphia: printed for the publisher, 1811.

Roberts, Kenneth and Anna (translators). *Moreau de St. Méry's American Journey (1793–1798)*. New York: Doubleday and Company, 1947.

Rogers, Meric R. *American Interiors*. New York: Bonanza Books, 1947.

Roth, Rodris C. *The Interior Decoration of City Houses in Baltimore 1783–1812*. Unpublished thesis, University of Delaware, Newark, Del., 1958.

Rumford, Count. *Essay IV: Of Chimney Fire-places, with Proposals to save Fuel; to render Dwelling-houses more Comfortable and Salubrious, and effectually prevent Chimnies from Smoking*. London: publisher unknown, 1796.

Sale, Edith Tunis. *Interiors of Virginia Houses of Colonial Times*. Richmond, Va.: William Byrd Press, Inc., 1928.

Smith, Oliver P. *The Domestic Architect*. Buffalo, N.Y.: Derby & Co.; Chicago, Ill., D. B. Cooke & Co., 1852.

Stotz, Charles Morse. *The Early Architecture of Western Pennsylvania*. Pittsburgh, Pa.: William Helpburn, Inc. for the Buhl Foundation, 1936.

Successful Fireplaces, A Book of. Farmington, Mich.: Structures Publishing Company, no date.

Swan, Abraham. *British Architect, or Builder's Treasury of Stair Cases*. England: 1745; Philadelphia and Boston: publisher unknown, 1775.

Sweeny, John A. M. *Winterthur Illustrated*. New York: Chanticleer Press, 1969.

Tallmadge, Thomas E. *The Story of Architecture in America*. New York: W. W. Norton & Co., rev. ed. 1936.

Ure, Andres, M.D. *A Dictionary of Arts, Manufactures, and Mines*. New York: D. Appleton & Co., 1856.

Vanderbilt, Cornelius. *The Living Past of America*. New York: Crown Publishers Inc., 1955.

Wertenbaker, Thomas J. *The Middle Colonies, The Founding of American Civilization Series*. New York: Cooper Square Publishers Inc., 1938.

Waterman, Thomas Tileson. *The Dwellings of Colonial America*. Chapel Hill, N.C.: University of North Carolina Press, 1950.

Westlager, C. A. *The Log Cabin in America*. New Brunswick, N.J.: Rutgers University Press, 1969.

Whiffin, Marcus. *Eighteenth-Century Houses of Williamsburg*. New York: Holt, Rinehart, and Winston, Inc., published for Colonial Williamsburg, Inc., 1960.

Index

Italics refer to pages of illustrations.